Days of Grace

Days
of Grace

a memoir by

ARTHUR ASHE and
Arnold Rampersad

ALFRED A. KNOPF   *New York*   *1993*

To the memory of my father and mother,
and to
Jeanne and Camera

. . . since we are surrounded by so great a cloud of witnesses, let us lay aside every weight, and the sin which so easily ensnares us, and let us run with endurance the race that is set before us . . .

—HEBREWS 12:1

Contents

Acknowledgments xi

1. My Outing 3

2. Middle Passage 33

3. Stars and Stripes: A Captain in the Davis
   Cup Wars 60

4. Protest and Politics 101

5. The Burden of Race 126

6. The Striving and Achieving 168

7. The Beast in the Jungle 195

8. Sex and Sports in the Age of AIDS 222

9. Stepping Up 249

10. The Threads in My Hands 272

11. My Dear Camera 293

Index 307

Acknowledgments

ARTHUR ROBERT ASHE, JR., died of pneumonia on the afternoon of Saturday, February 6, 1993, at New York Hospital–Cornell Medical Center, in Manhattan. He was buried the following Wednesday at Woodland Cemetery in Richmond, Virginia.

This memoir began with a telephone call from Arthur to me in June 1992. His call came as a surprise, because we had not been in touch with one another since our first meeting, at a children's book fair the previous November in Princeton. Arthur called to ask whether or not I would be interested in writing a book with him. In this book, he hoped to express his views on certain issues of importance to him, such as race, education, politics, and sports, as well as to give an account of his experience as a patient with heart disease and AIDS. I immediately agreed to do so. Such was the spirit of cooperation between us, and my sense of urgency, that we worked without a formal agreement from July until November, when we signed our contract with Knopf.

Although this book was nearly complete before Arthur's death, Jeanne Moutoussamy-Ashe has worked heroically since then to try to ensure not only its timely publication but also its accuracy and general soundness. I am grateful to her for her sacrifice in a time of profound bereavement.

My greatest additional debt, as was Arthur's, is to Jonathan Segal of Knopf. Although his interest was intense from the start, he took pains to ensure us freedom to write the book we wanted to write. He edited the text with sympathy and respect, and also suggested the title of the book.

I was truly fortunate to have as a copy editor Stephen Frankel, whose meticulous work on the manuscript improved it from start to finish.

For the transcription of many of my conversations with Arthur, I thank Judith Ferszt of the American Studies program at Princeton University. I also wish to thank Bruce Simon, also of Princeton University, who showed both zeal and imagination in researching a variety of issues arising from the manuscript. At *Tennis* magazine, Debra Fratoni assisted us enormously by providing many reports on Arthur's career as captain of the U.S. Davis Cup team.

I thank my wife, Marvina White, for her help and support in a time of intense activity.

Not least of all, I am indebted to Fifi Oscard and Kevin McShane of Fifi Oscard Agency, Inc.—Arthur's literary representative of many years—for providing invaluable advice that helped to facilitate the writing of this book. Although, sadly, Arthur did not live to participate in these acknowledgments, I feel certain I speak here for him as well.

ARNOLD RAMPERSAD
Princeton, New Jersey
March 1993

Days of Grace

CHAPTER ONE

My Outing

IF ONE'S REPUTATION is a possession, then of all my possessions, my reputation means most to me. Nothing comes even close to
it in importance. Now and then, I have wondered whether my reputation matters too much to me; but I can no more easily renounce my
concern with what other people think of me than I can will myself to
stop breathing. No matter what I do, or where or when I do it, I feel
the eyes of others on me, judging me.

Needless to say, I know that a fine line exists between caring about
one's reputation and hypocrisy. When I speak of the importance to me
of my reputation, I am referring to a reputation that is deserved, not
an image cultivated for the public in spite of the facts. I know that I
haven't always lived without error or sin, but I also know that I have
tried hard to be honest and good at all times. When I fail, my
conscience comes alive. I have never sinned or erred without knowing
I was being watched.

Who is watching me? The living and the dead. My mother, Mattie
Cordell Cunningham Ashe, watches me. She died when I was not quite
seven. I remember little about her, except for two images. My last sight
of her alive: I was finishing breakfast and she was standing in the side
doorway looking lovingly at me. She was dressed in her blue corduroy
dressing gown. The day was cool and cloudy, and when I went outside
I heard birds singing in the small oak tree outside our house. And then
I remember the last time I saw her, in a coffin at home. She was wearing
her best dress, made of pink satin. In her right hand was a single red

3

rose. Roses were her favorite flower, and my daddy had planted them all around the house; big, deep-hued red roses.

Every day since then I have thought about her. I would give anything to stand once again before her, to feel her arms about me, to touch and taste her skin. She is with me every day, watching me in everything I do. Whenever I speak to young persons about the morality of the decisions they make in life, I usually tell them, "Don't do anything you couldn't tell your mother about."

My father is watching me, too. My father, whose mouth dropped open when he first saw Jeanne, my wife. She looked so much like my mother, he said. He is still a force in my life. Some years ago, before he died of a stroke in 1989, I was being interviewed by the television journalist Charlayne Hunter-Gault in her home.

"Tell me, Arthur," she said, laughter in her voice, "how is it that I have never heard anyone say anything bad about you? How is it that you have never cursed an umpire, or punched an opponent, or gotten a little drunk and disorderly? Why are you such a goody-goody?"

I laughed in turn, and told the truth.

"I guess I have never misbehaved because I'm afraid that if I did anything like that, my father would come straight up from Virginia, find me wherever I happen to be, and kick my ass."

When I told that story not long ago on Men's Day at the West-wood Baptist Church in Richmond, Virginia, everyone smiled and some folks even laughed. They knew what I was talking about, even those few living in that little enclave of blacks surrounded by whites in Richmond who had never met my father. They knew fathers (and mothers) exactly like him, who in times past would come up and find you wherever you were and remind you exactly who you were and don't you forget it. You were their child, that's who.

My father was a strong, dutiful, providing man. He lived and died semi-literate, but he owned his own home and held jobs that were important to him and to people in the community where we lived. His love and his caring were real to me from that Sunday morning in 1950 when he sat on the bottom bunk bed between my brother Johnnie and me and told us between wrenching sobs that our mother had died during the night. From that time on he was father and mother to us. And the lesson he taught above all was about reputation.

"What people think of you, Arthur Junior, your reputation, is all that counts." Or, as I heard from so many older people as I grew up, "A good name is worth more than diamonds and gold."

What others think of me is important, and what I think of others is important. What else do I have to go by? Of course, I cannot make decisions based solely on what other people would think. There are moments when the individual must stand alone. Nevertheless, it is crucial to me that people think of me as honest and principled. In turn, to ensure that they do, I must always act in an honest and principled fashion, no matter the cost.

One day, in Dallas, Texas, in 1973, I was playing in the singles final of a World Championship Tennis (WCT) tournament. My opponent was Stan Smith, a brilliant tennis player but an even more impressive human being in his integrity. On one crucial point, I watched Smith storm forward, racing to intercept a ball about to bounce a second time on his side of the net. When the point was over, I was sure the ball had bounced twice before he hit it and that the point was mine. Smith said he had reached the ball in time. The umpire was baffled. The crowd was buzzing.

I called Smith up to the net.

"Stan, did you get to that ball?"

"I did. I got it."

I conceded the point. Later, after the match—which I lost—a reporter approached me. Was I so naïve? How could I have taken Smith's word on such an important point?

"Believe me," I assured him, "I am not a fool. I wouldn't take just anybody's word for it. But if Stan Smith says he got to the ball, he got to it. I trust his character."

When I was not quite eighteen years old, I played a tournament in Wheeling, West Virginia, the Middle Atlantic Junior Championships. As happened much of the time when I was growing up, I was the only black kid in the tournament, at least in the under-eighteen age section. One night, some of the other kids trashed a cabin; they absolutely destroyed it. And then they decided to say that I was responsible, although I had nothing to do with it. The incident even got into the papers. As much as I denied and protested, those white boys would not change their story.

I rode to Washington from West Virginia with the parents of Dickie Dell, another one of the players. They tried to reassure me, but it was an uncomfortable ride because I was silently worrying about what my father would do and say to me. When I reached Washington, where I was to play in another tournament, I telephoned him in Richmond. As I was aware, he already knew about the incident. When he spoke, he was grim. But he had one question only.

"Arthur Junior, all I want to know is, were you mixed up in that mess?"

"No, Daddy, I wasn't."

He never asked about it again. He trusted me. With my father, my reputation was solid.

I have tried to live so that people would trust my character, as I had trusted Stan Smith's. Sometimes I think it is almost a weakness in me, but I want to be seen as fair and honest, trustworthy, kind, calm, and polite. I want no stain on my character, no blemish on my reputation. And that was why what happened to me early in April 1992 hit me as hard as it did.

THE NIGHT BEFORE I met Jimmy Connors in the men's singles final at Wimbledon in the summer of 1975, I went to bed and slept soundly. That match was the biggest of my life. It was also one that just about everybody was sure I would lose, because Connors was then the finest tennis player in the world, virtually invincible. In fact, the match was supposed to be a slaughter, and I was to be the sacrificial lamb. Before going to bed I had talked and talked with various friends about strategy and tactics, but when it was time to go to sleep, I shrugged off all the nervousness and the worrying, as I usually do, and slept peacefully—as peacefully as that proverbial lamb.

The night of Tuesday, April 7, 1992, was another matter altogether. Try as I could, I was not able to deliver myself to sleep. Once again I had talked and talked, this time mainly with my wife at home but also with friends on the telephone. Once again we discussed strategy and tactics as I tried to make myself ready for another ordeal, but one far more threatening to me than four sets in the final at Wimbledon against Connors. This time I could not bring myself to sleep, except in fits and starts. From my windows on the fourteenth floor of my apartment building in Manhattan I saw the lights of the city and watched for the sun to come up through the murk and mist of Brooklyn and Queens to the east. Before six o'clock, with the sky still dark, I was dressed and ready to go, ready to hunt for a newspaper, to discover if my secret was out, exposed to the world. I knew that once that happened, my life and the lives of my family would be changed forever, and almost certainly for the worse.

In a shop across the avenue I found the newspaper I was waiting for, *USA Today*. I scanned the front page, then flipped back to the sports section. There was not a word about me. I felt a great relief. And then I knew that the relief was only temporary, that it was now up to me to take the matter into my own hands and break the news to whatever part of the world wanted to hear it. And I would have to do it that day, Wednesday, because the days—maybe the hours—of my secret were definitely numbered. I had to announce to the world that I, Arthur Ashe, had AIDS.

The afternoon before was supposed to have been a normal time for me: a visit from a boyhood friend; a medical appointment at the Westchester Diagnostic Center in nearby White Plains, Westchester County; a tennis clinic; then back home in time to play with my daughter, Camera, and then to have dinner with her and Jeanne. The medical appointment was all too normal for me. Since December 1979, when I had undergone a quadruple-bypass heart operation in New York, I had become a professional patient, although only my wife and closest friends, as well as my physicians, knew the full story of my career as a patient. So the medical appointment was normal, with me undergoing an MRI (magnetic resonance imaging) of my brain, which is like the better-known CAT scan (computerized axial tomography) but uses magnetism, not X rays, to capture its images.

Normal, too, was the visit from my boyhood friend Doug Smith. I make it a point to keep in touch with friends from my childhood in Richmond; I cannot help but think that childhood friends are the bedrock of all one's future relationships, and that you move away from them at your risk. There is an African proverb in which I believe: Hold on to your friends with both hands. I try to stay in touch. Doug was a longtime friend, newly remarried, and I was glad he was coming to visit. We had played tennis as teenagers. He had gone to Phoenix High School in Hampton, Virginia, and I had gone to Maggie Walker in

Richmond, but we had remained friends. He had gone on to Hampton Institute, as it was then called, and I had gone on to UCLA; but tennis had kept us together. Doug is a tennis writer for *USA Today*. When he called to ask if he could come to see me, I assumed that he wanted to discuss with me my three-volume work on African Americans in sports, *A Hard Road to Glory*. And we did talk about it for a while, sitting in my office at home. Then it became clear that something else was on his mind.

"Arthur, I've got to ask you something," he said. I could see that he was in pain, agonizing and wanting to be doing almost anything else than to ask me that question. "We have just gotten a lead at the newspaper, something about you, and my boss has asked me to follow up on the lead. I'm supposed to talk to you and ask you to confirm or deny it."

"What sort of lead, Doug?"

He didn't rush to answer, but he finally came out with it. "We have heard that you are HIV-positive, Arthur. That you have AIDS."

"Can you prove it?"

"No. That's the point. My editor wants to know, is it true? They sent me to find out. Is it true?"

Doug was a good friend and a good man, but right now he was the press, and I was not about to deliver myself to the press on this question without a struggle. In fact, I could feel my anger rising, slowly but steadily, although it was not aimed at Doug himself. I am not one to be plagued by fits or gusts of rage, and I try hard to keep calm and subdued at all times. I was taught to remain calm on the tennis court, no matter what the score or how questionable the call or discourteous my opponent. But the anger was building in me that this newspaper, *any* newspaper or any part of the media, could think that it had a right to tell the world that I had AIDS.

"I want to talk to your editor, Doug."

I could see that Doug was relieved at that point, happy to turn the matter over to his boss. From my office, as we sat there at home, I telephoned Gene Policinski, managing editor of sports for *USA Today*. Policinski couldn't talk right then, and Doug and I waited for him to return my call. He did so promptly enough, around four-thirty. We talked for between twenty and thirty minutes. He was fairly direct.

"Are you HIV-positive, or do you have AIDS?"

"Could be," I replied.

I could not lie to him. Sometimes, indirectly, I had to lie about AIDS. Now and then, I had to lie about it directly. In November 1991, when I wanted to go to South Africa, I lied on the application for my visa and said that I did not have an infectious disease. But I never lied without a sharp twinge of conscience, even in lying to the government of South Africa.

I also told Policinski flatly that I had no intention, at that time, of confirming or denying the story. I tried to argue with him, to make him see my position.

"Look," I said with some force, "the public has no right to know in this case."

As I saw this situation, the public's right to know really meant the newspaper's right to print. Of course, there would be people interested in, even titillated by, the news that I had AIDS; the question was, did they have a *right* to know? I absolutely did not think so. The law was on the side of the newspaper, but ethically its demand was wrong, as well as unnecessary.

"I am not a public figure anymore," I argued. "I don't play professional tennis anymore. I officially announced my retirement in 1980. I am not running for public office, so my health is no one's legitimate concern except my own. I haven't committed any crimes, so I am not fair game. And I haven't been caught in any scandals. Why do you think differently?"

"You *are* a public figure," Policinski insisted. "And anytime a public figure is ill, it's news. If he has a heart attack, as you did in 1979, it's news. We have no special zone of treatment for AIDS. It's a disease, like heart disease. It is news."

Match point had come, and I had lost it. All I could do now was try to control the announcement itself, to have it heard first directly from me and not as a blazing story in a national newspaper. I asked Policinski if I could have a little time, say, thirty-six hours, to call friends, talk to other journalists, and prepare a public statement. I reminded him that I had *not* confirmed his story, as far as I was concerned.

Policinski was polite but firm. No, it was not his role as the managing editor of a newspaper to help me plan a news conference, and he could not in good conscience withhold a story if he considered it newsworthy and if he had proof of its accuracy. However, *USA Today* had certain standards and practices which it would stick by in this story as in any other. In general, it did not print stories with elaborately vague sources—information attributed to "informed sources" and the like. And the newspaper did not approve of backing crablike into a story, by reporting a rumor and then declaring that the person or persons involved had denied it. Policinski and I ended the conversation without coming to any agreement, except that I stood by my refusal to confirm the story, and he stood by his determination to continue to investigate it, as well as his right to publish it if he could find confirmation. I fully expected to see the story in the next morning's edition.

I like *USA Today*. In fact, I have the paper delivered to my home every day. In its beginning and even now, some people deride it as *McPaper*, a kind of fast-food approach to journalism. The truth is that it is an extremely informative newspaper, attractive and dependable, and well written. And if you travel as much as I do, it keeps you abreast of events around the country and the world. At that moment, however, I hated the paper for what it was doing, although I was also glad that it was making a conscientious effort to determine if the story were true. It had given me time, much needed time.

I had to decide what to do next. First, I canceled my MRI. I canceled the tennis clinic, which was for my own Safe Passage Foundation, working with young people, in Newark, New Jersey. The next day, I was supposed to go to Washington, D.C., to be with my old tennis partner Stan Smith and Donald Dell, who is my lawyer and one of my closest friends, and speak to the Washington Tennis Patrons at the William G. Fitzgerald Tennis Center, where the center court is named after me. I canceled that appointment, too. Then Jeanne and I began to talk. We talked for hours that day, looking at the problem from every possible angle, trying to come up with the best plan.

In one way or another, Jeanne and I had already had this conversation many times. From the start, we had understood that the truth would eventually come out, and that basically we had three choices about the revelation: The first was to make the announcement ourselves, when and where we wanted. The second was to wait until the rumors began to build, until the story seemed about to break, then try to preempt the announcement ourselves. The third choice, easily the worst, was to wait until the announcement was a *fait accompli,* until one of us turned on the television or picked up a newspaper and saw a picture of my face and the report of a rumor, or until some reporter called on the telephone to say, "Mr. Ashe, sir, Associated Press is running a wire story about you. It says you have AIDS. Any comment, sir?" Then we would have totally lost control of our lives. We had decided long before that if we could not implement plan A, then we absolutely had to execute plan B. And now it had to be done the next day.

Although she later told me that I was wrong, quite wrong, I was sure Jeanne was relieved that the truth was finally going to come out. I suppose that I have a deeper commitment to keeping things to myself, bottling them up, suppressing them. I tend to be more on guard. But we both knew that our lives would be changed forever by the announcement, even if we didn't know exactly how and to what extent. I could see, too, that we were part of a larger pattern concerning AIDS and publicity, that our announcement could not be cleanly divorced from similar announcements by other persons of some celebrity. Although light needed to be shed on AIDS, very few people were willing to admit to being infected with the HIV virus, much less the disease itself.

Before Magic Johnson went public the previous November about his HIV infection, no prominent heterosexual had admitted publicly to being HIV-positive, or to having AIDS, unless he or she were on his or her deathbed. One could argue that Magic did not have much of a choice in making his announcement, in that he would have had to explain why he was retiring as a basketball player at the height of his game, apparently without an injury. He could not have feigned a career-threatening injury even if he had wanted to, because the integrity of his physicians would have been on the line. Rock Hudson admitted his infection only near the very end. Only after the death of Brad Davis, who starred in the movie *Midnight Express,* did anyone admit that he had died of AIDS. Willi Smith, the gifted black clothing designer, died without admitting he had AIDS. The entertainer Peter Allen died after my announcement but never came forward before his death to tell the world that he was infected. Rudolf Nureyev forced his doctor into the position of initially denying, after the dancer's death, that he had died of AIDS.

Public attitudes have changed and become more enlightened, and still AIDS patients who are public figures tremble at announcing their infection. Cancer, once almost as unspeakable, is one thing, but AIDS is quite another. One can be sure that there are many famous people who are HIV-positive, or who have full-blown AIDS, and are keeping it a secret. As for myself, I never worried as much about being a social outcast as I did about not being able to maintain my life's schedule. On visa applications, on job applications, in seeking medical treatment or insurance, and in myriad other ways, AIDS is enough in many cases to result in a blunt rejection. Brad Davis's wife confessed that Davis had kept his illness a secret so that he could continue to take whatever acting jobs came his way.

I love to travel, and I have to do so for business—such as going to Wimbledon as a television commentator. But several countries will not admit someone who discloses having AIDS, or even to being merely HIV-positive but without full-blown AIDS. The United States is one of those countries. One can get a temporary dispensation, but usually only if one is attending a conference about AIDS or the like. The infected person would then be accorded the same status as Soviet diplomats used to have in the United States during the Cold War, with severe limits placed on his or her travel. The major international conference on AIDS in 1992 was forced to move from Boston to Amsterdam in the Netherlands because of these restrictions. Because Great Britain also has restrictions connected to HIV and AIDS, I wondered if I would ever see Wimbledon again. I wondered about my commercial connections, my consultantships and other jobs in television, in the manufacture and sale of sports equipment and clothing, and in coaching. All of these connections went back a long way, and represented a tremendous human investment on my part as well as on the part of those companies. Would these connections survive the news?

For the news conference, Jeanne and I decided to appeal to Home Box Office (HBO), for whom I had worked regularly as a television commentator at Wimbledon. The president of Paramount Sports there is Seth Abraham, a close friend. He agreed at once to do it. We set the announcement for 3:30 the following afternoon. With HBO undertaking to notify the sports press, two major tasks remained. The first was to prepare a statement to be read at the conference, before I took questions from any reporters who showed up. The second, at least as difficult for me, was to call a number of people and break the news to them. To a few already in the know, I would be telling them only that I was going public; others would be hearing about my AIDS infection for the first time.

Between roughly 3:15 on Tuesday afternoon and 2:45 the following morning, I made between thirty and thirty-five telephone calls. I called several members of my family, including my brother in North Carolina, who is a retired Marine Corps captain, and my stepmother, stepsister, and stepbrother in Virginia; and I called many friends. Hearing the news that I had AIDS, two or three people burst into tears. I hastened to tell them, and others, that I was fine, that my spirits were up, that they should not worry about me. I called my lawyer Donald Dell, and he let me know at once that he would be present at the press conference. I called the chief of staff in the office of Dr. Louis Sullivan, the Secretary of Health and Human Services, in Washington, D.C. I asked him to inform Dr. Sullivan, and I wanted Dr. Sullivan himself to pass the news to Barbara Bush at the White House. I had been favorably impressed by Mrs. Bush's steadfast interest in AIDS and the generosity of her response to its victims when she visited children's hospitals. From the president of the National Commission on AIDS, I secured its list of medical reporters who might be interested in what I had to say. They, too, would be invited to the press conference.

Several of the people I called had either answering services or answering machines, but I was extremely cautious in leaving messages. I was guarded even in talking to certain spouses. Some I knew I could trust; others were less reliable.

To help me draft the text of my statement, I called my old friend Frank Deford, a veteran sports journalist and television personality and now a senior writer at *Newsweek* magazine. Deford is the spitting image of the handsome riverboat gambler, rakish mustache and all, but there is nothing hit-or-miss about his literary style or his common sense.

Co-author with me of *Arthur Ashe: Portrait in Motion*, which is an account of a year in my life on the professional tennis circuit, he had traveled with me to a number of places, including sub-Saharan Africa and South Africa. Together we had gone to Soweto, the most famous, or infamous, black township in South Africa. Although I would write a statement myself, I trusted Deford's judgment on what I should say at this particular time.

As I worked at my computer, the telephone rang steadily as word began to spread. Instead of Barbara Bush, President Bush himself called to express his sympathy and to wish us well. Another caller was Douglas Wilder, an old friend who had become the governor of the state where I was born, Virginia. I also heard from Andrew Young, the former mayor of Atlanta; Young, an ordained minister, had married Jeanne and me in 1977. I heard from my good friend David Dinkins, the mayor of New York and an avid tennis fan. I took every call, even those that had nothing to do with my announcement. I needed to feel that the world was still turning normally on its axis. Someone called about changing the bylaws of an organization of which I am a member; I listened patiently and talked the matter through as intelligently as I could.

As I talked and wrote, I was aware above all of one person's presence in the apartment: my five-year-old daughter, Camera. I could hardly look at her without thinking of how innocent she was of the import of this coming event, and how in one way or another she was bound to suffer for it. She is a beautiful child, if I say so myself. She was wearing yellow and pink barrettes in her hair and her smile went right to my heart. She had been tested and does not carry the virus. We had not told her about my AIDS, but now we had to do so, and soon—perhaps that night. We had to tell her before someone, most likely some other child, taunted her with the fact that her father has AIDS. In the apartment, where the phone was ringing more than ever and there were visitors in the middle of the morning, she knew that something was happening but didn't know what.

"Daddy," she said, and hugged me about my knees. She held out her right hand, which was closed. When she opened it, there was a chocolate kiss, in its bright silver wrapper. I kissed her on the cheek, and went back to my statement.

When I was finished I read the statement to Jeanne and Frank, and they approved of it. There was enough time for a quick lunch, and then I changed into a blue suit and red tie—just right for television, if anyone showed up from television. Jeanne, too, was dressed in a blue suit, with a white blouse and a blue velvet headband, as we went with Deford to the HBO office on the corner of Forty-seventh Street and the Avenue of the Americas.

We arrived just before the scheduled start of the conference at 3:30 p.m. Ross Levinsohn, who handles publicity for HBO, greeted us in the lobby.

"How's the turnout?" I asked him nervously. "Anybody here yet?"

"Anybody here?" he echoed. "The place is packed. It's been packed for an hour now."

I asked about the room. "You've probably seen it on television," Levinsohn assured me. "It's where we hold some of our biggest fight announcements. Evander Holyfield, George Foreman, Mike Tyson, they've all been in there, talking about their coming fights."

Oh great, I thought. Just great.

Almost exactly at 3:30 I entered the conference room on the fifteenth floor of the building. The room, warm and humid, was indeed jammed with reporters; the podium groaned with microphones. Like Holyfield, Foreman, and Tyson, I made my entrance with an entourage: my cardiologist, Dr. Stephen Scheidt, and my AIDS physician, Dr. Henry F. Murray, of New York Hospital–Cornell Medical Center; Edgar Mandeville, a close friend of mine who is also a physician; Donald Dell; Mayor Dinkins; and Jeanne. I half expected to hear the bell sound for Round One.

When I moved to the podium to explain why I had called the conference, I started with a joke. "George Steinbrenner has asked me to manage the Yankees," I said. (In the tumultuous reign of Steinbrenner as principal owner of the Yankees baseball team, so many managers had been hired and fired that it was hard to keep count.) "But I graciously declined."

Nobody laughed, which not infrequently happens with my jokes. Then I told my story. "Rumors and half-truths have been floating about, concerning my medical condition since my heart attack on July 31, 1979," I began. "I had my first heart bypass operation six months

later on December 13, 1979, and a second in June 1983. But beginning
with my admittance to New York Hospital for brain surgery in
September 1988, some of you heard that I had tested positive for HIV,
the virus that causes AIDS. That is indeed the case."

The virus had been transmitted through a blood transfusion during
one of my open-heart surgeries, almost certainly the second in 1983.
Testing for HIV in donated blood did not begin until two years later,
in 1985. In 1988, after I underwent brain surgery, it was confirmed that
I have AIDS. After my right hand had lost all motor function, a biopsy
of brain tissue detected the presence of toxoplasmosis, which is one of
the opportunistic infections that mark the presence of AIDS. Blood
tests had proved positive for HIV.

Why hadn't I gone public in 1988?

"The answer is simple: Any admission of HIV infection at that
time would have seriously, permanently, and—my wife and I believed—unnecessarily infringed upon our family's right to privacy. Just
as I am sure that everybody in this room has some personal matter he
or she would like to keep private, so did we. There was certainly no
compelling medical or physical necessity to go public with my medical
condition. I have had it on good authority that my status was common
knowledge in the medical community, and I am truly grateful to all of
you—medical and otherwise—who knew but either didn't even ask me
or never made it public. What I actually came to feel about a year ago
was that there was a silent and generous conspiracy to assist me in
maintaining my privacy. That has meant a great deal to me and Jeanne
and Camera."

Once I started to talk about my family, I could feel my emotions
bubbling and surging to the surface, and especially so when I thought
of Camera. I tried to continue reading, but her beautiful brown face
swam before me and I felt the tears flooding my eyes, and my throat
simply would not open to let out the words. I waited and waited but
I am not sure I would ever have been able to continue. I then asked
Jeanne to step to the microphones and read the words for me. "This
has meant a great deal to me and Jeanne and Camera," she read. "She
does already know that perfect strangers come up to Daddy on the
street and say 'Hi.' Even though we've begun preparing Camera for this
news, beginning tonight, Jeanne and I must teach her how to react to

new, different, and sometimes cruel comments that have little to do with her reality."

I did not want to be hard on *USA Today*, but I had to talk about what had caused me to break my silence. The newspaper had "put me in the unenviable position of having to lie if I wanted to protect our privacy. *No one should have to make that choice.* I am sorry that I have been forced to make this revelation now." I then revealed that Jeanne and Camera were in excellent health. Both had been tested and both were HIV-negative.

What of the future for me? "I have been an activist on many issues in the past—against apartheid, for education and the athlete, the need for faster change in tennis. I will continue with those projects in progress, and will certainly get involved with the AIDS crisis." I mentioned Earvin "Magic" Johnson and said that I thought we might work together. I ended with a reflection about what was to come: "The quality of one's life changes irrevocably when something like this becomes public. Reason and rational thought are too often waived out of fear, caution, or just plain ignorance. My family and I must now learn a new set of behavioral standards to function in the everyday world, and sadly, there really was no good reason for this to have to happen now. But it has happened, and we will adjust and go forward."

For about forty-five minutes more I took questions from the reporters and others present. "How do you feel?" someone asked. "I am not sick," I assured him. "I have good days and I have bad days. The good-day, bad-day ratio is about six-to-one." I mentioned some of the drugs I am taking for AIDS. Did I plan to sue the hospital where I received the tainted blood? No, I had no intention of suing anyone. I am not litigious by nature, and a lawsuit would serve no purpose, because I blamed no one. "Do you feel forced out?" some asked. "Absolutely. If the person hadn't called the newspaper, I'd still be leading a normal life." Did I have advice for AIDS sufferers? Yes, I did. "Take care, because you never know what breakthrough lies around the corner."

THEN IT WAS over. Flanked by Jeanne and David Dinkins, I left the room. A remark I had made to Doug Smith earlier in the day came back to me as I walked away. "In a way," I had said to him about the announcement, "it's sort of akin to walking out of the confessional booth in the Catholic Church. You're supposed to come out feeling better. Certainly there's a self-imposed burden when you keep something like this to yourself. It's one of those things that cries out for revelation, just to tell someone."

I indeed felt a certain sense of relief at having made the announcement, but in no way had I been "cleansed." The analogy between my statement and the Roman Catholic confessional was not a good one. I had not committed a sin, one that could be absolved either by a news conference or a priest. The truth is that I had been made to feel guilty without having committed a sin. First there was the sense of guilt that surrounds the acquisition of a disease, and especially a disease like AIDS that is linked sensationally in the public mind to "deviant" sex and drug abuse. Then there was the guilt implied in the newspaper's determination to break the story: my guilt in having deliberately kept a secret from the people. However, I had been guilty of nothing.

Doug, who is a Roman Catholic himself, understood what I meant in making the connection but still felt badly about his role in the affair. I thought I knew why my boyhood friend felt so bad. He could not be sure that I believed that his newspaper had received the tip that I had AIDS from someone else. Perhaps *he* had taken the rumor to his editor. But I believed him. In any event, he could console himself that he had acted completely aboveboard, from the viewpoint of journalistic ethics. He had not wormed the story out of me, then published it. I went out of my way to make sure that Doug understood that I bore him no ill will, none whatsoever.

About five weeks later, Doug sent Jeanne and me a touching letter about what he called "the fiasco in New York," in which he confessed to "the disturbance in my [Doug's] soul caused by my role in the experience." Nevertheless, he believed that "this traumatic event, and my role in it, were meant to be. The Lord, as my mother used to explain when logic was illusive, sometimes works in mysterious ways."

I couldn't bring myself to blame Doug himself for anything, and I certainly didn't have him in mind when I told the news conference that someone had "ratted" on me. Still, something in his letter didn't set well with me. Although he surely hadn't intended it in his letter, he had identified the role of the press, specifically *USA Today*, with the Lord. I was pretty certain at the time that Jesus Christ or Jehovah was not on the staff of that newspaper. In his appeal to scripture I thought I saw a claim to the divine right of the press. I am a firm believer in the freedom of the press, and in the First Amendment, broadly construed. I knew more than a little about the history of press censorship in the United States from John Peter Zenger down to our time. But I was still angry every time I thought about what the press had done to me.

Was I justified in claiming that I had a right to privacy? Or was *USA Today* justified in asserting its privilege? For the record, the newspaper had acted with some deliberation. The editors had decided at about eleven o'clock on Tuesday evening, the day before my announcement, not to carry the story. The decision had involved not simply Policinski but also Peter Prichard, the editor of the paper. With some accuracy, *USA Today* could assert, and did assert, that it never broke the story. Once I had made my decision, the newspaper enjoyed only a minor scoop of sorts. At one o'clock, before my conference, it sent the story to the newspaper's international edition, which mainly reaches Europe and Asia. The story was also sent to the Gannett News Service, which supplies a chain of eighty newspapers, including *USA Today*, as well as Cable News Network (CNN). "Tennis great Arthur Ashe has AIDS," the item began, "he will announce Wednesday afternoon at a New York press conference."

No one could doubt, however, who had forced my hand. To my surprise, and my satisfaction, this aspect of my announcement generated great controversy. More than seven hundred letters reached *USA Today* on the issue of my right to privacy, and about 95 percent vehemently opposed the newspaper's position. In other newspapers, the story created less of a stir but still attracted a suprising number of letters and comments, often angrily expressed. "I didn't want to turn on the television or read a newspaper ever again," a woman in Indianapolis wrote. "I cried last night, and I'm crying today. . . . Shame on *USA Today*." "I think *USA Today* is a villain this morning," one man from Charlotte, North Carolina, wrote. From a man in Sioux City, Iowa: "It seems to me that this story would be something I'd read in the grocery store sleaze journalism department, not *USA Today*." A man in Topeka, Kansas: "Linking AIDS with a public figure is titillating but rarely newsworthy. There is no compelling reason in this case to reveal Ashe has AIDS."

Among famous tennis players, long accustomed to the ways of the press, at least two had comments. "It's like the press has given up a touch of humanity," Chris Evert told a reporter. And Billie Jean King, who certainly had been burned badly by publicity, remarked knowingly: "It's almost like your life becomes a competition between members of the media."

A few readers felt differently. If Ashe had disclosed his condition earlier, a man from Huntsville, Alabama, wrote, "he might have saved a lot of people, including Magic Johnson. Because he is such a notable individual, especially in the black community, he could have done a lot of good work for minorities, since we make up 12 percent of the population, but 29 percent of those with AIDS." And another man, from Chattanooga, Tennessee, declared that Ashe "should have come out earlier and made his announcement when he discovered it or at least sooner than he did. Maybe he felt that his privacy would be invaded. I feel at the same time that AIDS needed a spokesman." A woman in Salem, Oregon, wrote the newspaper to "completely support your story on Arthur Ashe. He was not secretive about his life-threatening heart problem and the whole thing about his particular situation is the stigma attached. That stigma is the thing that needs to be changed. . . . I thank you for running the story."

A woman in St. Louis, Missouri, probably speaking for a lot of people, testified both to the solid reputation that *USA Today* had built in the few years of its existence and to the complexity of the issue. "You are really taking a public beating for breaking the Arthur Ashe story," she observed. "Good luck, and maybe something good will come of this somehow."

As the adverse criticism rolled in to *USA Today* (with 481 telephone calls, most of them negative, and 60 canceled subscriptions by 7:00 p.m. the following day), its editor took to its pages to defend the role of the newspaper in the affair. Not to have followed up the lead, argued Prichard, would have been to help me keep my secret. "Generally," he insisted, "I think it's a mistake for journalists to keep secrets—or to protect some friends who happen to be public figures, but not others."

Citing some famous instances of the American press keeping a secret, such as Franklin Delano Roosevelt's paralysis or Woodrow Wilson's stroke, he insisted that such a "conspiracy of silence has not served the public. Ashe is not a public official, but for many people, young and old, he's probably as influential as any president." By sharing the story, "Ashe and his family are free of a great weight."

I was flattered by his assessment of my influence, and by the comparisons to Roosevelt and Wilson, if only through our various infirmities. But my family and I did not now feel ourselves free of a burden. Camera, for one, had not been aware of any weight at all, but now had to assume one. Jeanne and I may have put down one heavy weight, but we had certainly picked up another, and one far more imposing.

One good result, at our expense but worthwhile on the whole, was the spirited discussion of the rights of the press and the right to privacy that echoed in the media itself. Inevitably certain cases were brought up. These were not references as arcane as Roosevelt and Wilson but of more recent vintage, about what the press had done to certain people in the name of its vaunted rights. Some had been presidential candidates such as Gary Hart, Bill Clinton, and Jerry Brown. Hart seemed to dare the reporters to find out something untoward about him, but Clinton's accuser was paid (reportedly $100,000) and prompted to tell her story of alleged marital infidelity on national television, to some 21 million viewers, according to *The New York Times*. Again on national television, Jerry Brown was accused by two men, unidentified and disguised, of allowing drugs to be used in his home while he was governor of California, even though the accusation seemed poorly founded. Then there was the case of William Kennedy Smith, of the Kennedy family, accused of rape and tried in a court of law; and of his alleged victim, whose name was revealed by one of the three major television networks in contravention of established journalistic practice concerning the victims of rape. And Senator Brock Adams of Washington, accused in the Seattle *Times* by eight women of sexual harassment—eight women who were not identified by the newspaper.

In the days that followed my announcement, several other newspapers, journalists, and organizations joined in the debate, quite apart from the many ordinary citizens who wrote to magazines and newspapers to express their opinion. *The New York Times* reported "a wave of public criticism of news organizations that was joined by some who have normally been among the press's staunchest champions." And indeed the executive director of the reporters' Committee for the Freedom of the Press said of the position taken by *USA Today,* "My visceral reaction was that this is the kind of thing that's going to get us regulated."

Several writers who defended my position used a special term— "outed"—to describe what had been done to me. The term refers to the growing practice among militant gays of deliberately publicizing the names of well-known individuals who are homosexual but live "in the closet." The aim, as I understand it, is both to discourage hypocrisy and to increase the power of gays by showing how pervasive gay culture really is. Ellen Goodman, the respected columnist and associate editor of the Boston *Globe,* called my case "the medical equivalent of an outing." She also called Policinski's explanation "pretentious." Another syndicated columnist, DeWayne Wickham, wrote that I deserved "the same privacy considerations" routinely given to rape victims; like them, I "should not be twice victimized by being made to suffer the harsh glare of the public spotlight." Michael Olesker in the Baltimore *Sun* declared that my privacy had been violated "because we in America live in a state of constant feeding frenzy now. Gossip is our snack food. The need for empty caloric titillation never goes away, it only arrives in a different wrapping each new morning."

Anna Quindlen, a syndicated columnist for *The New York Times,* eloquently went back and forth, caught in a dilemma that was evidently heartfelt. "I am disquieted by the Arthur Ashe story," she wrote. "I can't help but feel that in the medical sense we outed him, a practice that, in the sexual sense, I deplore. That's the human being talking. The reporter understands: public figure, big news." And: "Privacy, privacy. The white light of the press and the closed doors of our homes are two of the most deeply prized aspects of our lives as Americans. It just so happens that . . . they are often in direct opposition to each other." Raymond R. Coffey, editor of the editorial page of the Chicago *Sun-Times,* conceding that his position would be counted "treason" in some quarters, supported me. "What the news media (most specifically *USA Today*) did to Arthur Ashe," he argued, "was, in my view, something for all of us to be ashamed of." To Jonathan Yardley in the Washington *Post*, the editors of *USA Today* had gone after the story "with all the fury of a cur attacking a T-bone because the story had sensational potential. That Ashe had long ago ceased to be a 'public figure' as anyone in his right mind would interpret the term was entirely beside the point; the point was that red meat was there to be eaten."

Despite all of these vigorous attacks on the approach taken by *USA Today*, however, support for its position among editors and other journalists was clearly strong. One poll of seven editors who were then visiting Washington for the annual meeting of the American Society of Newspaper Editors revealed that six of the seven would have acted as *USA Today* had done. An editorial in *The New York Times* accused me of aiming my "barbs at the wrong target." Instead of being annoyed with the person who had put out the word about my condition, or with *USA Today*, I should have aimed at "the cruel and benighted public attitudes that compelled Mr. Ashe to keep his disease secret for three years." Needless to say, I considered the *Times*'s position self-serving.

The issue of privacy is far more important than one would think. The U.S. Constitution does not mention privacy, but the U.S. Supreme Court recognizes privacy as guaranteed by the Constitution. A long essay in the *Times*, prompted specifically by what had happened to me, pointed out that in a 1965 decision, *Griswold* v. *Connecticut*, the Supreme Court had validated the idea of a constitutional basis to the right to privacy. In that case, the state of Connecticut had tried to bar the sale of contraceptives; but the Supreme Court ruled that the law violated the privacy of married couples. *Roe* v. *Wade*, allowing abortion, has been one of the most controversial decisions of the Supreme Court in my lifetime, and few people know that the court based its decision on the concept of the right to privacy. Laws against abortion, according to the court, violate the right to privacy of women who happen to be pregnant.

Nevertheless, the court had definitely been on the permissive side in supporting the right of journalists to report on events in the lives of public figures. One of the most dubious decisions, I think, was that involving the young man who sued the San Francisco *Chronicle* after it published a news article referring to his having helped stop someone from trying to kill Gerald Ford, then president of the United States.

Instead of enjoying his status as a hero, the man had to cope with his inadvertent "outing" by the *Chronicle*. The paper reported that he was gay, and that was how his family found out he was gay. The man sued the newspaper, and lost. He had become a public figure when he tried to save the life of the president; therefore, he was fair game for the press.

The press, in effect, has to decide what is fair and what is not. It has to discipline itself. Obviously I thought that one important newspaper had not done so in my case. I am, when I wear one of my hats, a member of the press as a television commentator on tennis and as an irregular columnist in the Washington *Post*. I see both sides of the issue, but I do not believe that the line between the two sides is nearly as fuzzy as some people suggest. In a column in the *Post* right after my "outing," I tried to express myself on this point. "I know there are trade-offs in life," I wrote. "I understand that the press has a watchdog role in the maintenance of our freedoms and to expose corruption. But the process whereby news organizations make distinctions seems more art than science. I wasn't then, and am not now, comfortable with being sacrificed for the sake of the 'public's right to know.' Doctors, lawyers and journalists have gone to jail rather than expose a client or source without his or her permission. Perhaps sportswriters' organizations should take another look at the currently accepted rationale for making these decisions."

THE DAY AFTER my press conference, I made sure to keep the two appointments on my calendar because I was anxious to see how people would respond to me after the announcement. I was thinking not only about the people I knew personally, even intimately, but also about waiters and bartenders, doormen and taxi drivers. I knew all the myths and fears about AIDS. I also understood that if I hadn't been educated in the harshest possible way—by contracting the disease and living with it—I would probably share some of those myths and fears. I knew that I couldn't spread the disease by coughing or breathing or using plates and cups in a restaurant, but I knew that in some places my plates and cups would receive special attention, perhaps some extra soap and hot water. Perhaps they would be smashed and thrown away.

That morning, I accompanied Donald M. Stewart, head of the College Board testing service, on a visit to the offices of the New York Community Trust. We were seeking a grant of $5,000 to support the publication of a handbook aimed at student-athletes. The appointment went well; we got the money. And in the evening, I went in black tie to a gala dinner to celebrate the eightieth birthday of a man I had known for thirty years and regarded as one of my key mentors in New York City, Joseph Cullman III, a former chairman of Philip Morris. At the event, which took place at the Museum of Natural History in Manhattan, I felt anxiety rising as our taxi drew up to the curb. How would the other guests respond to me? The first person I saw was an old friend, John Reese. An investment banker now, in his youth John had been an up-and-coming star with me in junior tennis. He saw me, and hurried over. There was no mistaking the warmth of his greeting, his genuine concern but also his understanding of my predicament. We walked inside together and I had a fine time at the celebration.

Did I feel a sense of shame, however subdued, about having AIDS, although I was guilty of nothing in contracting it? Very little. I could not shake off completely that irrational sense of guilt, but I did my best to keep it in check, to recognize that it was based on nothing substantial.

I was glad, in this context, that I had not concealed my condition from certain people. I had reminded myself from the outset that I had an obligation to tell anyone who might be materially hurt by the news when it came out. I have been both proud of my commercial connections and grateful to the people who had asked me to represent them or work for them in some other way. Several of them had taken a chance on me when they knew full well, from the most basic market research in the early 1970s, that having an African American as a spokesman or an officer might cost them business.

Among these organizations, the most important were the Aetna Life and Casualty Company, where I was a member of the board of directors; Head USA, the sports-equipment manufacturer that had given me my first important commercial endorsement, a tennis racquet with my very own autograph on it; the Doral Resort and Country Club in Florida, where I had directed the tennis program; Le Coq Sportif, the sports-clothing manufacturer; Home Box Office (HBO), the cable-television network for which I worked as an analyst at Wimbledon; and ABC Sports, for which I also served as a commentator.

Not one of these companies had dropped me after I quietly revealed to their most important executives that I had AIDS. Now those executives had to deal with the response of the public. I would have to give them a chance to put some distance between their companies and me because I now carried the most abominable and intimidating medical virus of our age. In business, image is everything. And one would have to go back to leprosy, or the plague, to find a disease so full of terrifying implications as AIDS carries. AIDS was a scientific mystery that defied our vaunted claims for science, and also a religious or spiritual riddle—at least to those who insisted on thinking of it as possibly a punishment from God for our evil on earth, as more than one person had publicly suggested.

As far as I am concerned, these companies did not owe me anything. They had products and services to sell, and employees and stockholders and their families who were dependent on them. If I hurt their business, I believe, they would be obliged to revise our arrangements. I would not have waved my contract in anyone's face, or hidden behind an ingenious lawyer. I understand business and free enterprise. My university degree is in the field of business administration, and I have profited from business and the free-enterprise system.

I waited for the phone calls and the signs that my services were no longer needed. None came.

I READ SOMEWHERE that in the two weeks following his announcement that he was HIV-positive, Earvin "Magic" Johnson received thousands of pieces of mail, and that months later he was still receiving hundreds of letters a week. Well, I received nothing approaching that volume of correspondence following my press conference, but I certainly had a mountain of reading and writing to do in its aftermath. And every time I appeared on one of the few television interview shows I agreed to do, such as with Barbara Walters or Larry King, there was another surge of correspondence. I heard from the famous and the completely unknown, people I knew and people I had never met.

The most moving letters, without a doubt, came from people who had lived through an AIDS illness, either their own or that of a loved one. Often the loved one was now dead. These writers, above all, understood why I had made such a fuss about the issue of privacy. Many probably understood better than I did, because they were more vulnerable than I am, and had suffered more. One Manhattan woman wrote to tell me about her father, who had received HIV-tainted blood, as I had, through a blood transfusion following heart surgery. Without knowing it, he had passed the infection on to her mother. For some years, they had kept their illness a secret from their daughter. After they could keep the secret from her no longer, she in turn had worked to keep their secret from other family members and friends, and from the world. Although both parents were now dead, she wrote, "I share your anger at that anonymous person who violated either your trust or their professional ethics."

Another woman, writing from Toronto, told of her husband's similar infection. He, like me, had received a transfusion during his second bypass operation. One summer five years later, he was plagued by unaccountable bouts of fatigue and flulike symptoms. In the winter came a cough that would not go away. The spring brought pneumonia, and death. Virtually to the end, his illness seemed inexplicable. Only three days before his death was he finally tested for AIDS. The test was positive.

A grandmother in New England, HIV-positive after a transfusion, shared with me her terror that the company she worked for would dismiss her if they found out; she was awaiting the passage of a law that might protect her. From Idaho, a mother told me about her middle-aged son, who had tried to keep his AIDS condition a secret even from her: "My son kept it to himself for six months before he told me and I'll never forget that day as we cried together." His ordeal included dementia, forced incarceration in a state asylum, and ostracism by relatives and friends. But mother and son had spent his last "four difficult months" together. "I'm so thankful to have had those days with him."

I heard from people whom I had not thought of in years, and some of them had been touched by their own tragedy. A woman I remembered as a stunningly beautiful UCLA coed, as we called them in those days, told me about her younger brother, who had been diagnosed with full-blown AIDS about five years before. "He is gay," she reported, "and I saw how he lost so much self-esteem and hope" because of intolerance. "No one can speak as eloquently as you and Magic to allow the stigma to disperse regarding this situation." Another letter illustrated the power of the stigma. Signed simply, "Sorry I can't identify myself, but you understand," it came from a man who had been diagnosed with HIV three years ago. "I'm the father of six children and many grandchildren. I'm not into needles or the gay life. Don't know where it came from (really)."

As for my daughter, Camera, more than one writer underscored my fears about what she might have to undergo from insensitive people in the future. A woman whose son had died of AIDS about a year before, following the death of his wife, was now bringing up their young son: "I struggle with how this little child is going to deal with the insults and rejections that people will inflict on him when they find out that his father died from AIDS."

Perhaps the most unusual letter I received from someone with an ailing relative came from a woman in Florida who offered an anguished apology to me and others who had been infected from blood transfusions. As she told it, her mother had become HIV-positive two years before, following a personal history of drug addiction. "I realize that your situation, and [that of] many others who have contracted the virus, has been caused by people like my mother who have lived their lives with such disregard for the sanctity of human life."

Needless to say, I am grateful to all those who have taken the trouble to write. Most of the letters left me humbled. Among those famous people who wrote immediately after my announcement was Nelson Mandela, who is one of my genuine heroes, and whom I had met both in South Africa and here at home. He sent a long letter on the stationery of the African National Congress of South Africa. "I can never forget my own joy at meeting you," he wrote. "I hope you feel my embrace across the continents and that it serves to let you know that we love you and wish you well." Elizabeth Taylor, whose work on behalf of AIDS sufferers is to her eternal credit, sent a bouquet of tulips, and a lovely note: "My thoughts, prayers and admiration are with you and your family."

(I had never met her. Some months later, I read a story about her AIDS work in *Vanity Fair* and was startled to see my name. She had been annoyed when a colleague in their AIDS foundation, American Foundation for AIDS Research [AmFAR], contacted Magic Johnson after his announcement, to try to get him to join their effort. "I don't want to use him," she said about Magic. "It's the same with Arthur Ashe." She called my press treatment "appalling. The way [somebody] chooses to die is their own goddamn business.")

In addition to the telephone call from President Bush, I also received kind letters from former presidents Richard Nixon and Gerald Ford. An avid sportsman, Nixon had credited a meeting with me years before with stirring his interest in tennis. Given his wars with the press, I was not surprised that he backed my position against *USA Today:* "Your privacy should have been respected." Ford evidently concurred: "Betty and I congratulate you on your superb handling of a very difficult and personal matter. You and Mrs. Ashe have our highest admiration and affection."

Much more surprising to me was a letter from Supreme Court Justice Clarence Thomas, whose own television ordeal I had watched with dread fascination, and without being convinced of his guilt or, indeed, his innocence. "You have been an inspiration to me for most of my life," he wrote. "I admire & respect you; I will continue to remember you & your family in my prayers."

A woman who had cleaned my hotel room during a tournament in Tucson, Arizona, fifteen years before in 1975, wrote to Frank Deford after reading a story of his about me in *Newsweek.* She praised my "kindness, gentleness, and serenity." I was glad to get her letter.

Many tennis players called or sent me cards, notes, and letters, including Charlie Pasarell, one of my best friends from tennis and someone I've known since I was fourteen, and Pam Shriver, who generously sent a contribution in my name to the United Negro College Fund. I also heard from Tracy Austin, Brian Gottfried, Jeff Borowiak, Tom Okker (who had watched my news conference on CNN in Holland), and Rod Laver. I was a little surprised at the intensity of Laver's reaction. Rod and his wife, Mary, wrote about their "concern, emptiness, and yes, also anger" at the news. Since my tennis victories over him had been rare—two wins in twenty-one matches—I was pleased to be saluted by "the Rocket" now as a "great champion, both on & off the court."

A telegram came from the soccer star Pelé—Edson Arantes do Nascimento; two messages from the boxer Sugar Ray Leonard; a touching note from Lynn Swann, who had been a star wide receiver with the Pittsburgh Steelers football team and who always impressed me as being so much more than a professional athlete. John Thompson, the renowned basketball coach at Georgetown University, with whom I had sparred at one point on the telephone over the question of academic requirements for black student athletes, expressed the "good feeling that you'll be around to irritate me for a long time; this is my very sincere prayer." I received a card from the tennis team at the University of Chicago, and from Terry Donahue, the football coach, and various athletes at UCLA, my alma mater. I was pleased to hear from students at various elementary schools, including some I had visited, as I often do.

Many of these letters brought back powerful memories or associations, as did one from the outstanding golfer Gary Player. We had had our differences about his country, South Africa, where I had been banned twice, and about apartheid, which he could never bring himself to attack and which I found impossible for anyone to defend. Telling me about an educational foundation he had started in South Africa, he sent his sympathy and kind wishes: "Whilst we have perhaps at times had different views on South Africa in the past, I think we have both shared a common interest in people and mankind and have tried to contribute to society as a whole."

Race and politics crossing medicine and disease. One card I received called me "an inspiration to many people during your career. Our thoughts and prayers are with you and your family as you face this new challenge." It was signed: "A white family in Mississippi."

Believe me, these letters helped. I think I know better than to accept that all or even most of the praise heaped on me is deserved; but I felt good to know that so many people thought so highly of me. On the other hand, I know that sympathy clouds the judgment, especially when the object of sympathy has an illness we think of as terminal. Or an illness that *is* terminal. I began to have a sense in reading many of the letters and the essays on me in newspapers and magazines that I was reading my obituary, but I could not say, as Mark Twain did, that the reports of my death are greatly exaggerated. Exaggerated, but not greatly.

The sportswriter S. L. Price, in the Knight-Ridder newspapers, showed me that I was not imagining the funereal undertone. Price wrote:

> . . . People talk about beating cancer. No one talks about beating AIDS. These victims talk about living a full life, about the new treatments. They hope for a cure. But everyone else—even the wives and the parents and the good, close friends who want to believe—they cannot help but to begin placing them gently into the past.
>
> It began for Arthur Ashe on Wednesday. Testimonials. Tributes. Words on a tombstone. He was a great champion. He battled apartheid, he spoke eloquently on black issues, he was a fine man. All in the past tense. He *was*.

One Sunday evening that fall, I was reading to Camera when she was in bed, as I do every night when I can, and now she was drifting off peacefully to sleep. Then she opened her eyes, looked directly at me, and asked: "Daddy, how did you get AIDS?"

I shuddered. I hadn't expected the question at all, certainly not now, not dredged up, as it were, from her subconscious, where it obviously had been stirring awhile. In the wake of my public announcement—in fact, that very evening in April—Jeanne and I had tried to talk to Camera about my illness. As I said, we did not want her to find out about it through the taunts of a classmate or through the blunderings of some well-meaning adult.

Now and then she had asked Jeanne some casual questions about my medicine and my illness. But this was her first expression of arguably the most intimate question anyone could ask me about the illness.

"Well," I told her. "It was like this. I was in the hospital. I had to have an operation. During an operation, you can lose a lot of blood. And after the operation, to feel better, I got a blood transfusion to replace some of the blood I had lost. I was given blood that somebody had given to the hospital for people like me. The blood turned out to be bad."

"And the person had AIDS?"

"Yes."

Camera said nothing for a moment. Then she spoke again.

"Are you sure?"

"Yes, Camera. I'm sure. That's how I got it."

Her eyes remained open for a moment or two, and then she faded to sleep.

CHAPTER TWO

Middle Passage

ON JULY 25, 1979, in the picturesque Austrian hilltown of Kitz-bühel, I played the last tennis match of my professional career, and also one of the last tennis matches of my life. At the time, I had no idea that it would be so important. I lost, in only the second round of the tournament, to a virtually unknown French player named Christophe Freyss. Certainly I had recognized for some time that my career was winding down. The previous month, I had been ignominiously de-feated in the first round at Wimbledon by Chris Kachel, another player of whom nobody but his family, his friends, and a few local fans had ever heard. And this early Wimbledon exit repeated what had hap-pened to me there the previous year. The end was clearly in sight. Nevertheless, I saw no reason why I couldn't continue to play profes-sionally, with mixed success to be sure, for at least two or three more years.

Less than a week after losing to Freyss, I was in bed in New York, asleep before midnight, when I was jolted awake by the most intense chest pain I had ever suffered. After about two minutes, the pain subsided. Telling myself that I was suffering from nothing more than a severe case of indigestion, I tried to go back to sleep. I was almost there when the pain returned even more intensely than before. Breath-ing hard, I sat up in bed. I could not remember an attack of indigestion so acute. Again, the pain subsided; again I relaxed; and again, after about fifteen minutes, I was jolted by an excruciating pressure in my chest. Finally the pain ebbed and I returned to sleep.

The next day, July 31, I was conducting a tennis clinic just across the East River from Manhattan when the pain struck again. This time, it was far more intense and gave no sign of abating. A physician, Dr. Lee Wallace, who happened to be playing on a court nearby, asked me a few urgent questions. Then he insisted on escorting me personally to New York Hospital. Since then, I have come to know that institution well.

"I want Mr. Ashe admitted as a possible heart attack patient," he informed a resident physician.

This was my first indication that the pain I was suffering was the result of a heart attack. At New York Hospital, I spent two days in the intensive-care unit and most of the following eight days in the coronary-care section.

When I was released, I still hoped to resume my professional career. I missed the travel to foreign lands, the camaraderie of the players, the excitement of the matches themselves, and the prize money. In 1968, as an amateur, I had received exactly $280 in expense money after winning my country's most prestigious tournament, the first United States Open. Eleven years later, the stakes were much higher, and we were all professionals now. Most of all, though, I missed the camaraderie and the competition. In spite of my heart problem, and although my game was not what it once was, I still hoped to serve and volley a few more times against the mightiest names in professional tennis—Borg and Nastase, Vilas and Newcombe, McEnroe and Connors.

"Sorry, Arthur. Unless you have an operation, you can forget about playing tennis again. Certainly not professional tennis."

Two physicians, Dr. Mike Collins and Dr. Virginia Bouchard Smith, had scrutinized the results of a catheter examination of my arteries and heart and had laid down the law. Unless I underwent surgery, I could probably no longer think about playing tennis at the professional level; perhaps I would not be able to play any tennis at all.

I had enjoyed a wonderful career and didn't want it to end. I had never been the most dominant player the game had ever seen, or the most skilled. For example, my record against Rod Laver, who some experts call the greatest tennis player ever, is, as I have already said, just about all in Laver's favor. But I had certainly had my moments of triumph. I had been top ranked in the world once in my career and

co-holder of the number-one position at another time. I had won three
of the four Grand Slam tournaments that constitute the pillars of
international professional tennis: the United States Open, the Australian Open, and Wimbledon. I had shared the doubles crown in the
fourth Grand Slam event, the French Open, and also won, with Tony
Roche of Australia, the Australian Open doubles crown. In the decade since 1968—the start of the open era of professional tennis—I
had played steadily and won thirty-three events. That is quite a good
record.

Perhaps I was even more pleased by the way I had played than by
my results in terms of wins and losses, or even in terms of prize money.
I had done nothing, through scandal or bad behavior, to bring the game
into disrepute. And I was also proud that fans and other players had
found my game adventurous. As a junior player I had been a "pusher,"
mainly keeping the ball in play from the back of the court. Then, in
my senior year in high school, in St. Louis, Missouri, I had turned
myself into a serve-and-volley player. I became adventurous, sometimes
even reckless.

I liked being reckless, as long as I was reckless only on the tennis
court, and as long as I won. Fans deserve to see a player with flair,
someone for whom tennis is an art as well as a craft. Because I became
bored fairly easily I would try the difficult shot, or sometimes even the
impossible shot, just for the hell of it. I was known for being a winning
but frequently erratic player—or "liberal," as the proudly conservative
Clark Graebner once termed it in a genteel disparagement of my
approach. I admit that I was capable of following flights of exhilarating
tennis with bonehead misses. From time to time, my mind certainly
wandered on the court. On the whole, however, I was entertaining, and
I liked that.

Because I did not want my career to end in 1979, on December 13
of that year I underwent a quadruple coronary bypass operation. With
long, skillful incisions, my surgeon, Dr. John Hutchinson, removed
veins from my legs and implanted them in my chest to take over the
functions of my clogged arteries. He pronounced the operation a
success. If he could not assure me that I would be playing tennis
professionally again, he nevertheless gave me hope that my life might
be pretty close to normal.

Then, on March 9, 1980, I discovered that my life would never again be perfectly normal. That afternoon, in Cairo, during a long anticipated visit, I left my hotel near the pyramids for what I hoped would be a pleasant run. Three months had passed since I had undergone open-heart surgery. As far as I was concerned, I was completely recovered and only weeks away from a return to professional tennis. I was loping along gently, easing into the main phase of my run, when the angina struck. It hit me relatively softly, but hard enough to stop me dead in my tracks. I felt the world come to a halt. I walked slowly back to the hotel.

"Back already, Arthur?" Jeanne asked, half awake from a nap. "What happened?" She was cool as could be, but I could tell she knew something was wrong.

"Just a touch of angina. I thought I shouldn't go on with the run."

"Let's call Doug." Douglas Stein, a physician and one of our closest friends, had accompanied us on the trip.

When Doug came, he took my pulse and listened to my heart. Then he asked me to try some exercises, jumping jacks. As soon as I started, the angina returned. He checked my pulse again, and listened to my heart.

"You were right to stop running," Doug said. "Your heart wants no part of it."

"Should I be getting back to New York?"

"I think that's a good idea, Arthur."

"I'm sorry."

"There's nothing to be sorry about," Doug responded. "If your heart is acting up, you should definitely be close to your cardiologist and your surgeon. At the very least, you should be close to top-class medical facilities, where you would be recognized and taken care of at once. There are fine doctors here in Cairo, but we really don't know anyone. I don't think this is an emergency, but there is no point in taking chances."

As we flew out of Cairo, I knew one thing for sure: My career as a competitive tennis player was over.

We decided that instead of rushing back to New York, we would linger awhile in Europe, which I knew fairly well from years of playing tennis there. We stopped in Holland, a country I love. In Amsterdam, at my urging, we headed for the Rijksmuseum and its outstanding collection of Rembrandts.

Of the old masters, the work of Rembrandt moves me more than any other. At the Metropolitan Museum of Art, on Fifth Avenue in New York City, I have several times studied his celebrated *Aristotle Contemplating a Bust of Homer*. It evokes in me a wicked sense of the close kinship that exists between admiration and envy. In other museums in other cities around the world, taking time off from the tennis tournaments that usually had brought me there, I used to seek out his quiet, brooding self-portraits, or his wonderful group paintings, or his more modest but accomplished etchings. Having read a little about his life, I thought I saw a great deal of pain and suffering inscribed in those self-portraits. His paintings and etchings move me deeply, and yet I find them sublimely peaceful even in their dynamism. I own one of his etchings, called *The White Negress.*

Born in Leiden, Holland, the son of a prosperous miller, Rembrandt had married into a rich family and risen in the world to wealth and fame. Then, following the death of his first wife, Saskia, he had fallen slowly but irrevocably from that height. His last years found him poor and lonely. He saw his beloved mistress Hendrickje Stoffels, who was much younger, die, as well as his son Titus. But although his last years were unhappy, most critics agree that Rembrandt's art in this period was not only technically superior to that of his happier years but also much richer in spiritual and psychological insight. I wasn't surprised to read this judgment, because I have always been a firm believer in the therapeutic value of adversity. Of all people, athletes must reach an accommodation with losing, and learn to make the best of it.

Above all, I wanted to see one of his most famous works, *The Militia Company of Captain Frans Banning Cocq*, usually called *The Night Watch*. One of Rembrandt's earlier works, *The Night Watch* was also one of his most controversial. The picture fascinated me as much for the basic confusion surrounding it as for its intrinsic quality. I was always bemused by the fact that because soot and other grime had darkened Rembrandt's original work, it had been taken for something completely different. Rembrandt had painted the company of soldiers in brilliant noon sunshine, but the world had come to call the picture *The Night Watch*. I was sure there was a lesson of some kind to be learned in that.

I spent some time in front of *The Militia Company of Captain Frans Banning Cocq*, then moved on to other paintings. Unlike many of my friends who love art, such as the former tennis stars Tom Okker of the Netherlands and Wojtek Fibak of Poland, I have always been interested in biblical paintings. Here, too, Rembrandt was impressive. Of his 700 or so oil paintings, about 150 are on biblical subjects. In the Rijksmuseum, I found myself admiring several of his biblical pieces, including *The Apostle Peter Denying Christ.* Then I noticed one painting, *The Prophet Jeremiah Lamenting the Destruction of Jerusalem,* that riveted my attention. Its power over me at that particular moment had much to do with what had happened to me in Egypt. Rembrandt was speaking to my ill-fated attempt to jog near the Nile and the collapse of my dreams of returning in glory to the tennis court.

Jeanne, who is a professional photographer and—after years of classes at the Art Institute of Chicago and Cooper Union in New York—has a much keener eye for art than I do, also knows something about helping me keep my thoughts in perspective. Noticing me linger in front of the painting, she circled the room and came back to join me. She glanced at the painting, then at me.

"Oh my," she said, a chuckle in her voice. "Are we Jeremiah now?"

"Oh no, no," I replied quickly. "I just like the way the picture is laid out. Very interesting use of light and shade."

"Really, Arthur?"

"Really," I insisted, a little feebly. I didn't move. "Of course, Jeremiah does look a little depressed with this turn of events, doesn't he? I would say he is not entirely resigned to the destruction of Jerusalem. He is taking it pretty hard. In fact, I see a hint of disgust on his face."

"You know how he feels?"

"I know exactly how he feels."

"Let's go, Arthur. There are other paintings to see."

We joked about the end of my tennis career because the joking helped to take something of the sting out of the moment, which was painful. It hurt more than a little again when, later that month, in New York, I confirmed to the press that I had retired from playing the game as a professional.

In fact, I merely confirmed then what I had already admitted in a letter to twenty-two friends and associates. "A long time ago in my

Sunday school classes," I had written, "I learned that 'for every thing there is a season.' From today on, I will end my nonstop odyssey in search of the perfect serve and retire from competitive tennis. In case you were wondering about my health, I plan to live to be 100 years old."

When a reporter telephoned me about the letter, I was equally jaunty about how long I would live. "The doctors say I will live to be 100," I assured him, "but they won't put it in writing."

ONE LIFE HAD ended, and another had not yet quite begun. For some years I had known this moment would come, but now it was here in earnest. I had to negotiate the middle passage between the old and the new. Quite consciously, I gave myself a period of about three months simply to think about the past and about the future. At this crucial point in my life, I did not want to make any major mistakes.

Looking back on that period, I see only one thing clearly: that it seemed to me quite possibly a developing crisis. I felt a subtle but pervasive dissatisfaction with my life up to that point, and a deep confusion about what the rest of it would, and should, look like.

How could I be dissatisfied, even subtly, with my life to that point? I had lived, many people would say, a fantasy of a life. I had won a measure of international fame many people would die for. I had traveled all over the world, and often in grand style. Relatively speaking, I had made a great deal of money. I had won a large number of friends. How could I be dissatisfied?

But I *was* dissatisfied. Who knows what force gnaws at us, telling us that our accomplishments, no matter how sensational, are not enough, that we need to do more? Some psychologists, and some poets, talk about the rage for immortality that operates like a dynamo in the hearts and minds of men and women despite all we know about the transience of glory and the inevitability of death. I don't think I wanted to be immortal, not in any literal sense. Although I enjoy receiving honors and awards, I am not obsessed by the question of whether or not people would know my name a hundred years from now. But I did want to achieve something more than I had accomplished on the tennis court.

For one thing, I had been a professional athlete, and as far as I was concerned, few people took professional athletes seriously. At that time—perhaps it is somewhat different now—I thought that professional athletes were the modern counterpart to minstrels or *jongleurs* in the Middle Ages. All we needed, I sometimes believed, was the pointed hats and the curved shoes tipped by little balls to be complete fools. From start to finish we were entertainers, with essentially clownish roles assigned to us, for which we were handsomely paid. But the lavishness of the payment did not change the role.

I wanted to be taken seriously. In part, I had been instructed by the efforts of other athletes who had begun to tear themselves out of the clown's costume in my own time. From the social and racial remove of the almost entirely white, upper-class stratum that is the tennis world, I had looked with fascination on athletes who had stood up defiantly and protested against social injustice. Cautious about getting involved in politics and protest myself, I couldn't help but admire impetuous men such as Muhammad Ali, who struck me as menacing and purposeful even when he was amusing, a charming man but also unmistakably defiant; or the somber, black-gloved athlete-protesters Tommie Smith and John Carlos, who turned the victory stand at the Olympics in Mexico City in 1968 into a sacrificial altar, as they surrendered their victory to the greater good of downtrodden black people; or more scholarly but in some ways equally militant protesters such as Dr. Harry Edwards of the University of California at Berkeley.

Although I did not always agree with everything these men had said and done, I respected the way they had stood tall against the sky and had insisted on being heard on matters other than boxing or track and field, on weighty matters of civil rights and social responsibility and the destiny of black Americans in the modern world. For many years, even as I built my career in tennis, I had guiltily nursed the suspicion that I had not done as much as I should have in the arena of protest and politics, civil rights, and social reform. On the other hand, another part of me did not need a cue from other athletes, no matter how militant, about my duties as a citizen. I had been brought up to think that I myself was obliged to be a leader, and especially to help my fellow blacks. After years of caution, and with my tennis career over, I needed now to respond to those imperatives.

As I drew close to forty, I was aware of the special bind I was in, the dilemma that almost all professional athletes face when they come to retire. Most professional athletes leave their sport when they are in their twenties, brusquely cut by their teams or, in non-team sports, driven out by recurrent losses. The more successful, far fewer in number, leave professional sports in their thirties. A handful of stars remain into their forties. Then we all are gone, except for the "senior circuits" that have become more and more popular and viable. (I'm not sure that I could have brought myself to play any senior circuit in a serious, dedicated way.)

For most of the people in the world, retirement comes when old age or even death itself is on the horizon. Retirement then seems natural. At that point, the body and the mind are in relative harmony, both worn down from a lifetime of use. But athletes retiring at the age of thirty (or even at thirty-seven, as I was) are taking part in an unnatural rite. We may be tired of our individual sport or even injured, but our bodies are often, on the whole, still fundamentally fresh and vigorous. In no sense are we old. And with the amazing strides in scientific health care today, when men can look forward to living into their eighties, and women even longer, the retirement of a professional athlete is truly an anomaly as retirements go.

Most athletes, no matter how intelligent they may be, are almost totally unprepared to retire, as they are forced to do, while they are in their physical prime. I was at least as cautious and reflective as the next professional, but I know that I was not adequately prepared to take the step. Remove the glitter and glamour of the tennis world, I wondered, the endless stroking of the ego, the copious episodes of pampering and privilege, and where would I be? Would I end up like so many other ex-athletes I knew or have read about? Would I be haunting bars and picking up women, or loafing in my "den," swilling beer and playing videocassettes of the highlights of my career over and over to my "buddies," or to myself? That was not what I wanted.

Doubtless I wasn't the most intelligent person on the tennis tour, or the most sensitive; but my ideas and my feelings, as well as my principles, were at all times important to me. I guess I was different from most other athletes, especially in tennis, because I knew that a lot of people expected much from me, and that if I disappointed them, it would be extremely painful to them and to me. Some had sacrificed so that I might go forward with my tennis career. Most, however, I had never met. They were simply the masses—I suppose I was thinking mainly of the masses of poor black people—who idealistically expected a great deal from those, like myself, who had been given so much.

"Lord," W.E.B. Du Bois wrote, perhaps quoting someone, "make us not great but busy." I have long savored that little prayer. My father also believed in being busy, and he left his stamp on me. Not simply because he needed or wanted money, but because he believed in the therapy or balm of labor. When he was not on duty in his salaried job as a special policeman, he was working either as a caterer, cooking and waiting on tables in the homes of wealthy white families, or he was involved in the landscaping business, which meant taking care of the gardens of some of those people. No job was beneath Daddy, as long as it was honest. He took pride in being self-sufficient. And I know that my father did each job not merely to the best of his ability but very well.

He even erected a temple to his busyness: his home in Gum Spring, Virginia, some thirty miles from Richmond, where his widow, my stepmother, Lorene Kimbrough Ashe, still lives today. With my help, such as it was, Daddy built that house almost entirely out of scrap material, mainly cinder blocks and bricks, discarded when Interstate 95, which runs from Maine to Florida, cut its way in the 1960s through Richmond. Following in the wake of the destruction, Daddy picked up what he needed. To complete his house, he bought only certain material, such as tubing and wiring, when he absolutely had to. If he worshiped any deity in his temple besides his Presbyterian God, it was the god of hard work. And if Daddy took pride in what he had achieved, it was a quiet pride, the kind that is always wary of a fall, and that only more work appeases.

No matter how lofty or convoluted my ideas about hard work and fame were, I knew that my first responsibility was to support myself and my family. I did not need money desperately. Far from it. I was in no danger of becoming one of those tragic, or sometimes only pathetic, former professional athletes whose money vanishes even faster than their fame once they retire. Since the start of my professional career in 1969, I had had a financial manager, and I had made it my business to know my finances. After all, my finances were exactly that: *my business.* Unlike some of my friends in sport, I do not freeze with fright before a column of figures. In college, my major was business administration. I had intended to study architecture, but my coach and mentor, the late J. D. Morgan of UCLA, had wisely advised me that architecture courses probably left far less time for tennis than those in business administration. Later, while I was playing, I learned more, and in a practical way, about business. Now I would have to apply all that I was taught so that I could maintain the level of financial security I wanted for my family and myself. The idea of not working made no sense at all.

However, I was adamant about not giving myself over exclusively to making money. If God hadn't put me on earth mainly to stroke tennis balls, he certainly hadn't put me here to be greedy. I wanted to make a difference, however small, in the world, and I wanted to do so in a useful and honorable way. Having thought a great deal about the matter, I recognized that there were only a few ways, practically speaking, for me to begin to make a difference.

Although protesting black athletes like Muhammad Ali and John Carlos had challenged me with their example of defiance and militancy, I also had other models in mind for the kind of life I wanted to live after tennis. Frequently in the 1970s, after New York Knickerbocker basketball games at Madison Square Garden in New York, I would meet the Knicks star Bill Bradley to drink a glass of beer and talk about the game just ended and the important issues of the day; sometimes the Giants' quarterback Fran Tarkenton joined us. Born only a few days after me in 1943, Bradley had gone to Princeton, become an All-American player there, passed up professional basketball to take a Rhodes scholarship at Oxford, dutifully finished his Air Force military requirement, then returned to the United States to play for the Knicks, starting in the 1967–68 season. No longer a dominating force as he had been in college, he nevertheless played a crucial supporting role in two glorious Knicks championship seasons. But despite his fame and success, Bradley lived almost austerely. He also lived purposefully. In 1978, the year after he retired, he was elected to the U.S. Senate from New Jersey, where he has served with distinction ever since.

I hoped I could go on, as he had done, to a life of service and achievement after retirement. I also admired what Paul Robeson had done earlier in the century, after an All-American football career at Rutgers and graduation from the Columbia University Law School; Robeson had become first an acclaimed singer and actor, then grown into a charismatic political leader who in the end sacrificed his career for his beliefs. Yet another model for me was Byron "Whizzer" White, a football star who had become a respected U.S. Supreme Court justice; and Jackie Robinson, who moved on from baseball to a position of leadership both in the corporate world and in the African American community. I wanted to be like these men in what they had achieved beyond sport.

What could I myself do? First, I hoped I could continue to play a prominent role in tennis, although not as a player. Having compiled an outstanding record as a Davis Cup team member, playing for the United States, I wanted sooner or later to become involved in Davis Cup administration, preferably as captain of the squad, which was a great honor and responsibility. Second, I expected to do much more public speaking than in the past; I would try to share with diverse audiences, especially of younger people and people of color, some of my experiences and also my sense of the world. I knew that I also wanted to write, certainly about sport but also about broader social and political issues. Perhaps I could pen a newspaper column. I didn't think I could write a book—that is, that I would have the time to write one. Having collaborated with three writers on books about me, I suspected that a book would take more time than I could spare.

I might want to teach a course in a college, especially on the subject of sports and society. And I also hoped to become involved in voluntary public service. I don't like the word *philanthropy*, which often sounds condescending. But I know that it literally means "a love of humanity," and that was exactly the sentiment I hoped to express more freely in my retirement. I wanted to indulge and explore my love of humanity, and especially my concern for persons less fortunate than myself.

QUIETLY, FOR THE most part, Jeanne had been listening to me talk about my anxieties concerning this stage of my life as it approached.

She had been listening and watching me and anticipating my feelings through the many signals of distress I was obviously sending out, even if I was not fully aware of all or even most of them. In the fall of 1978, on a date that had no special significance for us, she presented me with a gift of a book, *The Seasons of a Man's Life*, by Daniel J. Levinson and four of his colleagues in the Department of Psychiatry at the Yale University School of Medicine. She inscribed it, "For my husband, with love, Jeanne." This was a timely gift.

I still have the book, and I still read it. It is where I found some of my fears and hopes written about with an almost uncanny degree of accuracy, illumination, and understanding. There I discovered, finely articulated, my basic fear: "Adults hope that life begins at forty. But the great anxiety is that it ends there."

I have kept rereading this book, and will probably do so as long as I live. Although I fastened on the chapter called "The Mid-life Transition," the book isn't simply about the so-called mid-life crisis but about all of the "seasons" of a man's life. Levinson introduced me to ideas I had hardly encountered in my readings in elementary psychology as an undergraduate at UCLA early in the 1960s.

Dr. Levinson takes issue with Freud's basic contention that the truly formative part of our lives is our early childhood and that our later life is mainly a reenactment of childhood conflicts, of which we are largely unconscious. For Levinson, a man's life is a succession of stages, and each stage involves its own conflicts and dramas. (The major underlying problem facing many athletes is that they wish to remain "forever young," which is impossible.) "Each phase in the life cycle," he writes, "has its own virtues and limitations. To realize its potential value, we must know and accept its terms and create our lives within it accordingly." Childhood is important, but so are the other stages. "No season," Dr. Levinson writes, "is better or more important than any other."

For most men, the basic long-term enterprise of life is the task of "Becoming One's Own Man." And at mid-life, we assess our success or failure in achieving this goal.

In the "Mid-life Transition," which is certainly where I was, three major tasks face a man as he prepares for the future. One task is to close out the period of early adulthood, and to assess what has been achieved in it. For an athlete, retirement dramatizes this moment. The second task is to begin to take steps toward the coming change of life, which I was doing, especially in terms of altering existing negative patterns. And the third task facing a man, according to Levinson, is "to deal with the polarities that are sources of deep divisions in his life." There are four of these polarities.

In the first polarity—Young/Old—a man must deal with the fact that he feels himself to be both young and old, and must resolve the conflicts involved. This was the most important polarity; Dr. Levinson calls it the one "most central to all developmental change." The terms *young* and *old* have little to do with actual age levels. After all, old people can and do feel young, and becoming old begins at birth itself. "Young" has to do with "growth, openness, energy, potential," and the like. "Old" has to do with "termination, fruition, stability, structure, completion, death." In this context, to have AIDS is to be instantly "old."

Complicating the Young/Old polarity for me was the fact that I had just retired from my career, which made me feel old; and the fact that I had undergone open-heart surgery, which made me feel older still. But I wanted to feel young; and in some ways I did feel myself young. "In all beginnings dwells a magic force," wrote Hermann Hesse in his poem "Stages."

In the second polarity—Destruction/Creation—a man is aware as never before of the pain and affliction that other people have wrought on him and also the pain and affliction that he has wrought on others, including his family. At this point, aware of his own mortality as never before, he also has a strong and assertive desire to become more creative. Dr. Levinson puts it this way: "In middle adulthood, a man can come to know, more than ever before, that powerful forces of destructiveness and of creativity coexist in the human soul—in my soul!—and can integrate them in new ways."

"Arthur," a friend asked me once, "do you regret having been mean to certain women in your life?"

"Mean to certain women? What are you thinking about?"

"Well, you must have been mean to some women. That's part of being a man."

"Look," I said to him, "I can't recall being mean to anybody, much less to women. Unless you and I have completely different ideas about what being mean is."

"Arthur, I don't believe you."

Still, I understand that one doesn't have to be overtly mean to other people to be destructive to them. As for creativity: Yes, I wanted to create. But what had I created thus far? How creative was winning Wimbledon?

The third polarity—Masculine/Feminine—asserts the need for a man to come to terms with the mixture of genders that exists in every human being. This polarity is not about homosexuality, latent or otherwise, but about the biological fact of gender blending that exists in each individual, and the changing social response to this blending. During my tennis career, I knew many people who thought that the feminine had no place in the masculine world. Feminine meant weak, to be dominated and despised; masculine meant strong, to dominate and despise. Gentleness was feminine. Reading and reflection might be feminine, too. I knew that, according to these reckonings, some of me is feminine. I like being gentle and reflective. I want to hurt no one. I consciously looked forward to probing this aspect of my life even as, in the 1970s and early 1980s, the words *feminist* and *feminine* took on radically new meanings.

And in the fourth polarity—Attachment/Separateness—a man must deal with the need and desire to attach himself to others and at the same time the need and desire to be apart and alone. All of my life I have been acutely aware of this polarity. I married at the age of thirty-three, and for the reason many people do so: I had found the perfect partner, and I no longer wanted to be alone. My marriage was working, but who knew what the next few years and pressures would bring?

The Seasons of a Man's Life gave me much to think about. I had always been an avid reader, but the life of a professional athlete is not always conducive to much reflection. Athletes should be smart, but thinking too much can be a handicap on the court or on the field. So, too, with feeling too much. Emotionally, one had to rise to certain moments but also be able to act on instinct in a nanosecond and to be placid, detached, coldly analytical in moments of danger. I knew a lot of physically gifted athletes whose volatile minds and emotions prevented them from achieving lasting success in sports.

Two close friends of mine, whose advice meant and still means a great deal to me, thought that my habit of reading and thinking, and the activities related to them, were bad for my career. Back in the 1970s, they were always urging me to be more single-minded. Now, however, with my playing days behind me, and the "real" world ahead, I had to try to tap into the depths of my intellectual and emotional powers, whatever they were.

Why couldn't I be satisfied with what I had done, with my tennis accolades and other rewards?

"Often a man looks forward to a key event," Levinson says about the mid-life transition, "that in his mind carries the ultimate message of his affirmation by society." The big score. I suppose that one might think that winning Wimbledon in 1975 must have been such a culminating event for me. Well, it wasn't. The victory was tremendously important, but not important enough to stop that nibbling in my soul. Perhaps that was so because I had been preparing almost all of my life to win Wimbledon, even though my career was almost finished when I finally won it, and could easily have ended without a victory there. More likely it was so because my "culminating event" could never be physical, never something athletic.

My "culminating event" had to be less personal and materialistic, more humanitarian and inclusive. As I approached forty, I could think of nothing important that I had ever achieved of that sort. I had been a professional athlete, strictly defined and recognized as such. That's what I put down on my income-tax form as my occupation: professional athlete. It was as simple as that. Perhaps I would never have that truly satisfying "culminating event." Nevertheless, I knew that, at the very least, I had to probe the roots of my dissatisfaction with what I had achieved as a tennis player. I had to examine the sources of my fixation on those "higher" goals that had so little to do with my life as I had lived it to that point.

And while I may not be the most profoundly self-aware person alive, I knew I had to start with that figure of a woman dressed in a blue corduroy bathrobe who watched me eat breakfast one morning in 1950 and then went off to die and left me alone. In search of her, I found myself going where I thought I would never set foot: into a psychiatrist's office.

"Dr. Aaron's office. May I help you?"

"Ah, yes," I replied, even though I felt distinctly like hanging up. "I would like to make an appointment to see the doctor."

"Very well. Who referred you to us?"

I gave her the name of a friend of mine, a doctor, who had suggested Dr. Aaron to me. "I live nearby," I also told her. "I walk by your office all the time."

"I see. Your name, please?"

This was my last chance to hang up.

"Arthur Ashe."

There was a distinct pause on the line. A tennis fan, I thought. "Would Wednesday at three be okay, Mr. Ashe?"

"Wednesday at three is fine."

When I was younger, I shared the suspicion of psychotherapists and psychotherapy that many people have. African Americans, in particular, seem to take a dim view of what goes on in the world of psychiatry. I had heard all the objections, including the opinion that all our problems could simply be traced back to racism. True, many of our problems can be traced back to racism; but many cannot.

In the macho world of men's tennis, too, as perhaps in every corner of the sporting world where men are involved, anyone who admitted being in psychotherapy risked being drummed out of the fraternity. You simply would not admit, under normal circumstances, that you had been to see a "shrink." Come to think of it, the prejudice goes well beyond African Americans and athletes in general. A report that a presidential or a vice-presidential candidate had undergone therapy would just about finish his chances, as happened with Senator George McGovern's first nominee for vice-president, Senator Thomas Eagleton, during the 1972 presidential race. In fact, such a report would hurt anyone running for any public office in the United States.

In spite of that nonsense, I went to consult Dr. Aaron not because I was depressed, but because I was curious about myself at a time I thought could easily become a crisis if left unexplored.

At the first session, I brought up the main topic on my mind: my mother. I wanted to know what Dr. Aaron thought had been the effects on me of my mother's death when I was just short of seven years old. I told him how I had heard my relatives, especially my aunts, say that

I had withdrawn after her death. One of my aunts even went so far as to say, "Arthur was so small and pathetic. He looked like a motherless child. It about near broke my heart." But I don't remember grieving over my mother. She died, and life moved on. My father told people how my response to the news, as he sat crying his eyes out between my brother Johnnie and me, was simple enough. "Don't cry, Daddy," I consoled him. "As long as we have each other, we'll be all right." I don't remember any of that. I only remember the last time I saw my mother, the fact that she died, and that life was going on.

Throughout my life, various people have called me cold. The idea has almost haunted me. In 1968, when I was honored with my picture on the cover of *Life* magazine, the accompanying line read, "The Icy Elegance of Arthur Ashe." I don't like being called cold, and I don't agree with it as a fair description of me. Before I was married, I would start relationships with women, then grow out of those relationships. When I broke them off, some of the women involved accused me of being cold and remote.

I would rather be seen as being aloof, which is not much better, but which I probably am sometimes. Certainly I am somewhat detached. For a long time now, I have understood that this quality of emotional distance in me, my aloofness or coldness—whatever the name I or others give to it—may very well have something to do with the early loss of my mother. I have never thought of myself as having been cheated by her death, but I am terribly, insistently, aware of an emptiness in my soul that only she could have filled.

As I considered the new beginnings I was facing, I felt the emptiness acutely. I also guessed that only my mother's return to me, which was an impossibility, could have filled the emptiness. In going to a psychiatrist, I was on a fool's errand, in a sense. I had no real hope of relief for whatever was aching in me, only for a plausible explanation.

I had never intended to be, nor did I become, a long-term patient of Dr. Aaron's. I visited him about ten times, which was enough to satisfy my curiosity. He didn't put up a fight. He didn't say that I should stay, that I had some sort of neurosis or psychosis and that we needed to work it out. He understood that I was there because of a curiosity on my part, and that I would move on with my life.

I am sure that part of my reason for giving up on psychiatry was simply that I didn't feel it necessary anymore. Was this attitude a "macho thing"? Maybe, although I have always had little time for macho posturing. A desire for self-sufficiency? Well, perhaps self-sufficiency is also a "macho thing." I suspect that if I had still been a bachelor, I would have relied far more on Dr. Aaron. As it was, I had Jeanne at my side, and on my side, and who could ask for more?

Marrying Jeanne-Marie Moutoussamy turned out to be a far wiser and more self-interested act than I had ever thought it might be. I had met her one day in New York City, at a benefit for the United Negro College Fund at the Felt Forum at Madison Square Garden in New York City. A graphic artist at NBC-TV in New York City, and a professional photographer, Jeanne was at the benefit on a press pass, to take photographs. She took several pictures of me that day. I took a mental picture of her as maybe, just maybe, what my heart desired. I said hello to her, and we chatted. That was on October 16, 1976. On February 20, 1977, we were married.

The night before, we visited Andrew Young and his wife, Jean, in their suite at the Waldorf-Astoria, where they lived. Andrew was then United States Ambassador to the United Nations. He was also an ordained minister, and he was going to marry us. He and Jean had asked us to come by so they could talk to us about marriage as a sacrament.

That night, Andrew told us about the six people who were to be married by him the next day.

"Six people?" I asked, a little puzzled. "You are marrying six people tomorrow?"

"Yes, and no," Andy replied. "You see, when you and Jeanne get married tomorrow, six people will be involved. With each of you, there are really three persons. First, there is the person you are. Next, there is the person you *think* you are. Then there is the person others think you are. This is true of all marriages, not just yours. And in every marriage, all of these six people have to get along with one another if the contract is to work."

Jeanne and I were married with me standing on crutches, a symbol of physical frailty and vulnerability, recovering from an operation ten days before to remove bone chips from my left heel. Little did Jeanne or I realize that those crutches were a portent of other maladies to come. She and I would be united in holy matrimony, but we would also be bound by a shared ordeal involving doctors and medicine, pain and suffering, and the threat of death at any time. And while we would both suffer, I would depend on Jeanne physically and emotionally far more than she would depend on me.

More irony: When we were married in 1977, it was Jeanne, not me, who seemed to be in greater physical danger. She knew at the time that heart disease was chronic in her family, most of whom lived in Chicago. It was a close-knit family, headed by her father, John Warren Moutoussamy, a quiet, strong man. In 1974, he had suffered a major heart attack. He survived the attack, but tests showed that the family shared a common predisposition to abnormally high cholesterol levels and clogged arteries. This was true of her father's sister and even more seriously true of Jeanne's brother John Warren Moutoussamy, Jr. John Jr.'s cholesterol level was ridiculously high—above 400—and you could literally see on his elbows and knees the buildup of calcium deposits that one day would affect the flow of blood to his heart and brain. He knew, and we knew, that he was living on borrowed time.

In the wake of John Moutoussamy's illness and the subsequent tests, Jeanne and her family lived on a sort of twenty-four-hour alert concerning heart attacks.

In 1978, the year after we married, her father's sister underwent an open-heart bypass operation. Her operation was successful, at least for a few years.

In July 1979, in Kitzbühel, Austria, a telephone call in the middle of the night from my stepsister Loretta Harris in Virginia brought the news that my father had just suffered a serious angina attack. Daddy was doing well and on the way to recovery, but I was put on notice. So, it should not have been a complete surprise when, days later, on July 31, back in New York, I had my own heart attack, and the following December I had a quadruple-bypass operation.

Six months or so after my quadruple-bypass operation, I watched Jeanne sink slowly, and against her will, into a tremendous letdown, a depression. It was sad to see her spirits droop, especially since she continued to do all the things that I needed to have done to help me.

Then we discovered, to our relief, that it is common for someone to become depressed in the aftermath of a spouse's serious illness—and that this usually occurred almost exactly six months after the illness. We both felt better when we discovered that it was normal.

With those events, I discovered that my own family, like Jeanne's, had a history of heart disease. I had known only that my mother had died of complications after surgery. Now, when I examined her death certificate, I saw that while it specified toxemic pregnancy as the cause of death, it also established hypertension and cardiovascular disease as the main contributing factors. She had been only twenty-seven years old when she died.

The single most devastating blow came on Friday, December 18, 1982. Jeanne and I were in Chicago on a weekend visit to her family. Her father received a telephone call while Jeanne's brother John, a lawyer in the district attorney's office in Chicago, was at a public function of some sort. John had collapsed at the dinner and was on his way to the hospital. Jeanne, her parents, and John's wife, Penelope, rushed to the hospital. I remained at home with John and Penny's two young boys, David and Jay. At the right hour, I made sure that they went to bed.

Eventually the telephone rang. It was Jeanne, and she was in tears, hurting pretty badly.

"Arthur," I remember her saying, "Johnny didn't make it." She didn't say anything else about his dying. Johnny Moutoussamy was thirty-nine years old.

At the hospital, her father had said only one thing when he heard that his first-born was dead: "Damn it!" So much grief and pain concealed behind one mild expletive.

On the phone, we decided that it would be best to let the boys sleep rather than wake them with the terrible news. Penny and Jeanne came back to the house at about two-thirty in the morning. Penny was almost overcome with shock and grief. Jeanne, too, was distraught, but striving hard to remain alert and controlled.

The next morning, I woke David, who is a deep sleeper, and told him that his father had suffered a heart attack and was dead. He took the news stoically. Not so with Jay, who had crept into his parents' bedroom, as many young children like to do. He had asked about his father. The news hit him like a blow. He rolled onto his back and kept up a piteous refrain: "I want my daddy! I want my daddy!" Looking at him, I was reminded of my father's tearful reaction to my mother's death in 1950.

Jeanne and I took the kids down to the glittering Water Tower shopping center to buy them new dress shirts and ties for their father's funeral. And I watched from a distance as the Moutoussamy family coped with this tragedy as only the immediate family must cope with a tragedy of such dimensions.

By the following year, 1983, when I had my second heart operation, a double-bypass, Jeanne was a seasoned veteran of these skirmishes between life and death. In 1988, when I had my brain operation and discovered that I had AIDS, she was a rock of stability.

So, too, when my father died of a stroke on March 19, 1989. Jeanne and I were at our Florida home, on the Gold golf course at the Doral Resort and Country Club. I was sitting on a couch in our living room, with Camera on my lap, when the phone rang. I answered it. My stepsister, Loretta, wanted to talk to Jeanne. Afterward, Jeanne hung up the telephone, then turned to me.

"Arthur, your father just died." Daddy had collapsed while at Loretta's home in the suburb of Glen Allen, outside Richmond. He had gone there for a Palm Sunday dinner. Loretta was afraid the news might affect my own heart. My heart withstood the shock but I cried and cried when I heard the news. Dominating, stern, protective, my father had loved me and taken care of me when I needed him the most.

And Jeanne was strong again when I had another heart attack late in the summer of 1992. This one came just after I had taken part in a demonstration in Washington, D.C., to protest what I considered the inhumane treatment of Haitian refugees by the federal government under President Bush. The police had arrested and handcuffed me and others, according to our plan. Maybe I had put too much strain on my heart. I had felt the attack coming on and I had even taken some of the nitroglycerin pills I carry around with me for just such an emergency. Unfortunately, I had held on to this batch of pills too long—they were useless.

As we cope with my AIDS, Jeanne has been even more remarkable in her steadfastness. In the face of impending disaster, she has been unflappable. Or almost so. One fact I can depend on: Whatever happens, Jeanne is not going to panic. She will know what to do.

If medical problems have dominated our marriage, the illnesses have bonded us in a way that good fortune could not have. But binding or not, they have also created their own tensions. In the various episodes of my illnesses, many people called to ask how I was doing. A few people, not many, asked Jeanne, "How are *you* doing? I can read in the newspapers how Arthur is doing, but what about *you?*" She is grateful for all the calls, but she remembers those few people with a special gratitude. And I do, too.

Our marriage, I think, has been a very good one—very good for me, and I think very good for Jeanne. Of course, we had some difficulty in the beginning adjusting to one another, as all couples do, even couples in an old-fashioned marriage in which the husband dominates. In the beginning, Jeanne was bothered by people who saw her as an appendage to a famous man. She detested being called Mrs. Arthur Ashe, as if she had no identity of her own and had brought nothing to our marriage. But I never intended to marry a nobody, and Jeanne was not that. She is bright, independent, a graduate of probably the finest and most competitive art school in New York, and from a good family, in addition to being beautiful.

Some of my older friends told me that she would care less and less, as time passed, about whether people called her Mrs. Arthur Ashe, and the implications of such a title, and that is exactly how it worked out. It doesn't bother her much any longer, if it bothers her at all. Her passport still identifies her as Jeanne-Marie Moutoussamy. After she published two books, *Daufuskie: A Photographic Essay*, about the inhabitants of one of the Sea Islands off South Carolina, and *Viewfinders: A History of Black Women Photographers*, she became more confident, more able to shrug off the slights of those who could not appreciate her for what she was.

In any marriage, there are smooth phases and troubled phases. Committed couples reach an understanding, a rapprochement. Successful ones develop a formula for success and stick by it. Not all the formulas are for me, or us. We have found ourselves in situations with other couples where we have said, "Oh my goodness, I could never do that! That's embarrassing!" But every couple has to find what it takes to keep them going. And I do think, as Andrew and Jean Young tried to tell us, that marriage is sacred. You treat it casually at your peril.

My love for Jeanne has grown deeper with every passing year. It has become deeper with every medical crisis. My emotional attachment to her has become tighter. So, too—at least in some cases—has my emotional dependence. I started to lean on her, to let myself depend on her. It took me a while to realize this fact, because I had taken pride for so long in being self-sufficient. But too much happened, and no sense of self-sufficiency could prevent me from realizing that, in many ways, life would be difficult without her. I think about certain situations in the past, then try to take Jeanne out of the equation, so to speak, and I wonder how I would have survived without her.

The disappointments we shared could have driven us apart. Instead, they have brought us closer together. We will be together till death do us part.

THE FACT THAT Jeanne and I had a history of heart disease in both of our families naturally made us tense and intimidated when we thought about having children. How could we justify bringing a child into the world knowing that he or she most likely would be born with a predisposition to death at an early age?

For a while, we assumed that we would not have any. That seemed the best way to proceed, no matter how much we regretted not experiencing the joys of parenthood. Around 1984, however, we decided that we wanted and needed a child. Steadily the thought became more and more important to us.

On December 21, 1986, Camera came into our lives. We pulled out a bureau drawer in a walk-in closet and that's where she slept her first night home. Like many first-time parents, we were obsessed by the possibility of sudden infant death (also called crib death) or another mysterious ailment that would take away from us the fragile little body that represented our hopes and dreams of the past few years. We kept popping up in bed and going over to the bureau drawer to make sure she was well—to make sure, I think, that she was still there.

Of course, the next morning she was alive and well. And she has been well ever since. I think if Jeanne and I prayed for anything in connection with our new baby, it was only that he or she be healthy. Whether it was a boy or a girl didn't matter. And we have been blessed with a child as robust as any parents could ever hope for. Typically, whenever the pediatrician examines Camera, he throws up his hands in mock exasperation and exclaims, "This is one healthy child!" For which we thank God.

From the first day, she altered the patterns of our lives. We knew that her coming would do so, but the extent to which she changed things was nevertheless something of a shock. In fact, our lives revolve around Camera.

We were then living in Mount Kisco. The previous year, Jeanne and I had moved there from our duplex apartment in a building on East Seventy-second Street in Manhattan. To tell the truth, Jeanne had been less interested than I in moving out of the city; in fact, she loves New York City. However, I had become tired of its pressures. I guess I began to feel my age. The sheer volume of singles' bars and trendy restaurants in my neighborhood on the Upper East Side, where I had been living for fifteen years, began to get to me.

In 1990, however, we returned to the city. In fact, we came back to an apartment only four blocks away from our old place, so I guess we liked the old neighborhood. We came back in part because of Jeanne's preferences, but perhaps the overriding reason was my health. Northern Westchester Hospital Center is an excellent facility, and being on the board certainly assured that I would get extra-special treatment; but with the twin conditions of heart disease and AIDS, I felt more comfortable at New York Hospital.

I have watched and am watching Camera grow. With all my own physical problems, her positive robustness has been a godsend to me, a daily reaffirmation of the power of life. Like all children, she has her naughty side. For example, I am amazed to see how easily a lovely, sweet child can turn unashamedly vindictive. But that is life. I marvel at the way she has no interest in being the center of attention but still enjoys being with other people.

I had no idea that I would love fatherhood as much as I do. I have an acute sense of responsibility for her—to help her, teach her, protect her, and (most of all) to love her.

In matters of discipline, I know I can't go the way of my father.

He was of the old school; his word was law, and he enforced the law with his thick police belt. You disobeyed at your peril. He was never in any way brutal to us, but I don't think I can be the same kind of father. Times have changed. I am not like my father, and Jeanne is even less so. I also watched my brother, Johnnie, and his wife, Sandra, bring up their daughter, Luchia, and I have tried to learn from them. I have also learned from my stepsister, Loretta, and her husband, David Harris, whose children, LaChandra and David, Jr., are outstanding young people.

Among the youngsters in our family, Luchia is probably the star. She will graduate with excellent grades from the North Carolina School of Science and Mathematics, which is a highly competitive institution. I saw how Johnnie and Sandra tried to expose her to enriching experiences, so that Luchia was able to pursue her love of dance and also to take part, when she wanted to, in beauty and talent competitions. I also watched carefully to see how Johnnie exerted discipline over her—very carefully. Johnnie was a career Marine officer, but when it comes to a father and his daughter, the Marine tradition often goes right out the window, apparently. Love and compassion take over. If Camera can be like Luchia, we would be very pleased. But she doesn't have to be. We are simply not going to put undue pressure on her to succeed. She loves her mommy and daddy, and we are ecstatic about her.

I do not take her or her health for granted. Children seem immortal. But I know how quickly they can be taken away. Like many well-known athletes, I have been to my share of children's hospitals, trying to cheer up the sick. Often you meet kids who are going to be well, but just as often you meet kids who you know are going to die soon. It is heartbreaking.

I have experienced some sad days in my life, but few as harrowing as the day in Westport, Connecticut, only a few years ago when I was a pallbearer at the funeral of Alex Deford, the daughter of my good friend Frank Deford. Alex died of cystic fibrosis, at the age of eight.

So I take nothing about Camera for granted. I guess by now I take nothing about anything for granted. Few things have worked out exactly as I thought they would, and my life has taken curious turns.

This is my middle passage, but because of my illnesses I have to face the fact that it is both a middle passage and probably a terminus.

I can't avoid the fact that AIDS is a terminal disease. No doubt science will one day come up with a vaccine, or even a way to reverse the effects of AIDS itself in the human body. But that will be a cure for other people, too late for me.

Meanwhile, I keep sailing on in this middle passage. I am sailing into the wind and the dark. But I am doing my best to keep my boat steady and my sails full.

CHAPTER THREE

Stars and Stripes:
A Captain in the
Davis Cup Wars

EVER SINCE ONE fateful afternoon in 1950 or 1951, tennis has been at or near the center of my life. On that day, when I was seven, I had spent the greater part of an hour quietly watching Ron Charity, the most accomplished black tennis player in Richmond, practice his serve alone on one of the tennis courts my father supervised at the eighteen-acre Brook Field playground where we lived. At some point, Charity stopped his practice. Walking over to me, he gently asked, "Would you like to learn to play?"

"Yes, I would," I replied. As casually as that, my life was transformed.

Diligently over the next year or two, Charity laid the foundation on which I built my career through the junior ranks, then as a college player and an adult amateur, then finally as a full-fledged professional. Now, thirty years later, as I retired from the circuit under strict orders from my doctors, I knew that tennis, above all, could provide the sturdiest bridge from my old life to the new. If I could no longer play the game, I could certainly teach it. In my capacity as director of tennis at the Doral Resort and Country Club in Florida, I would continue to do so. But I also knew that my richest reward would come from my continued involvement in the Davis Cup campaigns, where teams represented their country in the most distinguished international competition in tennis.

Once Charity's lessons and a love of the game had taken hold of me in Richmond, three stars shone brighter than all the others in my sky. One of them was Pancho Gonzalez, who was not only the best player in the world but also an outsider, like me, because he was a Mexican American. The second was the West Side Tennis Club in Forest Hills, New York, sacred ground to me because it was the home of our national tennis championships. The third star, at least as bright as the others, was the Davis Cup, the international competition in which one day, with luck, I might be allowed to play for my country. (The original thirteen-inch silver cup was named for Dwight F. Davis, an American who donated it in 1900 both to stimulate international competition and to promote goodwill.)

Segregation and racism had made me loathe aspects of the white South but had left me scarcely less of a patriot. In fact, to me and my family, winning a place on our national team would mark my ultimate triumph over all those people who had opposed my career in the South in the name of segregation. As a junior in Richmond, I was barred from playing on most of the public tennis courts, which were reserved for whites; and the most powerful local tennis officials had tried to kill my game by shutting me out of any competition involving whites.

But my game hadn't died, because other people had given it the chance to grow. Finally, in 1963, when I was twenty years old and a sophomore at UCLA, Bob Kelleher, then the U.S. Davis Cup captain, invited me to join the team. Even as race relations in America became increasingly stormy, and I started to feel the attraction of more militant approaches to segregation and racism, I nevertheless saw my Davis Cup appointment as the outstanding honor of my life to that point. Since no black American had ever been on the team, I was now a part of history. Despite segregation, I loved the United States. That year, I played only one Davis Cup match, a "dead rubber" match (one played after the best-of-five series has been decided), in which I defeated Orlando Bracamonte of Venezuela. And at the moment of my victory, it thrilled me beyond measure to hear the umpire announce not my name but that of my country: "Game: United States," "Set: United States," "Game, Set, and Match: United States."

Over the next fifteen years, I played thirty-two Davis Cup matches and won twenty-seven of them, more than any American in the history of the Cup to that point. I had some stirring victories, but so demanding is Davis Cup play that I remember most clearly my losses, especially two singles defeats against Ecuador in 1967. I remember them vividly because they were national as well as personal defeats, and thus hurt me more. I played my last Davis Cup match in 1978.

To my surprise, the opportunity to lead the team came sooner than I had expected, indeed, the very year I retired. Between 1980 and 1985, I served as captain of the United States team. Although other involvements marked that period of my life, my captaincy was its highlight. My captaincy also proved to be much more challenging than I had anticipated. Those five years turned out to be, on the whole, a disorganized, sometimes exhilarating, sometimes frustrating and even humiliating epic of victories and defeats, excitement and tedium, camaraderie and isolation. At a mature age, I learned a fair amount about my strengths and my weaknesses, my principles and my moods.

I also learned much about other people, including the two finest players in the world, Jimmy Connors and John McEnroe, and a generous selection of the other memorable personalities who then made up the elite of men's international tennis competition. I learned about the sharp differences between individualism and leadership, playing and coaching, the younger generation and the old guard, of which I was rapidly becoming a member. In my middle passage, nothing shoved me along so rudely into the future as my experience as a captain in the Davis Cup wars.

IN THE SUMMER of 1980, I was at the U.S. Open at the National Tennis Center at Flushing Meadows, New York, when I received word that the incoming president of the United States Tennis Association, Marvin P. Richmond, wanted to see me. When I found him, Richmond was with the outgoing president of the USTA, Joseph E. Carrico. They wasted no time.

"Tony Trabert wants out," Richmond said. "He can't take it any longer." Trabert was our current Davis Cup captain. He had been serving since 1976, and there had been no hint that he might step down soon.

"Take what?" I asked.

"The behavior of the players. McEnroe. Gerulaitis. Peter Fleming. They are driving him nuts."

"Well," I said. "I've been reading a little about all that. But I didn't think it was all *that* bad."

"You don't know the half of it," Richmond assured me. "Anyway, Trabert's out."

"Am I on your short list?" I asked.

The U.S. Davis Cup captain is chosen by the president of the USTA. The captain then chooses the team.

"No," Richmond replied, a grin on his face.

"What?"

"No, because we don't have a short list. We want you."

I felt so happy and proud I could have jumped into the air—the job meant that much to me.

"Gee," I said, "it's quite an honor, but this is rather sudden. I need to think about it. Can you give me twenty-four hours?" I was buying time from the inevitable onslaught of the press. I wanted to anticipate the questions and prepare for them, as well as talk to a few players.

I had played Davis Cup tennis under Trabert's captaincy in 1978 and knew him fairly well, so I sought him out immediately. In his prime, starting at his hometown University of Cincinnati, Trabert had been an extraordinary player. He had won the national collegiate singles title, then had gone on to compile one of the most distinguished records in American tennis. Until Michael Chang won the French Open in 1989, no American had been victorious at Roland Garros since Trabert earned the title, for the second time, in 1955. That year, he also won at Forest Hills and Wimbledon.

Trabert had played Davis Cup tennis for four years, between 1951 and 1955. Then he had turned professional, touring with Gonzalez. Once he turned professional, of course, all the major amateur tournaments and events were closed to him, including the Davis Cup. He returned to the Cup as captain of the team, and under his coaching they won fourteen matches, a better record than any of his predecessors. Trabert is a Midwesterner in the best sense of the term—solid, dependable, principled. He had collided with a generation of players who had a different and far less reverential concept of what it meant to play for the Davis Cup.

"I'm happy for you, Arthur," Trabert told me. "You would have been my first choice, too. But good luck to you with some of these guys. It's just not the way we were brought up."

I liked him for saying that. On the other hand, we really were not of the same generation. Trabert was thirteen years older than me. I considered myself to be one of the younger guys, even though my attitudes and values were more of Trabert's generation than McEnroe's.

"Well," I responded, "some of them certainly are high-spirited."

"High-spirited? I can take high-spirited. But what's been going on is really offensive. I find too much of the behavior distasteful. It's just not fun anymore, Arthur."

Trabert was progressive and fair, I knew, but he also had the deserved reputation of being a law-and-order man. I myself certainly believed in law and order, if the laws were just; but I thought I could sympathize more readily with the younger players, to whom I was closer in age and with whom I had played. Vitas Gerulaitis, for example, was a good friend. The previous summer, in 1979, Jeanne and I had rented a car with him for a week and driven from Munich to Kitzbühel. I had played against McEnroe twice in the 1979 Masters tournament at Madison Square Garden in New York and admired the sheer genius of his play. "I'm a little closer in age to the players," I told *Tennis* magazine, "so I'm hoping that my brand of friendly persuasion will work." With my fingers crossed, I sincerely believed so.

In my day as a player, and for a long time after, Davis Cup play was the most exciting, the most demanding competition in the world of tennis. It remains probably the most challenging competition for the players involved. Almost every player would readily admit that playing for his country in the Davis Cup is much more nerve-wracking than competing for himself in a Grand Slam final, including Wimbledon. "It takes at least a week to prepare for the thing," Boris Becker once said about a typical Cup series or "tie," as it is called, "another week to play it, and a week to recover."

In Cup play, the captain's role can be crucial, especially as it has evolved in the United States. In some other countries, a committee chooses the players. The American captain selects the squad of players, and then sets the tone for the entire effort. The strong sense of responsibility I brought to Davis Cup play was keenly supported by my first captain, Bob Kelleher, and indeed by all the others I played under—George MacCall, Donald Dell, Edward Turville, Dennis Ralston, and Trabert. Kelleher, who went on to become a federal judge in Los Angeles, constantly emphasized the lofty ideals inherent in the Davis Cup that I had and still have. In fact, Kelleher seldom passed up a chance to let his players understand that no matter what the event—a Davis Cup match, a Grand Slam event, or a city tournament in the south of France—as team members we represented the United States of America. Therefore, we had an obligation to act accordingly. We not only had to try to win, but we had to try to win with grace. We could not besmirch our country's honor. My father had brought me up to think exactly like that, and I would not have dreamed of behaving any other way—not in any tournament, but above all not in the Davis Cup, where I was representing all of America.

In 1980, I was well aware that I was taking over the U.S. captaincy at a particularly significant time in the eighty-year history of the Cup, with its national and international prestige waning. The best players did not care to play, and attendance had dwindled at many matches. As much as I regretted its loss of prestige, I knew that I had certainly had something to do with the evolution in tennis that had weakened the Davis Cup. I had been one of the leaders in expediting changes that had altered the face of tennis.

Tennis had needed to change, because the world had changed. When my international career began around 1963, very few players earned a living from the sport. Amateurs could not play with professionals, who were shut out from the Davis Cup and from all the major tournaments. After mounting pressure, all of that ended one day in April 1968 in Bournemouth, England, when Mark Cox played Pancho Gonzalez in the British Hard Court Championships, the first sanctioned tournament for both professionals and amateurs. The Open era of tennis began. Later that year, when I won the first United States Open and received only $280 in expense money, I was still an amateur and a gentleman player, a second lieutenant in the U.S. Army happy to be able to make the payments on my beloved Ford Mustang. Tom Okker lost to me in the final, and took home $14,000. Tom was a gentleman, too; but he was also a professional who could accept prize money.

Between 1968 and 1981, professional tennis exploded in popularity. As a leader of the Association of Tennis Professionals (ATP), the players' union founded in 1972 (I was president in 1974–75), I saw the fireworks intimately. No one was well prepared for the transition from the closed amateur (or "shamateur," as some called it) to the open era—not the International Lawn Tennis Federation (ILTF), as it was then called, nor the Big Four (the governing bodies of the American, French, Australian, and British championships). Fearful that they would lose control of the game and the players, the ILTF (later shortened to ITF) and the Big Four pursued a reactionary strategy, impeding us at almost every turn. In my judgment, they resisted change in defense of privilege and a stuffy conception of the traditional. In the end, they lost control.

If the governing bodies were not ready, neither were most of the players. For many of us, the deluge of money led to confusion and an unholy scrambling after dollars. Certain values and standards that had bonded players in my earlier years as a professional—certain codes of honor and a spirit of cooperation and camaraderie—disappeared. In some ways, the youngest players arrived in a world in which the very concept of values and standards was unknown or quaint and obsolete, like wooden racquets or the white tennis balls on which Wimbledon insisted long after the superiority of color had been demonstrated.

I wonder how much we, the leaders of the players during this transition, contributed to the fall. I can't forget, for example, in light of my concern for the Davis Cup, that one of the main blows struck by the ATP in the name of freedom for players was at the expense of the Davis Cup. In 1973, we boycotted Wimbledon after Nikki Pilic of Yugoslavia was barred from taking part in the tournament by his country because he refused to play in a particular Davis Cup match. The ILTF, reactionary to the core at the time, backed the Yugoslavian Tennis Federation's banning of Pilic. Our view in the ATP was that a tennis player had the right to play or not to play in the Davis Cup. The ILTF and Wimbledon would not budge from their position of supporting the suspension, and the British courts refused to intervene. We carried out the boycott.

Aided by private promoters such as Lamar Hunt and power brokers such as Donald Dell and Jack Kramer, we prospered. The number of tournaments increased to such an extent that it was difficult to keep track of them. The prize money grew amazingly. (Some people would say obscenely; I wouldn't. Although I missed out on most of the huge purses of later years, I have never heard of any prize money in tennis that I consider excessive, certainly not compared to what individuals make in other sports and activities, such as rock music.)

Meanwhile, the top players were expected to play Davis Cup for expense money only. Increasingly, they found reasons to be elsewhere or flatly refused to play. At last, starting in 1981, the Davis Cup leadership decided to award prize money. A giant Japanese electronics firm, Nippon Electric Company (NEC), put up one million dollars to sponsor the competition in 1981. This piece of news, striking in itself, was followed by the announcement that NEC intended to give $2.5 million dollars to the Davis Cup in 1983. The winning team would collect $200,000, plus its usual share of the gate receipts. The U.S. committee announced that after meeting our expenses, we would distribute most of the remaining money to the players.

The ancient unwieldiness of the Cup format was also a problem. Up until 1972, the defending champion did not play until the other nations had fought among themselves for the honor of meeting the previous winner. Then the challenger met the defending champion in the final, called the Challenge Round.

Reaching the Challenge Round could take the greater part of a year of sometimes rough campaigning. Matches were normally scheduled without any regard for the players' plans. Many of the ties were totally uncompetitive (resulting in 5–0 scores) and unprofitable for the more powerful nation involved; yet they had to be played. And after all that effort, the final result was actually quite predictable. From the first match in 1900 until 1973, only four nations had ever won the Cup: the U.S., Britain, France, and Australia. Between 1937 and 1973, only the U.S. and Australia had won it. Under the venerable captain Harry Hopman, the Australians had played in the finals every year from 1950 to 1968. Fortunately for the rest of us, Hopman retired that year. Since

1974, there has been greater diversity among the winners, with the Cup going to South Africa, Sweden, Italy, and Czechoslovakia, as well as to the Aussies and to us.

In 1980, the system was overhauled. When I assumed our captaincy, under the new rules only sixteen countries would play for the Cup—the top four nations in each of four international zones formed for the competition. The following year, twelve of the sixteen spots would be taken by the eight first-round winners from 1981 and the four winners of a relegation match between the eight first-round losers from 1981. The remaining four spots would be taken by 1982's four zonal winners. Now the winning country would have to play only four ties to claim the Cup. And every effort would be made to schedule matches at sensible times, to avoid any conflicts with lucrative tournaments elsewhere. The main pieces were now clearly in place for a revival of the Davis Cup.

Despite Trabert's solid record, the United States effort in the Cup also needed revitalizing. Between 1968 and 1972, the U.S. had won the cup five straight times. Since then, we had lost to Australia, Colombia, Mexico (twice), and Argentina. Between 1976 and 1981, the U.S. had won the Cup only twice, most recently in 1979. In 1980, the U.S. had lost to Argentina in Buenos Aires, a defeat that hastened Trabert's departure. We needed a win in 1981.

MY INITIAL TASK as captain was to select a squad to play the first match, against Mexico in Carlsbad, California. I was determined to field the strongest team possible. I needed two singles players and a pair of doubles players. Everyone knew that the two best singles players in the United States were John McEnroe and Jimmy Connors. Whatever trouble Trabert had experienced with the fiery McEnroe, I fully expected McEnroe to be the mainstay of the new team. Connors was a more difficult proposition. McEnroe had committed himself from the start of his career to the Davis Cup concept; Connors had not. He had played in two Davis Cup matches in 1976 but had stayed off the team since then. I soon discovered that he would not be available against Mexico. To play the four singles matches, I named McEnroe and another left-hander (and at that time the possessor of perhaps the fastest serve in professional tennis), Roscoe Tanner. To play the doubles match, I selected Stan Smith and Bob Lutz, who had compiled a Davis Cup record of fourteen victories and only one defeat. When Smith developed arm trouble, I named another veteran duo, Marty Riessen and Sherwood Stewart, to play instead.

As our squad assembled in Carlsbad, I began to see that the job was more challenging than I had imagined. I had to instruct the players but also keep them happy, respond to their questions and requests, supervise practices, and be ready to make instant decisions during the matches. I soon discovered that even players who believed wholeheartedly in the team concept had egos that sometimes required the balm of special favors. The squad was a collection of individuals, each of whom was something of a star in his own right. To emphasize the team concept, I never spoke about "my" team, but always about "our" team and what "we" hoped to accomplish or had accomplished. I found myself being called upon to apply both diplomacy and psychology to keep everyone happy. I also found that I did not enjoy this aspect of my job much. Dutiful myself, I disliked being a nursemaid or a babysitter for my fellow adults.

Assuredly, McEnroe was the center of attention, as befitting the kind of tennis player the world might see only once every fifty years. Several other players also had his amazing array of shots, but no one else could consistently select each shot at precisely the right moment under intense match pressure, execute the shot, and make it look as easy as John routinely did. No one had the disguised swerve of his highly unorthodox left-handed serve, or the tantalizingly soft touch of his volleys and drop shots. No one was more genuinely self-confident, or could raise his game on demand with the smooth, swift overdrive that John commanded.

With relatively little effort, McEnroe won his first singles match. Then Roscoe Tanner lost a long, five-set match to the cat-quick veteran Raul Ramirez. Suddenly the doubles match became far more important than I had anticipated. In selecting my doubles team, I had relied on the theory that the singles players should be kept fresh to play singles; they should avoid playing doubles if at all possible. Thus I had discounted the wisdom of a little joke that had been making the rounds of the tennis world:

"Who is the best doubles team in the world?"

"McEnroe and Peter Fleming." Fleming was McEnroe's regular partner.

"Who is the second best?"

"McEnroe and anyone else."

No matter how good he was as a singles player, McEnroe was probably the best doubles player who had ever lived. His court sense was uncanny. And yet, after the withdrawal of Smith and Lutz, I had stuck to my theory and turned to Riessen and Stewart, who promptly fell in five sets to Ramirez and an unknown seventeen-year-old player, Jorge Lozano. We were down 1–2. What was supposed to be a breeze was now a cliff-hanger. Fortunately, Tanner then won his match and McEnroe easily defeated Ramirez in straight sets to win the tie for us.

We broke out the champagne to celebrate not only the win but also the fact that the tie against Mexico had been a sellout, with the stadium packed for each match. Ever since McEnroe had joined the team, Davis Cup tennis had become a popular attraction once again.

Among those present at Carlsbad was Pancho Gonzalez. At one point, he took me aside for some words of advice concerning my theory about not mixing singles and doubles play.

"Your theory is bulldust, Arthur," said Pancho. "Nothing but bulldust. You should play your best doubles players even if they are playing singles. If they are fit, they are not going to be too tired. McEnroe would not have lost that match."

Gonzalez had a point. I needed to be more practical, less dogmatic perhaps.

"And another thing, Arthur."

"Yes?"

"You've got to be more involved in what's going on on the court."

"But I *am* involved, Pancho," I said. "Sometimes my heart was thumping away out there."

"Well, we don't want your heart to thump too much, Arthur. But you have to *look* more involved, I guess."

Far more than my doubles theory, which I was ready to alter, this business of seeming to be involved would be a sore point over the coming years. I did not want to interfere with the play of international tennis stars by seeking to coach them on camera. I had been Tanner's first doubles partner when he turned professional, and he welcomed my advice; other players seemed to resent it. Tanner, whose powerful game could suddenly become erratic, needed hours of practice to groove his strokes; McEnroe found anything more than two hours of practice redundant. I had to indulge both players. At courtside, I tended to be restrained. I did not intend to leap up at every point during a match merely to assert my presence or authority. And I was determined not to join the players automatically in their protests and tantrums, as football and basketball coaches routinely do. I would back the players if I thought they had a point, but I wouldn't become enraged on demand.

Connors created a stir when he showed up in Carlsbad and offered to practice with McEnroe and Tanner. We took him up on his offer. His arrival was a significant development because of his repeated refusal to play on the Davis Cup team since 1976, when he lost a deciding fifth match to Ramirez. That defeat of the United States by Mexico had been one of the most ignominious in U.S. Davis Cup history. Soon after I accepted the captaincy, I had called Connors and asked him to join the team, and he had said that he would do so, but not against Mexico. No matter; I knew that he would be invaluable against our next opponent, Czechoslovakia, and its best player, Ivan Lendl, whom he had beaten in all seven of their matches.

Watching Jimmy and John hit at Carlsbad, I was looking at not only the two best players in American tennis but also the two most brash and stormy personalities in our tennis world. In some ways, as a tennis phenomenon, Connors was by far the more extraordinary. Unlike McEnroe, who came from the affluent community of Douglaston, Queens, in the city of New York, Connors had been born in Belleville, Illinois, a town adjacent to East St. Louis, a name now almost synonymous with urban blight. If Connors was sometimes ill-mannered, brusque, and downright truculent, he seemed to have the approval of his mother, Gloria Connors, and her own mother. The women had obviously wanted to shape a fighter, and they succeeded brilliantly.

Physically unprepossessing, even a little frail, Connors nevertheless wore an air of such arrogance that he regularly intimidated his opponents even before he had hit a ball. Then he proceeded to smack the ball with a force that bordered on vindictiveness. His two-handed backhand shot from midcourt, when he had time to play it well, was among the most damaging strokes ever seen in tennis. It rivaled the famed two-handed forehand shot of Pancho Segura, who was once a mentor to Connors. Jimmy's return of serve was unbridled aggression. His overhead smashes were awkward but decisive. And in his prime he never seemed to tire, much less become despondent on the court. His heart was always in it, and his readiness to fight never left him.

His career was also unusual. In the early 1970s, his clever manager at the time, Bill Riordan, had created an entire mini-circuit around Connors, with the immensely gifted but always mercurial Rumanian player Ilie Nastase as his comic counterpart. Then, in 1974, Connors launched his first major attack on the tennis citadels of the world. That year, he won Wimbledon, the U.S. Open, and the Australian Open.

As a player, I admired him. In other ways, Connors disturbed me. He refused to join the ATP even though he, like all the professionals, profited from its labors. He never helped in our ongoing struggles with the national and international governing bodies. He seemed to care little for what most people expected of him—or his advisers didn't care, and he was loyal to them. Above all, I never did understand his refusal to play Davis Cup tennis. There had never been an American player of his caliber who, when asked, had consistently refused. Jimmy's stand had antagonized a number of us, including not only the USTA but also players like Stan Smith and Charlie Pasarell, who had grown up with different ideas.

Actually, I considered the Davis Cup his Achilles' heel, because it raised questions about his patriotism. In 1975, choosing my words carefully, I commented that James Scott Connors was "seemingly unpatriotic" in refusing to play for his country. Connors was outraged. Just before the start of Wimbledon that year, he filed a libel suit against me, requesting damages from the court in the amount of millions of dollars. Obviously Connors considered himself to be a *very* patriotic fellow. After I defeated him in the singles final at Wimbledon that year, he quietly dropped the suit.

Now, six years later, he was ready to play under me for his country. He seemed not to have forgotten his defeat at the hands of Ramirez and Mexico. "I'd like to help the team win the Cup back," he announced. "Being on a winning Davis Cup team is important to me, because I haven't done that."

In July, at the National Tennis Center in Flushing Meadows, New York, we met Czechoslovakia, the defending champions, in the quarterfinals. Connors agreed to play the second match, against Tomas Smid. McEnroe would play the first, against Lendl, who was then ranked number four in the world. Smith and Lutz would play doubles against Lendl and Smid. A more formidable tennis team had never before represented the United States. Davis Cup tickets, once difficult to sell, suddenly became precious.

Unfortunately, unlike at Carlsbad, McEnroe arrived at Flushing Meadows with his nerves sorely frayed and his emotions drained. The previous Saturday, he had won Wimbledon by defeating Borg. However, he had behaved so execrably during various matches that the Wimbledon committee had fined him $2,250. It had also threatened, in scathing language, to levy an additional $12,500 in fines and to suspend him from playing in the future. The British press had treated him savagely. Then, in some respects the most shocking punishment came later in the week, after his victory. For the first time in the history of Wimbledon, the club refused to grant honorary membership to a reigning singles champion.

I myself would have been devastated by this highly personal form of censure and ostracism. Although John was less affected than I would have been, he was definitely not elated at the news. He was an unhappy young man, hardly ready now to launch himself against powerful Czechoslovakia, when he joined us in New York for the Davis Cup tie.

In the first match, under a fiery July sun and before 17,445 fans, the largest home crowd for a Davis Cup match in American history, McEnroe lost to Lendl. John's usually lethal serve never locked onto its target and his volleys were often tentative, while Lendl was muscular and imposing. McEnroe behaved impeccably, but good manners were not enough; they seldom are. He lost in three sets: 6–4, 14–12, 7–5. (In those days, tiebreakers were not used in Davis Cup play.) "I wanted to do well," he explained afterward, a little plaintively. "I tried. It's hard to explain. In retrospect, I wish we didn't have to play this particular week. . . . The mental thing of the last couple of weeks wore me out."

Connors, perhaps not entirely displeased that McEnroe had lost, proceeded to smash Smid 6–3, 6–1, 6–2. "Knowing John lost made me go out a little more eager, a little more up," he told *The New York Times.* Of course, he avoided any suggestion that he had wanted to show up McEnroe. "I didn't want to end the day 0–2, especially on Arthur's birthday."

The next day, Smith and Lutz crushed Lendl and Smid in straight sets. Only once in the match did an American lose a game on his serve.

On Sunday, McEnroe returned to form. He also stayed on his best behavior. The crowd, most of whom must have been his fellow New Yorkers, cheered his every point. Intimidated before the first ball was served, Smid did not put up much of a fight. McEnroe's mastery was such that in the last two sets, he lost only two points on his serve. "I try my best," Smid groaned, "but he's too good for me."

With that victory, we won the tie and ousted the defending champions. In the "dead rubber" match, shortened to the best of three sets, Connors defeated Lendl 7–5, 6–4.

I was happy for the team, and especially for McEnroe. He and I had fairly different temperaments, but he had been through an ordeal in Britain, even if much of it was of his own making. "I need a rest," he told a reporter. "I'm going to sit back, relax, and get away from the tennis scene. I'm going to see if people can forget who I am, so I can be left alone like everyone else."

Connors, too, should have been happy, but he was not. He seemed uncomfortable, even out of place, on the team. He was a great player, with a wide following among the fans. In my opinion, however, he was somewhat envious of McEnroe and hated the fact that John was the center of so much fuss and commotion. As Peter Fleming once astutely observed, "Jimmy might not be able to stand the idea of being star No. 1-A behind Junior." Jimmy sometimes seemed to want all the publicity for himself, no matter how it was earned. This was part of the reason he was so captivating; under pressure, he was a superb player. As far as I could tell, McEnroe never sought the notoriety that accompanied his outrageous behavior. At heart, he was a shy soul who simply couldn't control himself at certain times. Connors envied the fame that accrued to McEnroe with his combination of bad behavior and astonishing play. But while Connors could put on a memorable tantrum, he lacked McEnroe's edge of genius in this department, too. He simply didn't have McEnroe's awful gift of rage.

I don't mean to deny Connors his rightful place in tennis history. Looking back from the early 1990s, with Connors still playing well, I see that he was the greatest male tennis player, bar none, in the two and a half decades since the Open era began in 1968. No top player lasted longer as a major attraction or so thoroughly captured the admiration and sympathy of the public for the same length of time. Only Billie Jean King, with her mixture of dedicated feminism, general gifts of leadership, and athletic brilliance, has been more important among all tennis players since World War II.

After his two victories, I was sure that Connors would be at my side in the Davis Cup for a long time to come. He had promised to play in other matches in 1981. In the hour of victory, however, he packed his bags and strolled away from us. The next time he played Davis Cup was in 1984.

IN OCTOBER, WE played Australia in the semi-finals in Portland, Oregon. In recent years, the U.S. had stumbled badly from time to time, but the decline of Australian tennis had been precipitous. In Cup play, the Aussies showed no sign of fully recovering. We shut them out, 5–0. Once again, with McEnroe (though without Connors), we enjoyed a sellout crowd. In fact, the Portland crowd of 34,900 paying spectators over three days was a U.S. record for Davis Cup attendance.

I had also discovered, by this time, exactly what had sent Trabert over the edge and out of the captaincy the previous year. In various little ways that added up to a chronic headache, McEnroe was difficult to take at times. As captain, I was for protocol; he was not. John showed up for his matches but seemed to wait three minutes before starting play even if he was ready; it was a matter of utter indifference to him if he kept an international television audience waiting. And yet he was our heart and soul, the model of dedication to the Cup, and a patient, attentive, forgiving teammate. The following year, Gene Mayer, one of his teammates, published a tribute to John's sterling qualities as a team player: "He's there trying to do whatever he can, he's helpful, sincere, not cocky or carried away with himself as many of the young players are when they start to play so well at a young age." I would endorse all of those accolades. But McEnroe hated any form of authority, at least in tennis. I wasn't a linesman or an umpire or a referee, but as captain I represented authority, and he clearly felt an obligation to rebel.

I responded at first by keeping some distance between myself and John; I thought he needed room to commune with his demons and keep them at bay. In the doubles match that October against Peter McNamara and Phil Dent, however, the demons were all over the court. McEnroe and Fleming behaved so badly and uttered so many obscenities and profanities, and so insulted their opponents, the officials, and some spectators, that I was left embarrassed, enraged, and bitter. When I told the two of them that they had behaved disgracefully, they were unapologetic. I found myself withdrawing even more from them. In *World Tennis* magazine, the writer Richard Evans speculated about "the seemingly unbridgeable gap that existed between Ashe and two of his players—a gap that had more to do with upbringing than difference in age." (I thought about Trabert when I read that remark.) Evans ventured that I might be "simply too low-key for McEnroe—and, it must be said—for other members of the team as well." McEnroe, on the other hand, "was operating at a pitch of emotional endeavor that Ashe could barely understand."

Perhaps Evans was right, but John knew that he had been out of control, simply outrageous. After the match, he showed a twinge of remorse, although he did not share it directly with me. "We blew it," he told Evans. "I know, don't tell me, man, we blew it."

As much as possible, I avoided trying to coach John, or John and Peter when they were playing doubles, during a match. At one point, during a changeover, Fleming had told me flatly not to try.

"John and I have played a million doubles matches," Peter said agitatedly, as he himself later recalled. "We don't need advice or coaching."

I took him at his word, and kept my mouth shut. I coached players who wanted to be coached, and kept my distance from the others. I found it hard, however, to desist from coaching but perform as a cheerleader, which all the players evidently expected of me. It wasn't,

I hope, a matter of pique. I had enormous respect for John's court intelligence; I couldn't imagine that he or anyone else needed me to cheer him on. But a number of people, including finally John and Peter themselves, thought I should have become more active during the matches. Eventually this criticism reached the magazines. "Maybe I didn't expect Arthur to take me so literally," Fleming remarked. So much for obedience.

The tension between McEnroe and me reached a climax not against Australia but at the finals against Argentina in November. We were playing at Riverfront Stadium in Cincinnati, Ohio. Before the match I let it be known that I was prepared to surrender and default the match if we misbehaved again. When word reached McEnroe, he chose to attack the reporters: "Why do you guys write about that stuff? All you want to do is sell newspapers!" John never fully accepted the fact that if he persisted in misbehaving, he could not win battles with the print media.

Once again, incidentally, Connors had teased and then eluded us. Apparently he had planned a ski trip for the same time as the final; or was it that he needed to rest? He had the cheek to call a cable television call-in talk show where I was a guest and wish us well. "It would be a lot easier," I told him, "if you were with us." Which is about my limit in sarcasm. After the match, I said that we would invite Connors again, "but we won't chase him anymore, that's for sure."

There was great tension among the players in Cincinnati. The glamorous and talented Argentinean stars Guillermo Vilas and Jose Luis Clerc, egged on by their Latin brand of vanity, which seemed almost limitless, made it clear that they could barely stand one another's presence; yet they were to represent their country not only in singles matches but also as doubles partners. For McEnroe, however, this was a grudge match *par excellence*. The previous year, in Buenos Aires, he had lost Davis Cup matches to both Vilas and Clerc. He had lost on clay—his least favorite surface—before a tumultuous, heckling crowd that he obviously had not forgotten or forgiven. Now, at home and on a fast synthetic surface, he wanted blood.

In the first match, he overran Vilas in straight sets, 6–3, 6–2, 6–2. Vilas had trouble with his first serve, and McEnroe pounded his second without mercy. A brilliant player and a famously sensitive man who wrote poetry, Vilas was so wounded by this thrashing that he refused to come to the interview room. Instead, he pouted and sulked in his tent. "Tell him to send us a poem," one wag in the press corps jibed. Then Roscoe Tanner, fighting hard but with his game clearly unstable against a wily, resourceful opponent, lost to Clerc, also in straight sets. The doubles match became crucial.

Although Vilas and Clerc disliked one another, and seldom played together, they stepped on the doubles court primed for the match. They were an artful, intelligent duo. On the fast surface, they decided to try standing back deep when receiving the powerful serves of Fleming and McEnroe and to lob over the Americans at the net. They would try switching sides after each set, as they were allowed to do. And they would also use little tricks of gamesmanship, including subtle delaying tactics and polite but needling remarks. The Argentineans hoped to rattle McEnroe and perhaps even provoke him into a ballistic explosion. They succeeded perfectly. Well, almost perfectly.

By the end of the third set, with the U.S. leading 6–3, 4–6, 6–4, McEnroe's temper was at white heat. In addition to needling by Vilas and Clerc, a group of Argentinean fans had goaded him throughout the match with insults in English and Spanish; John seemed to understand insults in both languages. "We'll see who wins!" he screamed at one point to the foreign fans in a classic display of the passion that drove him both to victories and to unpardonable lapses in behavior. Most of what he said to Vilas and Clerc is unprintable, at least by me. Then, just after the third set, he reached a flash point. Because of an earlier delay to repair the synthetic surface, the referee canceled the usual ten-minute break after the third set, a feature of Davis Cup tennis. Everyone knew that. But as McEnroe prepared to serve, Vilas and Clerc devilishly packed their bags as if on their way to the locker room. McEnroe exploded in anger. "Let me know when you're ready, all right?" he yelled. "We got all afternoon." The four players closed at the net, railing at one another and obviously close to exchanging blows. I rushed up to McEnroe, literally to protect him. I also thought of the millions of television viewers who were now momentarily transfixed.

"John, get to the line and serve! Now!" I pointed at the base line.

John glowered. No doubt he thought for a split second about smacking me with the racket, then stamped over to the line. He served and won the game. Then, changing ends, Clerc and McEnroe went at it verbally.

"John. Peter. You have to quit now," I insisted. "This is a disgrace. You cannot continue like this. I do not want to hear another obscenity out here. You are playing for the United States. Remember that!"

I thought I saw John pull himself together. But then, as he walked onto the court, Clerc looked at him sweetly and lisped, provocatively, "You're so nice!"

"Go fuck yourself!" McEnroe screamed.

I was stunned. I stormed onto the court, and John and I exchanged some bitter words for a few seconds. This time I thought I might punch John. I have never punched anyone in my life, but I was truly on the brink of hitting him. I had never been so angry in my life. I couldn't trust myself not to strangle him. Of course, if I had, any jury would have acquitted me.

I was by no means the only person appalled. Philippe Chatrier, the elegant president of the International Tennis Federation and a former Davis Cup captain of France, walked out of the stadium. "I felt so embarrassed for my hosts," he said, "I eventually got up and left." McEnroe was out of control. Once he even deliberately insulted a middle-aged black linesman by calling him "boy," as if he had searched hard to find something unusually insulting to say to an official.

At the same time, I could hardly believe the quality of tennis John and Peter were playing. Their volleying was spectacular and they refused to die. Vilas served for the match at 7–6, but John and Peter scorched him with four blistering returns, from which he and Clerc never quite recovered. We won the last set, 11–9, to take the match. "If people don't think Davis Cup is different from a regular tournament," McEnroe pronounced, "then they didn't see what happened out there today." The umpire, Bob Jenkins of Britain, spoke for most of the spectators: "I don't think I've ever been involved in a more exciting match."

Still, my anger wouldn't abate. It was so powerful, it astonished me. I thought of one of my favorite lines of verse, from a poem by John Dryden: "Beware the fury of a patient man." I tossed and turned that night. Then, getting up at six-thirty the next morning, Sunday, I placed telephone calls to Marvin Richmond and to Gordon Jorgensen, the chairman of our Davis Cup committee. I got them out of bed.

"I've had it," I told Richmond. Once more, I thought of Tony Trabert. "This cannot continue. What John and Peter did out there was absolutely inexcusable. In thirty years of competitive tennis I have never seen anything like it. Even *close* to it. It makes us look bad, all of us, including the United States as a nation. I want to forfeit the match if McEnroe acts anything like that again. I need your support."

"You have it."

A few hours later, when I sat face to face with McEnroe, we were barely polite to one another. In an icy tone, I told him I had spoken to Richmond and Jorgensen and had their backing. If he acted as disgracefully in his match today as he had behaved yesterday, the United States would default the match. I told him flatly that our national honor was at stake.

McEnroe listened stonily. He never said a word until I was finished. Then he asked, "Is that all?"

"Yes, that's all."

He got up and left the room. Later, on court, he kept his distance from me, and I from him. We, captain and player, were like total strangers. I wasn't happy about the situation, but I had no stomach for fake camaraderie or ersatz shows of friendship.

Secretly I wanted John to act badly again, so that I could lower the hammer on him and forfeit the match. No one had ever stood up to McEnroe, and I was sure that his behavior would have been different if someone had done so when he was younger. Of course, he was still young—only twenty-two years old—which is one reason I thought he could learn something from a default.

Holding his emotions in check, McEnroe proceeded to play an extraordinarily gutsy, magnificent match against Clerc. John lost the second and the fourth sets, then somehow fired himself up for one last, titanic effort in the fifth. He attacked Clerc's serve relentlessly, and on his own serve he surrendered only four points in the last set. He won the match 7–5, 5–7, 6–3, 3–6, 6–3.

Later, I called our differences "intrafamilial fights." Clearly McEnroe, too, was sorry about the bad blood that had arisen between us. He complained about my demeanor, which he found too placid. "Not too much needs to be said," he ventured. "But I think there's a happy medium. You don't want him to say too much but it's almost uncomfortable if he says nothing at all."

LOOKING BACK ON my Davis Cup captaincy more than ten years after it started, I think I am starting to understand exactly what McEnroe and his fiery personality may have meant to me. Neil Amdur, who collaborated with me on my book *Off the Court*, suggested in an essay in 1983 that McEnroe and I were poles apart in personality, perhaps even irreconcilable, because he freely expressed his rage while I repressed mine. Neil traced my repression back to the death of my grandfather and mother in the span of one year during my childhood, and especially my father's grief when my mother died when I was seven. "The sight of adult family members sobbing and wailing," Amdur wrote, "admittedly frightened Ashe. To protect himself, he built an emotional wall that extends to his friends, family and tennis. Each time McEnroe loses control on the court in a Davis Cup match, it forces Ashe to deal with the most delicate frames in his psyche."

Perhaps this is true. I suspect now that McEnroe and I were not so far apart, after all. Far from seeing John as an alien, I think I may have known him, probably without being fully aware of my feelings, as a reflection of an intimate part of myself. This sense of McEnroe as embodying feelings I could only repress, or as a kind of darker angel to my own tightly restrained spirit, may explain why I always hesitated to interfere with his rages even when he was excessive, although I sometimes had to do so. Now I wonder whether I had not always been aware, at some level, that John was expressing my own rage, my own anger, for me, as I never could express it; and I perhaps was even grateful to him for doing so, although his behavior was, on another level, totally unacceptable.

Perhaps my sense of kinship with him also explains the trance—totally inappropriate in a captain, I'm sure—that I sometimes slipped into when I watched John play, and that many people took to be remoteness or indifference, which it could never have been. At one point, speaking to a reporter who was intent on probing the nature of our relationship and who was puzzled by my apparent aloofness at courtside, I used some telling words (unconsciously, I am sure) to describe my odd state of mind as I watched John. "I know it looks funny when John's playing and I'm just sitting there, staring into space most of the time," I told the reporter. Then I quickly had to cancel out the image of myself as a dreamer. "But what am I supposed to do, put on a show and ask him the time, or what the weather's like?"

I developed a deep affection for McEnroe, and also a genuine respect for his character and integrity that defused my outrage at behavior often so different from my own. I found ways to forgive him, and I tried to give him what he asked for. Some critics chose to interpret my attitude as obsequiousness before a star. I was blamed for indulging McEnroe instead of cracking the whip—as if one could crack the whip on a multimillionaire genius of a tennis player. The charge of obsequiousness makes no sense to me. I myself had been a star. I had never been a star of John's magnitude, but I can't imagine myself being obsequious to another tennis player. What bound me to McEnroe was not simply his rage but also his selflessness in making sacrifices to play for our country, and his artistry on the tennis court. I couldn't resist that combination. I began to see him as a brother. He was, in some ways, an incorrigible brother; but our fights were indeed, in my mind, "intrafamilial."

OUR NEXT CAMPAIGN, in 1982, was far less controversial, yet it had its share of drama. With McEnroe again loyal, together with an excellent supporting cast, we were supposed to be almost invincible against most nations. We duly defeated India easily. We were then supposed to roll over Sweden in the quarterfinals in July in St. Louis, Missouri. The commanding Borg, after all, had retired. Unfortunately, no one told Mats Wilander and Anders Jarryd that they were supposed to lose.

Five days after losing a long match in the singles final at Wimbledon to Connors, McEnroe beat Jarryd in the first match. Then Wilander, seventeen years old and the recent victor in the French Open, scored an upset over Eliot Teltscher, then one of the top ten players in the world. The United States won the doubles, to make the score 2–1. During the night, however, Teltscher developed severe back spasms. I replaced him with Brian Gottfried, also in the top ten. His opponent, Jarryd, was in the top forty. Although he tried hard, Gott-fried then played the worst Davis Cup match of his career as Jarryd prevailed 6–2, 6–2, 6–4. The tie came down to McEnroe against Wilander.

This deciding match lasted 6 hours, 39 minutes, as Wilander and McEnroe played 79 games. If anyone could fully appreciate what the players were enduring, I certainly could. In 1970, I had played in the longest singles match in Davis Cup history: 86 games, against Christian Kuhnke of West Germany. That match was an ordeal I will never forget. Once again, the sustaining element for me was the fact that I was representing my country. I couldn't lower the flag because of physical fatigue or a lack of willpower. I was determined that the United States would prevail. I won that match.

McEnroe won the first two sets, then Wilander took the next two (the third went 15–17 against John). The struggle in the fifth was wondrous to behold. This was one of the few times when I ventured to advise McEnroe about his playing. "I know you're tired but you've got to be patient," I told him. "Don't come to the net and try to hit a crazy shot like you would against somebody else in some other match. You've got to be patient and wait to hit a good shot." John listened intently, as in fact he always did on those few occasions when I offered him tennis advice.

Both men held serve until the fourteenth game, when McEnroe broke Wilander's serve and closed out the fifth and deciding set. We embraced, he wept, and I whispered my congratulations.

"John, that's the greatest match you have ever played in the Davis Cup."

To the press, he was generous in praise of Wilander, and character-istically modest and self-effacing about his own effort: "I thought this match would go on forever, and it was frustrating. I should have won the match easier. It was a mental effort just to stay out there."

I was certain that my admiration for McEnroe's mental resilience could not possibly grow after that match. Then he took my breath away against Australia, down under in Perth. After enduring a terrible three-day flight from San Francisco, he and Fleming arrived at Perth two days behind schedule, at night. At midnight, he went out and practiced. Then he defeated Peter McNamara in four sets, teamed with

Fleming to take the doubles, and dispatched John Alexander to complete a 5–0 rout of Australia by the United States. Playing well, Gene Mayer won the other singles matches.

The 1982 final took place indoors in a happy, festive atmosphere in Grenoble, France. Although the French were justifiably proud of their young team, which included the ascendant Yannick Noah and the promising teenagers Henri Leconte and Thierry Tulasne, they adored McEnroe and above all were happy to be in the Cup final. I was happy to see the French doing well. Philippe Chatrier, who had been a very good friend to tennis professionals and the ATP when the old guard still obstructed our path, had almost singlehandedly reversed the French fortunes in tennis. When I telephoned him one day in 1971 with the news that I had just seen a remarkably gifted eleven-year-old boy playing on a court in Africa, Chatrier responded in his typically generous way. He acted on the tip, and the brightest star in French tennis since the famed "Musketeers" of the 1920s was born: Yannick Noah.

In Grenoble, Yannick was a remarkable sight. At six feet four inches, he had always been commanding and yet sweet and gentle. However, he had just dreadlocked his hair (for his sister's wedding), and it radically altered his image; the classically featured Yannick now looked like a Rastafarian, rather fierce. McEnroe, of course, was not about to be intimidated by anyone. "The only thing I'm scared about," he assured a reporter about Noah, "is his hair."

Against Noah and his dreadlocks, John stared down Medusa and took the first set, 12–10. Then, John lost the next two sets before lifting his game almost effortlessly, winning the last set 6–2. I was never worried much, even though John did not care for the clay surface. Seeking an edge, our hosts had trucked in about three hundred tons of rock, soil, and crushed brick to simulate the clay at Roland Garros stadium in Paris. Fortunately for us, the surface was not particularly slow. "When it gets to the fifth," I told reporters later, "I feel confident John's going to win, on anything—even popcorn."

Our team spirit was so high in Grenoble in part because our other singles player was Gene Mayer. Gene and his brother Sandy were both fine players, well prepared by their father, a professional coach. Like McEnroe, both brothers had played at Stanford University for coach Dick Gould. Friendly and generous, Gene also possessed one of the sharpest minds I have ever known in the tennis world; he was a brilliant student who excelled at intellectual tests. Far from being bookishly aloof, Gene was a happy chatterer, who lifted his teammates' spirits with his endless stream of talk. Oddly enough, as a tennis player Mayer was full of little fears and insecurities. The playing conditions had to be just right for him to play his best. They were good enough in his first singles match of the 1982 final and he won easily in four sets against the gifted but erratic teenager Leconte.

McEnroe never fell asleep in the doubles match with Fleming against Noah and Leconte, unlike in his singles match against Noah. In the ten games in which he served, John lost only eleven points. And thus we won the Davis Cup for the second year in a row. Champagne flowed in our locker room. One of the happiest persons in the room was Gene Mayer's father, Alex Mayer, who had emigrated to the United States from Hungary, where he had played Davis Cup tennis. One of his dreams had been to see one or both of his sons help win the Cup for the United States. At the presentation ceremony I delivered my little speech, jokes and all, in French. The crowd loved it, and even laughed at my jokes. (I hope they weren't laughing at my French.) I have always believed that learning a second language must be a goal for any educated person. I could never understand why we Americans blithely expect other people to speak English but make little or no effort to learn foreign languages. Years later, I was pleased to see Jim Courier speak French as he accepted the singles trophy at Roland Garros after winning the French Open.

We had hardly digested our victory before we learned that in the next Davis Cup competition, we had to open by playing the Argentineans in Argentina. The previous year, Argentina had lost to France in the first round, so they were at the bottom of the draw although they were certainly one of the top four teams in the world. And because they had last played us in the United States, they could now play us at home. This was a far cry from the days of old, when the champion nation rested and waited before playing in the Challenge Round of the Cup at home.

In March 1983—on clay, of course, and outdoors—Argentina crushed the United States, 4–1. Again, McEnroe showed extraordinary heart. Vilas and Clerc, both ranked in the top ten (as were McEnroe and Gene Mayer), called a truce in their endless bickering about who was Argentina's darling and took full advantage of the blazing Argentinean summer sun. Vilas defeated Mayer 6–3, 6–3, 6–4. Then Clerc bore down on McEnroe. He took the first two sets, 6–4, 6–0, and all seemed lost. John was nursing a bad shoulder, which our trainer and I massaged whenever we could. Under a cloudless sky, his face sunburnt, his nose as red as Rudolph's, John fought off a relentless Clerc and a heckling, hectoring crowd of 10,000 to take the next two sets.

At 2–2 in the fifth set, with darkness enveloping us, everyone on our side wanted me to insist that play be suspended for the night. But I let it go on, then spoke up finally when the score reached 5–2, with McEnroe trailing but about to serve. "The most pressure is trying to *serve out* a match," I explained later. The next day, I was vindicated. John held his serve, then broke the nervous Clerc. Next, John held his serve to even the score at 5–5. But the effort was too much. The fire went out of McEnroe's game, and he lost the set 5–7.

John and Peter won the doubles, but again we played five sets, and with explosions from McEnroe, who had been dubbed "El Irascible" by the national daily newspaper *La Prensa.* At one point, El Irascible started to climb into the stands to attack one persistently rude fan. He twice loudly denounced the people of Argentina as a nation, and in the process of picking up a penalty point he dismissed Nicola Pietrangeli, the referee and former Italian tennis star, as a "moron" and a "jerk."

In the second round of singles, Mayer lost again. So did John, to Vilas. This was the only tennis match I ever saw in which John was utterly dominated. He tried everything he knew, but Vilas was simply better. John was not humiliated, but he was outclassed on a clay court in a foreign country, with a bad shoulder and a severe case of fatigue. By the middle of the third set, he and I understood that there would be no fifth-set miracle, that he was probably going down. McEnroe battled bravely on, but in front of all those hostile, jeering fans, he seemed a lonely figure, yet brave and brilliant, heroic.

He sealed my feeling for him by uttering a few simple words. As he was about to trudge back to the baseline, down 1–4 in the third set, facing his and our team's worst defeat in the Cup competition in many years, John turned to me. A smile that mocked us both flirted with a jaunty smirk.

"Well, captain," he said, plucking at his racquet strings, "do you have any pearly words of wisdom for me?"

I smiled, and he went out on the court to be beaten. I thought it was our finest moment together. Sometimes, a defeat can be more beautiful and satisfying than certain victories. The English have a point in insisting that it matters not who won or lost, but how you played the game.

Thus, a few months after popping open bottles of champagne following our victory in Grenoble, the United States was bounced from the next Davis Cup competition in the first round.

ON JUNE 21 of that year, 1983, I underwent a double-bypass heart operation at St. Luke's–Roosevelt Hospital in Manhattan, where my first heart surgery had taken place in 1979. Once again, my surgeon was Dr. John Hutchinson. I had been suffering from chest pains for a while, notably at a business meeting I had attended in April in Hartford, Connecticut, not long after returning from Argentina; after extensive testing, my doctors decided that I needed further surgery. Because of the tough scar tissue from my first operation, entry into my sternum was far more difficult the second time. I also came out of this new operation in worse condition than after the first. I felt weak, even anemic. That was when I made the decision to receive two units of blood. This transfusion indeed picked me up and sent me on the road to recovery from my surgery; it also, unwittingly, set in motion my descent into AIDS.

Four days after I left St. Luke's hospital and went home, I turned forty.

On July 10, Jeanne organized a little birthday party at home for me with a few of our closest friends, including Doug Stein and Donald and Carole Dell. For a birthday present, she gave me a pair of roller skates, which I loved and looked forward to using. To my mortification, however, the main surprise of the party was a performance by a striptease artist who proceeded to bump and grind her way around my living room, dressed in precious little, while I hung my head in sheepish embarrassment. I had loudly scolded every man in the room for inflicting this spectacle on me when the stripper completed her act and read the birthday message from the real culprit: Jeanne.

Jeanne knew that I needed something unusual to cheer me up. My second operation, coming as it did only four years after the first, was a major physical and psychological setback, one that left me on the brink of depression. I had assumed that my quadruple-bypass surgery would be far more effective and lasting than it turned out to be; was the second but a presage of a decline that would virtually cripple me? More than ever, I became aware of my mortality.

Tennis, even the Davis Cup, receded from my mind. As for the captaincy, I certainly considered resigning from it. Perhaps I would have done so if my illness had prevented me from carrying out my duties, which it could easily have done. In the previous two years, moreover, my life had taken certain other turns that had led me into satisfying new activities: I had just started serving as a board member of the Aetna Life and Casualty Company, an association that had already proven more rewarding than almost any other I had had outside of tennis; I had taught a course at a college in Miami, where Jeanne and I had a second home; and I was thinking of starting work on a book on black athletes in the United States, which would consume much of my time.

In the Davis Cup, our loss to Argentina meant that we did not advance to the quarterfinals. Our next match would be in October. Thus I had sufficient time—four months—to recover from surgery and to pursue other matters besides tennis before resuming my duties as captain. I put the thought of resigning out of my mind. By the end of the summer, I was once again eagerly looking forward to the campaign.

IN OCTOBER, OUR team assembled in Dublin, Ireland, to qualify for the group of sixteen by playing Ireland. Here I saw yet another side of McEnroe. With the Irish emotionally welcoming John as a native son come home, I was prepared to have him play the part, wax nostalgic about the old sod, and milk his visit for what it was worth. As an African American in the 1980s, I knew all about the allegedly magical powers of one's "roots." To his credit, however, John refused to indulge in ethnic romanticism. "I don't have a special feeling competing here because I'm Irish," he stated bluntly. "You're playing for your country and trying to win regardless of where you come from." Many of the Irish loved him for his apparent dislike of British snobbishness as represented by Wimbledon, but he himself was unsentimental. Dublin, he told one reporter, "looks like London to me, only drearier. I hope the people are nicer."

The Irish forgave him his truculence; perhaps they considered it characteristically Irish. I myself didn't. In the United States, I have had people say to me about McEnroe and Connors's excesses, "Gee, what do you expect? That's the Irish in them." Such ethnic stereotyping makes me uncomfortable. In any event, McEnroe drew a record crowd to watch tennis at the Royal Dublin Society's Simmonscourt Pavil-ion—a fancy barn, really, where horse and cattle breeders showed their stock. The place had been cleaned out, fumigated, and a carpet set down for play. It was all a little odd. Still, during and after our victory, the Irish were ebullient, gracious hosts. And with his victories in Dublin, McEnroe broke my record of twenty-seven wins for the U.S. in singles matches. I did not begrudge him the record.

For our next match, in the first round of the 1984 Davis Cup, against Rumania, in Bucharest, we finally had the services of Jimmy Connors. Since the last time Connors had played for us, Donald Dell had become his manager. Dell, a former Cup captain, had argued to Jimmy and his mother, Gloria, that no American had ever achieved legendary status in tennis without playing Davis Cup, and so Jimmy agreed to play. But he had evidently heard negative remarks about my captaincy. We had a meeting at a tournament before Bucharest, and he was blunt.

"Look, Arthur, I don't need anyone sitting on the sidelines telling me how to play tennis."

"I understand, Jimmy."

"One thing I want to know, though, Arthur. Are you going to fight for me?"

"What do you mean, Jimmy?"

"I mean, am I going to be out there by myself? Will I be doing my own arguing?"

"I'm out there, Jimmy," I replied. "I'm on your side. I'm going to be working for you."

Twice during Jimmy's first match I made sure that I jumped up and made my presence known to Jimmy and the assembled gathering. I am not sure what I accomplished by these moves, except for making Connors happy. But that was reason enough, I suppose.

Connors's effervescence, the stellar quality of his magnetism and drive, lifted everyone. "That Connors doesn't like losing *in practice*," Jimmy Arias said to me one day as we watched Connors go after McEnroe on the court. I thought I saw a remarkable spirit of camaraderie, of genuine affection, kindle between Jimmy and John, and ignite among the other players. Then Connors's old discomfort with the Davis Cup began to surface. To Mac and me, that silver cup was the Holy Grail. To Jimmy, it seemed that it might have been made of Styrofoam, he had so little sense of, or interest in, Davis Cup legend and lore.

One day, at practice just before the opening match, he yelled out to me with a question. "Arthur, this match is best of three sets, isn't it?"

I could hardly believe my ears. "You mean this practice?"

"No, I mean the matches." He was serious. Stupefied, I shook my head and looked up into the empty stands.

Once again, as much as he tried, Connors couldn't stomach the fact that everyone was in McEnroe's shadow, as far as publicity and fame were concerned. McEnroe welcomed Jimmy, but I sensed that he also nursed a lingering resentment about the fact that Jimmy had indicated that he would play Davis Cup in 1981 and then changed his mind. Still, John had such a genuine interest in our fortunes as a team that he wanted Connors to play. The previous year, he had even accused me of not being firm enough with Connors. "He says he's a friend of his," John told a reporter about Connors and me, "but I don't think he pushed Connors enough. Arthur doesn't press him." Of course, I believed that I had pressed Connors as much as I could, or should, have. I was not going to force anyone to play Davis Cup tennis.

Bucharest in 1984 was a dreary city, with shops that had nothing to offer, and with a repressive, intrusive secret police that resulted in our party, including wives, attending a briefing at the U.S. embassy in a room draped with aluminum foil, or some similar substance, to frustrate eavesdropping. The only spark of warmth and friendship emanating from Rumania came from the unforgettable personality of

Ilie Nastase. Still a member of the national team, Nastase evoked bitter memories of the Davis Cup tie in Bucharest in 1972 between the U.S. and Rumania, when cheating by local officials reached an abysmal low. In the decisive match between Stan Smith and Ion Tiriac, judges called foot faults to negate Smith's aces, Tiriac orchestrated crowd noises to disturb Smith's game, and a linesman at one point openly massaged Tiriac's cramping legs and urged him on. Smith, always the epitome of self-control, kept his temper in check and eventually won the match. At the end, he gravely shook Tiriac's hand. "Ion," Stan said, "I must tell you that I will always respect you as a player. But I will never again have any respect for you as a man." Tiriac was left speechless.

Nastase had been, in his prime, fantastically gifted as a player, almost on a level of uncanny ability with McEnroe. He was also given to outrageous behavior on the tennis court, including crude and vicious teasing of opponents, such as accusations about their sexual preferences and abilities. He liked to call me "Negroni," and once, in the heat of battle in a tournament in Hawaii, even called me a nigger. I myself didn't hear the remark but was told about it. In 1975, at the Masters tournament in Sweden, I had walked off the court in a match against him after his taunting had become unbearable. Refusing to answer him in kind, I deliberately defaulted. (The supervising committee decided later that day to award me the match, 6–0, 6–0. After the tournament, which he nevertheless won because its format did not allow for elimi-nation after one loss, Nastase sent me a bouquet of roses.) Since then, I have always counted Nastase as a friend. In 1977, he showed up at my wedding. "You didn't invite me," he said, grinning and offering his hand in congratulations. "But I came anyway."

Nastase was always a little mad. Now, thirty-seven years old and fifteen pounds above his best weight, he showed flashes of his genius of old, firing thirteen aces past McEnroe in the opening match. He stalled and argued, abused the umpire, and was duly penalized. To our cadre of supporters from the U.S. embassy who waved little American flags to encourage our effort, he genially offered the finger from time to time. He worked on McEnroe, seeking to arouse him; but John remained calm. The Rumanians did not win a set until the last match of the tie.

We beat Argentina and Australia, and then in mid-December,

faced the Swedes in the Cup final in Göteborg. This encounter turned out to be one of the more dismal points of my tennis career. From our arrival, nothing seemed to go right. Inside the Scandinavium, the nation's largest indoor facility, the Swedes had prepared a clay court to give themselves an advantage. We needed to accustom ourselves to the surface, but none of us seemed ready to make the supreme effort. Meanwhile, everyone on the Swedish team except Mats Wilander diligently arrived in Göteborg ten days before the tie and worked out hard for four hours daily. Wilander was away only because he was chasing his second Australian Open, which he won. Then, match fit, he hurried home.

In contrast, McEnroe and Connors were both badly off their stride. Unshaven and unkempt, McEnroe looked exhausted and depressed. He had recently been suspended for twenty-one days for outrageous behavior in a tournament in Stockholm. Viewers around the world had seen the film clip of McEnroe engaging in a vile, murderous tirade, smashing racquets and cups and abusing officials. Now, rusty from his enforced rest, he had to return to Sweden to play Davis Cup tennis. With the press he was first testy, then surly, and finally bitter and contentious. Connors, too, hadn't played competitively in a while. With his wife, Patty, expecting their second child any day, he was also distracted. He asked me if he could arrive a day late and I agreed, which was a mistake. When he got there, all his hostility to the Davis Cup and to team play seemed to return. Everything about our arrangements appeared to anger him, and nothing I said made any difference.

Relations between us crumbled after an incident one night. Practice was scheduled for seven in the evening between Connors and Arias, whom I had selected as an alternate singles player all year. Connors, on time, was already at the stadium; I was supposed to bring Arias over. Our car was late in arriving, and we reached the stadium about ten or fifteen minutes after seven. By this point, Connors, who is nearly always punctual (when he shows up for an event), had worked himself up into a sweaty rage. As I walked through a door onto the court, I saw a message he had scrawled in large letters in the soft clay, presumably for me. His message read: FUCK YOU.

I felt exactly as if he had slapped my face. I wanted to replace him on the spot and send him home, but I knew our chances of winning would have dropped precipitously. I swallowed my pride and endured the insult.

In the tie, played before enthusiastic, sellout crowds, the Swedes defeated us decisively, 4–1. Wilander, tanned, lithe, and fleet of foot after his Australian campaign, crushed Connors 6–1, 6–3, 6–3. Jimmy was sadly out of shape, and the clay court set up by the Swedes caused a few odd bounces that frustrated him as he struggled to find his form. At the end of the first set, he resorted to unspeakably vile language, cursing both the umpire and referee Alan Mills (who was also later the Wimbledon referee). Mills was outraged. Connors was fined $2,000 and came within a penalty point of being defaulted. Mills let us know that he was thinking seriously of recommending that Connors be banned from further competition.

Donald Dell, who had come in for the matches, convinced Connors to apologize to Mills. As Donald put it, Jimmy had to apologize to preserve the honor of the United States. I don't know if Jimmy fully appreciated this concept, but he understood it sufficiently to make what Mills called a "very genuine and personal apology" to both him and the umpire.

By this time, Henrik Sundstrom had defeated McEnroe, who also found the clay surface daunting. McEnroe's rustiness showed, and he had also injured his wrist. The next day, in the doubles, McEnroe and Fleming fell to Jarryd and nineteen-year-old Stefan Edberg in four sets—and we had lost the Cup. We had prepared shabbily, and had paid the price accordingly. For this I bear most of the blame.

The tie now decided, Connors asked to go home to his wife. I gave him permission to do so, and Arias finally had his chance to play. I had named Arias to our team after he had become one of the top ten in the world, then stuck with him when his ranking slid into the twenties. Then I heard from agents for other players who couldn't understand why he was on the team and they were not. I believed that I had to be loyal to Arias, and not dump him simply because he had slipped a little. Meanwhile, Arias himself made it clear that he did not enjoy being a backup player, even to Connors and McEnroe. He wanted to play singles. Now he had his chance in a best-of-three-sets "dead rubber" match.

Against Sundstrom, Arias took the first set and seemed on his way to an easy triumph. Then, inexplicably, with no sun or wind to contend with, and on his favorite surface, clay, Arias began to hyperventilate. He simply became too excited. As I watched in deepening embarrassment, he began to cramp up badly. Sundstrom won, 3–6, 8–6, 6–3.

THE WAY WE had lost to Sweden, more than the loss itself, truly hurt me. Whatever their reasons, Connors and McEnroe had not come prepared to play at their best. I suppose I could have demoted them just before their matches, but I don't think anyone else would have done so. Above all, I hated being associated with the vile language Connors flung about on the court, and the flagrant abuse of the officials. I was also taken aback at the awards dinner when Hunter Delatour, the president of the USTA in 1983 and 1984, apologized to the Swedes for the Americans' conduct during the tie. I know that I would not have done so, and some of the American players were livid. I took it as another rebuke, although one not unjustified, when the incoming president of the USTA, J. Randolph Gregson, promised to make a "complete evaluation" of our Cup effort. Then Harry Merlo, chairman of the Louisiana-Pacific Corporation, the sponsor of our national team, threatened to withdraw its support if such misconduct continued. "Unless we can be assured that such constructive changes will be made," he insisted, "we will move to withdraw our sponsorship."

We were heading toward a crisis. Public criticism of the players became widespread; I received about fifty letters asking me to banish McEnroe and Connors, at least for a year. In a syndicated column, William E. Simon, a former U.S. Secretary of the Treasury, called their behavior in Sweden "one of the most disgusting and vulgar displays of childishness ever seen in a world-class sporting event." The column was entitled "America's Punks." A highly respected Washington *Post* sportswriter called for the two players to be "kicked off the U.S. Davis Cup team immediately."

Then Merlo and Gregson came up with a plan. In January 1985, the USTA sent out letters to the top thirty or so American players asking them to apply for Davis Cup selection only if they were prepared to abide by a list of guidelines for good behavior. If they applied for a spot and were chosen, they would have to sign a Davis Cup "contract" that required them to behave like gentlemen.

To me, the idea seemed like a loyalty pledge. The U.S. Davis Cup committee had a right to expect good behavior, but umpires and referees already had the power to discipline players. Some players were scornful. "I could have written the proposed guidelines in third grade," Fleming jeered. "They aren't exactly revolutionary." And one prominent tennis writer compared them "to the Pledge of Allegiance sleepy kids recite every morning in school."

I couldn't bring myself to take a resolutely hard line against the players even if they needed it, and even if they behaved in ways that I detested. In January, at an event I attended to promote a new line of sports clothing, most of the questions put to me were about the players' behavior. I tried to put the burden of disciplining them on the umpires and referees. "If I feel a player is wrong," I told a reporter, "I'll let the umpire nail him. Then, if it gets too embarrassing, I'll tell the players to stop or we'll roll down the nets. But if the umpire doesn't nail the player, then . . ." Even I could see that this was hardly an adamant statement.

McEnroe hated the pledge and made it clear that he would not sign it. "I don't see why I should have to sign it," he said, "simply because they [the USTA] were backed into a corner by some sponsor who wasn't even involved the first six years that I played." Earlier, he had announced that he would skip our next match, against Japan—the first Cup tie he would miss in seven years. His aim, he said (and I believed him), was to give other players a chance to shine. He would then return to the team, if selected. But he would not sign the pledge. "What if I signed," he asked insouciantly at one point, "then went on a rampage in the next match? Would I have to sign again?"

In the final analysis, I faced the fact that I had been chosen captain by the president of the USTA and had an obligation to enforce its decisions or else resign. And I did not want to resign in apparent defense of the right of players to misbehave. Publicly I called the guidelines enforceable, and looked to the future: "A more disciplined U.S. team should emerge."

As for coarse language on court, I tried to point out that "all athletes curse at times—at themselves, at opponents, at officials, and sometimes at the public." However, tennis players would have to realize that the presence of microphones on the court, as well as the traditional gentility of tennis, meant that the players would have to learn to restrain themselves, although their tirades boosted television ratings for tennis matches. "Tennis players are not going to stop cursing," I said, "but they are going to have to learn to do it *sotto voce* or else they will be defaulted. In the future, audible coarse language will not be tolerated from our team members." I believed I had taken as firm a stand as I wanted.

IN MARCH 1985, in Kyoto, Japan, and in the absence of Mac and Jimmy, I named Eliot Teltscher and Aaron Krickstein to play singles, and Ken Flach and Robert Seguso to play doubles. Now I had to endure the anger of Arias and his agent.

"You kicked Jimmy in the teeth!" he screamed at me. "In the teeth!"

"I gave him a chance in a match that didn't really matter," I countered. "And he blew it."

In *Tennis* magazine, Arias complained bitterly (but not very effectively, I thought) about me. "I went to Bucharest in the middle of the winter," he said. "I've attended every single match as a water boy, practically. I just felt I'd paid my dues." He would play Davis Cup tennis again, he offered, "but with Arthur as captain, it's questionable." (He failed to mention, apparently, that he was paid $60,000 as a team member for the year.) Teltscher, too, criticized me. My "indecisiveness" annoyed him. "He asked me if I'd be available to play," Eliot explained to the press. "I said, 'Are you asking me to?' He said, 'No, I just wanted to see if you'd be available.' I just want him to make a decision and let me know."

I didn't take such criticism too much to heart. Most players want to play, even if they don't deserve to do so ahead of other players. Rookies seldom like watching veterans enjoy the fruits of their years of labor. I thought John had earned the right to expect a favor or two, but lesser players often complained about that. I remember one heated exchange with Arias.

"How come Mac can show up a day late for the tie," Jimmy fumed, "and I have to be here on time? How come, Arthur?"

"Go win three Wimbledons and four U.S. Opens like John," I snapped back, "and then we'll discuss it." (In 1986, Arias redeemed himself by winning the decisive fifth match against Ecuador.)

In Kyoto, we dropped only one set and moved past Japan, 5–0.

Next we faced a tougher opponent, West Germany. We needed to field our best possible team. The USTA still stood by its pledge, and McEnroe and Connors still refused to sign it. I made it clear that I wanted McEnroe. "If John doesn't sign," I told a *New York Times* reporter in May, "there may be other ways to put him on the team. His willingness to play might be acceptable. And if he makes himself available, I'll pick him whether he signs or not." Although I knew that this statement would not sit well with the USTA or with Harry Merlo of Louisiana-Pacific, I wanted to make it clear that I thought we should have McEnroe with us.

Connors's refusal was more symbolic than substantial. He had never really been one of us. Then he announced that he would not play Davis Cup anymore. At least he was honest enough to admit his shortcomings. "I've never been a team man," he conceded. "That's why I never joined the Association [of Tennis Professionals] and why I don't play doubles anymore. I've always taken full credit for my success and full controversy for my failures."

Later in the year, in *World Tennis* magazine, my journalist friend Bud Collins stoutly defended McEnroe and Connors: "It was an insult to be asked to sign." He went further: "I guess I'm even more disappointed by captain Ashe and the Davis Cup players other than McEnroe and Connors. Their failure to stick together against the imposition of a loyalty oath, and in defense of their comrades, Mac and Jimmy, by refusing, en masse, to sign the undemocratic pledge, tells me that the team was not really a team."

In August 1985, in Hamburg, I assembled the same team that had defeated Japan: Teltscher, Krickstein, Flach, and Seguso. (We didn't have McEnroe, but we received a telegram from his family wishing us luck.) The Germans had an ace waiting for us: redheaded Boris Becker, who had electrified the tennis world the previous month by winning Wimbledon at the age of seventeen. I had never seen a tennis prodigy built like Becker; he reminded me of some overgrown high-school basketball superstar suddenly thrown in with the top professionals, making some mistakes but dazzling his elders all the same. Six feet three inches tall, powerful, athletic, and impetuous, he promptly subdued Teltscher, 6–2, 6–2, 6–3. Like some infant unaware of his own strength, Becker marveled afterward at how easily he had disposed of a higher-ranked player. "I thought it would be a tougher fight," he said. "Like maybe four sets."

Then followed one of the most frustrating matches of my Davis Cup captaincy.

As a tennis player, young Krickstein had a great deal going for him. Blessed with big shoulders (he had started out as a swimmer), Krickstein had mighty groundstrokes, excellent control, and abundant stamina. He had everything except the so-called killer instinct, if the killing had to take place at the net. He was a decent volleyer, but even on drop shots, Aaron would often rush in to retrieve the ball, then scurry back to the baseline, where he felt much safer. The result was that he seldom finished points quickly—or games, or sets. In fact, he didn't finish matches quickly. In a mixture of respect and derision, Aaron came to be known among the players as "the King of the Five-Setters."

In Hamburg, against low-ranked Hansjörg Schwaier, Aaron played his royal game. He won the first set (6–2), dropped the second (1–6), won the third (6–2), dropped the fourth (1–6). Midway through the fifth, however, he started to cramp up, and then lost the match. He had dominated most of the points but refused to come to the net to finish them off. A win in the doubles and the first of the reverse singles kept our hopes alive, but then Becker blasted Krickstein, 6–2, 6–2, 6–1. Becker started the match wearing a sweater, and never bothered to take it off. Urged on by cries of "Bravo, Boris!" and "Deutschland!," he needed only an hour and a half to win.

West Germany, hardly a major power in world tennis just two months before, had beaten us. For the third straight year, I had led the United States to defeat in the Davis Cup. I understood that my days as captain were numbered.

THAT SUMMER, IN a personal consolation, I was inducted into the International Tennis Hall of Fame at Newport, Rhode Island. As happens only on rare occasions, the committee inducted me as soon as I was eligible, five years after my retirement. I would like to think that my heart operations had nothing to do with their decision. Inducted along with me were Fred Stolle of Australia, an old tournament companion from my playing days who excelled above all in doubles play, and Ann Haydon Jones of Britain, who had won a Wimbledon singles crown in 1969. I made a family affair of this honor of a lifetime. Jeanne and her parents attended the event with me in Newport, as did my father and stepmother, as well as my brother Johnnie, his wife, Sandra, their daughter, Luchia, and other members of our large family.

On October 22, *The New York Times* carried a story headlined: "Ashe to Be Dropped as Davis Captain." The usual "informed sources" said I had been advised that I would be let go, and that Randy Gregson had lost confidence in me "for a perceived lack of discipline and organization on the team." The sources were well informed. A few days previously, at a meeting in midtown Manhattan, Gregson and Jorgensen had informed me that I was finished. I made it clear that I wanted to stay on, but they had made up their minds.

At noon on the day after the *Times* story appeared, I called Gregson in Arizona and tendered my resignation. I underscored my continuing loyalty to the Davis Cup competition by accepting the essentially ceremonial position of vice-chairman of the Cup committee.

Not long afterward, Tom Gorman, an old friend and former Davis Cup player, was named to replace me. I wished him well, although I was a little hurt by the headline of an editorial (by Steve Flink) in *World Tennis* magazine: "Can Gorman Raise the Cup From Ashe?" Had I really brought it so low? Looking back on my career as captain, I can point with some pride to my record of 13 wins against 3 losses. I am also proud to be only the second captain in thirty years to lead the U.S. team to consecutive victories (1981 and 1982). However, as I had led some of the most talented teams ever fielded by the United States, we should have done better, and some of the blame must rest on my shoulders.

To be more effective, I suppose, I should have been more gregarious at times, and at other times more aggressive. I should have tried harder to impose my will on the players. But I couldn't do that, and I have to live with the consequences. I accepted the fact that as much as I want to lead others, and love to be around other people, in some essential way I am something of a loner.

Nevertheless, that knowledge did not make me more reclusive. My setbacks in connection with the Davis Cup helped me to understand that to be effective, I would have to step more boldly into the spotlight, especially if I wished to be effective in the crucial area of social and political progress. My Davis Cup captaincy was a rich, challenging, and also satisfying experience, not least of all because of that simple lesson.

CHAPTER FOUR

Protest and Politics

AS I HAD hoped, my captaincy in the Davis Cup proved to be a bridge—albeit one with some broken planks, and one that sometimes swayed ominously in the wind—between my glory years as a player and the obscurity of retirement. The Cup kept me in the public eye and in the sports pages much longer than I otherwise would have been. This exposure probably also brought me a few endorsements and other financial opportunities that I would not otherwise have earned. I was lucky, I knew, to have had this bridge; as I have said, the sudden darkness of retirement is for some professional athletes, including tennis players, a shock to the nervous system from which they never completely recover.

However, my Cup captaincy did not fully satisfy my desire to make the most of my retirement years, or give me an entirely settled perspective on my new life. In the first place, I had been less than triumphant as a leader, after my initial successes. More important, even the most impressive record in tennis would not have stilled certain disquieting feelings that ran deeper in me than patriotism or sporting fame. I am an African American, one born in the iron grip of legal segregation. Aside from my feelings about religion and family, my innermost stirrings inevitably have to do with trying to overcome racism and other forms of social injustice, with the search for dignity and power for blacks in a world so often hostile to us. Not the tennis court but the arena of protest and politics would be the single most significant testing ground for me in the middle years of my life.

* * *

A DAY OR so after the announcement that I had resigned from the Davis Cup captaincy, I received a telephone call from the sports editor of *Jet* magazine. *Jet*, a sister publication of the better known *Ebony*, is a lively little magazine of news about the African American world. Like most journals and newspapers devoted to black Americans, it examines most developments with a focus on race and politics.

"Arthur," the editor began, "according to various reports, including *The New York Times*, you didn't want to give up the captaincy. Is that true?"

"I think it's fair to say that. No, I did not want to give up the captaincy. No one wants to go out on a losing note."

"You were forced out?"

"Yes, I was forced out, I suppose," I answered, "although it certainly was done according to law."

"Do you think that politics had anything to do with it?"

"What do you mean by politics?" I asked.

"I mean your interest in human rights. For example, your ongoing opposition to the practice of apartheid in South Africa?"

I thought about the question, but only for a moment. I did not want to misrepresent the situation and embarrass the United States Tennis Association, but I also did not want to avoid telling the truth.

"I think so," I answered. "I believe that my role in publicly protesting against apartheid probably had something to do with the USTA deciding not to ask me back for next year. Some people probably think I've gone too far."

"Did the president tell you that?"

"No, he didn't. No one at the USTA said so to my face. But I've heard so from other sources."

"Could you tell us about these sources? What did they say?"

"No," I replied. "I can't tell you about them and what they said. I was given certain information on a confidential basis, and I can't reveal anything more. Besides, I don't believe that politics was the only reason, so I don't want to make too much of what I was told."

The story duly appeared, headlined "Ashe Says Activist Role May Be Part of His Ouster as Davis Cup Team Captain." Happily, it was accurate and fair. I certainly did not want to exploit the situation and make Randy Gregson and the USTA appear to be villains in a political drama. However, I sincerely believe that Gregson and others in the USTA saw me as someone far more concerned with politics than a Davis Cup captain should be. And by politics, I'm sure they meant "radical" politics.

I was then, and I am now, no radical, but many people in the tennis leadership, as in other sports, are terrified of taking a stand on political affairs, or on controversial questions of social justice. Although certain exceptions come to mind, the prevailing political ambience of tennis has always been a wealth-oriented conservatism of the kind associated in this country with staunch Republicanism and exclusive country clubs. The idea of apartheid in South Africa undoubtedly is abhorrent to some of these people, but the idea of demonstrating in the streets against it might be even more abhorrent, in practical terms. I respect many of the values of conservatism and Republicanism, but I hate injustice much more than I love decorum.

The previous January, I had been arrested in Washington, D.C., while taking part in a demonstration against South Africa. Quietly, innocently, South Africa had come into my life on an exquisite June afternoon in 1968, at the Queen's Club in London. For forty years or more, and until recently, the Queen's Club tournament was notable among tennis lovers mainly as the last competition for top players in Britain before Wimbledon; Queen's offered the final chance to hone one's skills on grass courts before participating in the premier tournament in the world. In the clubhouse, I was sitting next to John Newcombe in a meeting with a group of top players, all bound for Wimbledon. Only two months after the first open tennis tournament, we were talking primarily about the possibility of forming an association of professional tennis players, a kind of trade union, and about the reception we could expect from various governing bodies around the world. The first open Wimbledon was at hand. The first U.S. Open would be held later in the summer.

One of the South African players, Cliff Drysdale, mentioned that the first South African Open would be held in the fall. He and his compatriots, top players like Frew McMillan and Ray Moore, were eagerly looking forward to the competition, which hoped to attract a stellar field to Johannesburg.

Turning to me, Drysdale said casually, "They'd never let you play."

I was startled. "Is it *that* bad?"

"Oh, the Lawn Tennis Association would let you play," Cliff explained. "I'm pretty sure of that. In fact, they would love to have you come. But you would need a visa to enter South Africa, and the government would never let you have one."

"Are you serious?"

"Try them. You'll see."

The following year, 1969, I mailed an application for a visa to allow me to play in the Open. My application was rejected.

At that time, South Africa was not a major political issue for American voters, white or black, or indeed for many people outside South Africa itself. The United Nations had not yet voted to impose social and cultural isolation on the nation of apartheid. Portugal still held the territories of Mozambique and Angola, which served as effective buffers between South Africa and independent black Africa. South Africa still played in the Davis Cup. In fact, it would win the Cup in 1974, when India defaulted in the final rather than compete in sport with South Africa. The bloody Soweto student uprising of June 16, 1976, which transformed the image of South Africa for many people, and which I learned about while I was at Wimbledon, had not yet taken place.

I tried again for a visa in 1970, and was rebuffed again. Finally, in 1973 I was allowed in. I visited South Africa again in 1974, 1975, and 1977. On each occasion (except for 1977, when I was there on assignment for ABC Sports), I insisted that there be no segregated seating at my matches, and my request was honored. In 1973, my appearance there in the Open created a sensation, especially when I proceeded to do well on the court. I made my way to the men's singles final before losing to Jimmy Connors, and I won the doubles title with Tom Okker. Tennis, however, was only one aspect of my visits. I was eager to learn as much as I could about the conditions of people there, especially the "nonwhite" peoples held in bondage by apartheid. And there was no shortage of people, white, black, Colored, or Indian, just as eager to share with me their lifelong experience of apartheid and their vision of the future of South Africa.

I looked apartheid directly in the face, saw the appalling WHITES

ONLY and NONWHITES ONLY signs, the separate and drastically unequal facilities very much like those of my childhood in Virginia. I saw the sneer of superiority on the faces of many whites, and the look of obsequiousness, fatalism, cynicism, and despair on the faces of many blacks. I saw the rigid divisions between the black and Colored and Asian and Jewish and English and Dutch peoples, with the Dutch holding the highest ground of apartheid. I met educated, kindly, but dedicated apologists for apartheid. I met liberal whites troubled by the system that sustained their privilege, and I even stayed in the home of one of them, a Jewish businessman. I was also befriended by Indians, Coloreds, and blacks.

I will never forget one black boy, about fourteen years old, who in 1974 seemed to follow me around Johannesburg's Ellis Park, the most hallowed site in South African rugby, the national sport, and the site also of the South African Open. Every day, he was there when I arrived, and he seemed to be there when I left. He was watchful but shy as he shadowed me around the park. It was as if I exuded some precious, mysterious quality that he wanted to possess. Finally I confronted him, though gently.

"Tell me something," I said. "Why are you following me around?"

"Because you are the first one I have ever seen," he answered.

"The first what?"

"You are the first truly free black man I have ever seen."

When I heard these words, I felt a distinct chill. Nothing anyone else said or wrote during my stay captured as poignantly for me the abyss of inhumanity that was South African apartheid. The major aim of the system was to prepare, to program, and to destine young blacks like this boy for a lifetime of servitude. He was obviously yearning for freedom, and I was touched to be a rallying point for him in his struggle.

Other young blacks were not so accepting. They saw my playing in the South African Open as an act of complicity with the white racist government, although the government itself obviously saw me as something of a threat, or at least a nuisance. In 1973, at Pfepfeni Park, outside Johannesburg, the site of a train station and sporting facilities, I actually felt myself in physical danger among young blacks who bristled with hostility to apartheid, and to me for seeming to condone it; their rage was almost palpable. My only solace was that I was sure the place was full of informers and undercover policemen, and that I would be defended if attacked. Nothing I said made any favorable impression on these desperate young blacks. I never felt so much an outsider, a meddling outsider, in that country.

The difficulty of my position, from their point of view, was underscored by an incident that occurred at Jan Smuts Airport as I was leaving Johannesburg once after a visit. On the plane, I received a message that had been smuggled aboard in a newspaper slipped surreptitiously to Carole Dell, who had accompanied her husband to South Africa in our party. Inside the folded-up newspaper was a moving poem ("An Anguished Spirit: Ashe"), about me and my visit, by Don Mattera, a banned Colored writer, and a note from Winnie Mandela, who had sent the messenger, together with a photograph of her. Her note thanked me for coming to South Africa, but also warned me, and Americans like me, not to believe that we could think for black South Africans. "The best thing you can do," Winnie wrote to me, "is ask the South Africans what you can do to help in their struggle."

Among my friends and advisers in the United States, my visits were also controversial. Some felt that I should not appear to give comfort to the government by visiting South Africa; others counseled that I needed to go and see for myself and then spread the anti-apartheid word in the United States. Opposition at home to my going to South Africa surfaced most unpleasantly during a speech I delivered at predominantly black Howard University in Washington, D.C., after one trip. As I spoke, I noticed two black students, their hands in their pockets, pacing back and forth in the back of the hall, obviously more than a little agitated. I knew that my words were stirring them in some way, and I naturally assumed that they liked what I was saying. Suddenly, they were yelling from the back of the hall, trying to drown me out.

"Uncle Tom! Uncle Tom! Arthur Ashe is an Uncle Tom and a traitor!"

I was stunned. From their accents, I recognized that they were Africans.

"You betrayed us in South Africa! You betrayed your black brothers!" they insisted. "Shame on you, Arthur Ashe! Sit down and shut up!"

I stopped speaking, and they delivered a few remarks bitterly attacking my visits to South Africa. Once I recovered from the shock of being shouted down, which had never happened to me before, I became incensed. Without thinking, I broke one of my cardinal rules as a public speaker. I take pains to try never to embarrass a questioner, no matter how poorly phrased, inappropriate, or even impertinent the question. This time I decided not to hold back.

"Will you answer two questions for me?" I asked into the microphone. "Just two questions?"

They didn't answer me, but I went on all the same.

"Why don't you tell everybody in this hall tonight why, if you are so brave and militant, you are hiding away in school in the United States and not confronting apartheid in South Africa, which is your homeland?"

The crowd murmured. No sound came from the two protesters, except perhaps for a grinding of teeth.

"And also tell us how you as radicals expect to win international support for your cause when you give vent to your anger and rage as you have done here tonight in disrupting my speech. What do you expect to achieve when you give in to passion and invective and surrender the high moral ground that alone can bring you victory?"

They made no attempt to answer my questions, but they also made no further attempt to disrupt my address.

Despite such opposition, from the early 1970s I consciously made South Africa the focus of my political energies inside and outside the United States. Although I had visited South Africa and had also opposed the decision of India to forfeit its Davis Cup final against South Africa in 1974 (questioning why India should allow South Africa to win the Cup without playing), I was in favor of international sanctions against the country. Not only did I play a major role in having South Africa banned from Davis Cup play, I also worked hard to convince individuals not to play there. Ironically, my first important challenge in this respect came at the start of my Davis Cup captaincy, before we played our first match. It also carried the risk that I might alienate our top player, John McEnroe.

On December 6, 1980, McEnroe was supposed to play Bjorn Borg in Bophuthatswana in South Africa, in an exhibition organized by a hotel-casino organization there. Bophuthatswana is one of the phony "independent" states set up by South Africa; unrecognized by almost all nations, these states were designed to accommodate the major African tribes of the country but in reality are rigidly controlled by the white government. I did not want McEnroe to appear to collude with apartheid by playing in this patently fraudulent state. The United Nations had imposed a cultural ban on South Africa.

The proposed match had stirred much interest. At Wimbledon in June, Borg and McEnroe had played a stupendous match, in which the fourth-set tie breaker had lifted their tennis to dizzying heights of drama and athletic prowess before John won it, 18–16, only to have Borg win the match in the fifth set. Then, in the finals of the U.S. Open in New York, Borg lost to McEnroe in another five-setter. The match in South Africa, I suppose, was to decide on the tennis court who was the best player in the world in 1980. The purses for the match were also stupendous: each player was guaranteed $600,000, with the winner to receive an additional $150,000—far more than the top prize at any of the Grand Slam events. According to reports, this money would come mainly from NBC-TV in the United States, which had agreed to televise the match, and the hotel-casino group located in Bophuthatswana.

Determined to stop the match, I approached John McEnroe, Sr., who is a lawyer and his son's principal adviser. I did not want to make a public fuss about the matter. However, I let the McEnroes know that a public fuss was bound to ensue if the match were played. Recently, heavyweight boxers Mike Weaver of the U.S. and Gerrie Coetzee of South Africa had fought in Bophuthatswana, and Weaver had been criticized for fighting there. The outcry against Weaver was nothing compared to what would probably be visited on McEnroe. Weaver might claim that he needed the money; but most people would think that John either had already made a fortune in prize money and endorsements or would do so soon. The huge sum of money might make playing there excusable, but it also seemed to put a price on McEnroe's integrity.

No one could accuse McEnroe of being mercenary. For one thing, his commitment to Davis Cup play meant a financial sacrifice no matter what sum the U.S. committee awarded him. John lost a great deal of money every time he played Cup matches by forgoing exhibition matches elsewhere at the same time. Now I was asking him to sacrifice more money by canceling the match against Borg. The family didn't hesitate, and the event was canceled. "John and I," his father announced soon after, "felt it was neither the right time nor the right place for that match." I was pleased, too, that this episode had no adverse effect on my relationship with John when Cup play started.

IN OPPOSING APARTHEID, I made a careful distinction between the government of South Africa and individual white South Africans. I always opposed the idea of banning individual South Africans from tournaments in the United States. Ironically, as a player I had found the men from South Africa—Cliff Drysdale, Ray Moore, Frew McMillan, and others—by far the most intelligent and the best educated of all the national groups. I was fondest of the Australians, but the South Africans were much more cultivated, and they were friendly, too. Almost certainly, few tennis professionals have ever set a higher standard of courtesy and exemplary behavior on the court than Drysdale. I don't know if he was consciously trying to compensate for his country's tarnished image, but Drysdale was a model competitor.

In 1985, while I was still captain of the Davis Cup team, I insisted, in the face of some opposition, on the right of South African–born players who had become U.S. citizens, notably Kevin Curren and Johan Kriek, to play for the United States. I did so even though Curren, for one, made little effort to hide the fact that his U.S. citizenship was mainly a convenience. When he played (and lost) in his 1985 Wimbledon final against Boris Becker, most people regarded the match as South Africa facing West Germany; Curren was no more American in spirit than Nastase, for example. However, he was legally a U.S. citizen and, therefore, as far as I was concerned, entitled to all its rights and privileges. I would certainly have selected one of these players to represent the U.S. if the situation called for it.

However, I did not approve of *all* white South African athletes. I disliked the extreme caution of the golfer Gary Player (much as I admired his game) in facing the question of apartheid. I wanted him to say where he stood on this burning issue, even if he ended up defending apartheid. I would have accepted his defense more readily than I accepted his fence-sitting on an issue so charged with moral implications. In my book *Off the Court* I called Player a hypocrite. No doubt he is a fine fellow; certainly he sent me a generous note after my AIDS announcement, and informed me about certain educational programs he was pursuing in South Africa of which he thought I might approve. That was the problem: because it was so lucrative for whites and so demoralizing for blacks, apartheid made even fine fellows, white or black, look sometimes like villains.

In my adamant opposition to apartheid I felt, at first, in the early 1970s, as one among only a handful of people in the black American community. But other people were starting to fight this potent vestige of white supremacy in Africa. Almost from its inception, I was involved in TransAfrica, the organization set up by the Black Congressional Caucus as a sort of think tank and lobby for African and Caribbean affairs—the first and still the only think tank controlled by black Americans and with a focus on foreign affairs. Its first executive director was Randall Robinson, a childhood friend of mine from Richmond.

For several summers as boys, Randall and I had played baseball together. His father had been the leading coach and sports administrator in the black community, and a fixture at Brook Field, where I lived. Randall went on to graduate from Virginia Union in Richmond and then from Harvard Law School. As adults, we worked closely on developing TransAfrica Forum, which raises tax-exempt money for TransAfrica. I have served for many years as co-chair of the Forum. In addition, I became a founding member of Artists and Athletes Against Apartheid, which I co-chaired with Harry Belafonte. One of our main goals, as we stepped up our pressure on South Africa, was to persuade athletes and entertainers not to perform there. I had gone to South Africa to play tennis after United Nations sanctions against the nation had been voted; now we worked to enforce those sanctions.

On January 11, 1985, I was arrested outside the South African embassy in Washington, D.C. Although this was not a particularly risky act, I nevertheless found it disturbing. Because I had spent my life making sure no one would ever have cause to arrest me for anything, the experience of being handcuffed, carted away, and booked was daunting. I also knew that, in certain circles, my arrest could cost me some influence and prestige. I have always assumed, as I told *Jet* magazine, that it had been a sore point (perhaps the last straw) with the president of the USTA, Randy Gregson, as he pondered my future as Davis Cup captain. Very few professional athletes, let alone captains of national sporting teams, are arrested for taking part in political demonstrations. The cause itself seemed not to matter.

By 1985, I was at last satisfied that the anti-apartheid movement, once exotic, was blossoming in America. Arrested along with me that January 11 were sixteen other demonstrators, including teachers, municipal workers, and trade union officials. And we were only one small part of an ongoing national effort since November of the previous year, when three prominent blacks had staged a sit-in at the South African embassy in Washington. Behind the national effort was the Free South Africa Movement, coordinated by Randall Robinson, who had been one of the three people in that sit-in. Since November, a host of well-known figures, including Belafonte, Coretta Scott King, and myself, had walked the picket lines outside the embassy complex. The picketing continued long after my arrest, with demonstrations and arrests taking place in other cities. When Jesse Jackson was arrested in March, the police had charged almost 1,500 people in Washington alone; by August, 3,000 had been arrested.

The core of my opposition to apartheid was undoubtedly my memory of growing up under segregation in Virginia. The WHITES ONLY signs in Johannesburg shocked me back to the days when I could play tennis in Brook Field park with other blacks or with a visiting white player looking for a good game, but not in the many better-equipped public courts reserved for whites. It reminded me of going with Ron Charity, who had taught me to play tennis, to try to convince Sam Woods, the white man who practically ran tennis in Richmond, to allow me to play in a city tournament. Charity asked respectfully on my behalf, but Woods, a kindly, gracious, gray-haired man, said no. I was twelve years old. After my arrest I told the Washington *Post,* in explaining my opposition to apartheid, "I speak with a great deal of personal experience. I went through a segregated school system and a segregated society."

I had also gone through that school system and the society that sponsored it without a protest. Blacks did not publicly protest much in Virginia when I was growing up; and they protested even less in my father's household. If I had left the matter to my father, I probably would not have been arrested in 1985. Before going on the picket line in January, I had telephoned him in Richmond.

"Daddy, I want you to know that I'm probably going to be arrested tomorrow, in Washington."

He paused before answering. When he spoke, I could hear a nervousness in his voice. "In Washington? Is this about that South Africa business, Arthur?"

"Yes, Daddy."

"Well, son, I don't know. South Africa's an awful long way from us here. But if you think you have to do it, then I guess you have to do it."

"I have to do it, Daddy."

"All right, son. Just be careful."

"Yes, Daddy. I'll be careful."

And I was. I was careful again when I received other requests to put my body on the line, even in this largely symbolic way, against apartheid. Sometimes I acceded to the requests, but most often I did not. Much as I admire certain well-known entertainers who are quick to respond to calls to the barricades, I did not want to become a fashionable protester giving photo opportunities, as they are called, to journalists.

I also wrestled with a far more perplexing question. To what extent was I trying to make up, with my anti-apartheid crusade, for my relative inaction a decade or more earlier during the civil-rights struggle?

No one knew better than I that a demonstration such as the one in Washington, when I was arrested, was mainly a staged or token affair, a piece of political choreography. I did not feel in any way like a hero for taking part in it. Indeed, I was painfully aware of the difference between, on the one hand, the symbolic punishment that I had allowed myself to be subjected to, and, on the other hand, the terror that the Ku Klux Klan and thousands of white Southern vigilantes and law officers imposed on the black men, women, and children who risked their lives during the civil-rights movement. While blood was running freely in the streets of Birmingham, Memphis, and Biloxi, I had been playing tennis. Dressed in immaculate white, I was elegantly stroking tennis balls on perfectly paved courts in California and New York and Europe. Meanwhile, across the South, young men and women of my age were enduring pain and suffering so that blacks would be free of our American brand of apartheid.

I certainly had been offered more than one opportunity to stand up for the movement. The black social revolution definitely reached UCLA. I remember one long conversation with the intense, argumentative, but likable Ron Karenga, a cultural nationalist who was the head of an organization ingeniously called US, which stood for "Us Slaves." A passionate man, Karenga was driven by the need for blacks to learn their own history and develop their own rites and rituals as part of the building of a black nation. He even invented Kwanzaa, a ritualistic celebration for blacks based on a crossing of African beliefs and rituals with beliefs and rituals from other parts of the world; celebrated around Christmastime, Kwanzaa is obviously designed to rival or even supplant it, although some nationalists claim differently. Karenga was persuasive, and I listened with genuine respect. But I was never able to cross the wall that separated athletes with scholarships at UCLA from the other students. Besides, there was an irrational edge to US, as there is perhaps in all extreme cultural nationalism. In conflicts with the Black Panthers, two US members were killed at UCLA about this time, and the organization never recovered. Those killings did nothing to ease my misgivings about militant politics.

Some of my friends tried to assure me that I, too, was playing my part in the revolution, but they never convinced me of it, not completely. There were times, in fact, when I felt a burning sense of shame that I was not with other blacks—and whites—standing up to the fire hoses and the police dogs, the truncheons, bullets, and bombs that cut down such martyrs as Chaney, Schwerner, and Goodman, Viola Liuzzo, Martin Luther King, Jr., Medgar Evers, and the little girls in that bombed church in Birmingham, Alabama. As my fame increased, so did my anguish. I knew that many blacks were proud of my accomplishments on the tennis court. But I also knew that some others, especially many of my own age or younger, did not bother to hide their indifference to me and my trophies, or even their disdain and contempt for me.

In 1968, that year of death in America, when first Martin Luther King, Jr., and then Robert F. Kennedy died at the hands of assassins, I spoke out for the first time in public about race and politics. About three weeks before King's death, on March 10, I spoke at the Church of the Redeemer, Presbyterian, in Washington, D.C., on the role of the black athlete in the wrenching changes taking place in American society. I had been invited to speak by the minister of the church, the Reverend Jefferson Rogers, an intelligent, influential black man deeply concerned with trying to merge religious conviction with the imperatives of race consciousness and progressive politics.

I was more nervous about my coming speech than about any tennis match I had played in a long time, especially after the Washington *Post*, a few days before the event, ran a story about my decision to speak. The headline said: "Ashe Becomes Activist, Plans Speech Here on Civil Rights." A subheading read: "Negro Tennis Star Emerges from Shell." I recognized the extent to which I was hemmed in by authority. A second lieutenant and a systems analyst in the data-processing department at the U.S. Military Academy at West Point, I was very much under army control, as I admitted before speaking. My speech was limited by "what I can say and do as an army officer under army regulations," I conceded to the *Post*.

What I told the packed hall assembled that Sunday was hardly revolutionary or militant. With self-confidence and a desire to help others, the black athlete, whether of average ability or a superstar, must make a commitment to his or her community and attempt to transform it. I cited the example set by certain major black athletes, such as the basketball star Bill Russell and the baseball pioneer Jackie Robinson, as the model for what must be done by others, even those less gifted or famous. In assigning blame for our condition, I pointed in two directions, not just in one, as many nationalists insisted on doing. "There is a lot we can do and we don't do because we are lazy," I insisted. "This may be brutal, but poverty is half laziness." I committed myself to work for the improvement of African American life. Many ghetto youths knew little about tennis and might not even recognize my name, but I would still try to make a difference, as we all should.

"We must forget ourselves" and work for others, I declared, even if "what we do today may or may not bear fruit until two or three generations."

When I returned to West Point, I was promptly invited by my superiors to explain myself and my actions. I was warned not to make any more speeches of even a vaguely political nature. I took the warning to heart, because I understood the Army's reasoning. Army officers must be above or outside politics, and if silence was the price for maintaining that distance, then so be it. When I left the Army not long after, however, I did not suddenly become a firebrand. Like many people with even a modicum of conscience and intelligence, I was too confused about what was going on among the leaders of black America, especially the younger leaders, to know precisely where to tread. South Africa was a clearer issue, and I turned to it almost with relief.

As I have said, I was acutely aware at times that some people saw me as not having done enough for the cause. Should I have done more? It was hard for me to act when I could see that what some people wanted me to do would have clashed violently with the principles I had evolved for myself over the years, principles having to do with a love of peace, morality, moderation, and religion. My character was set in this way, and I would not change for anybody. I will never forget something that Jesse Jackson said to me one evening in the 1970s in Atlanta. We were in the basement playroom of the home of Walt Hazzard, then an Atlanta Hawks basketball player, who had been a star at UCLA during my time there. Several other young blacks were in the room, in addition to Jackson, Hazzard, Andrew Young, and myself. (Donald Dell was the only white there.) We were in the middle of a warm discussion of race, politics, and protest, and I was defending my principles, or trying to explain them, when Jackson stuck me with a needling comment.

"The problem with you, Arthur," he declared, "is that you're not arrogant enough. You're just not arrogant enough."

"You're right, Jesse," I answered. "I'm not arrogant. But I don't think that my lack of arrogance lessens my effectiveness one bit. I really don't think so."

I had heard this complaint before, expressed in various ways. At best, the arrogance Jackson seemed to want in me was not a purely self-serving arrogance but one that employed ego for some larger goal. The trouble, however, is that, once empowered and turned loose, egotism and arrogance are hard to control. I am not sure that Jesse, in his own life, has ever understood this lesson fully, despite the good work that he has done. As for myself, I found out a long time ago that I am best when I keep my ego under tight control and try to reason and look ahead, beyond temporary, flashy victories at some other human being's expense, to the future. One consequence of my commitment to reasoning and reconciling would always be to have some people think of me as conservative, or opportunistic, or even a coward. So be it.

Needless to say, there were times when I asked myself whether I was being principled or simply a coward. While I was growing up, I was undoubtedly timid away from the tennis court. I was not only my father's child; I was wrapped in the cocoon of tennis early in life, mainly by blacks like my most powerful mentor, Dr. Robert Walter Johnson of Lynchburg, Virginia. They insisted that I be unfailingly polite on the court, unfalteringly calm and detached, so that whites could never accuse me of meanness. I learned well. I look at photographs of the skinny, frail, little black boy that I was in the early 1950s, and I see that I was my tennis racquet and my tennis racquet was me. It was my rod and my staff.

Looking out for his two motherless sons, my father tried to keep us out of harm's way, and the possibility of harm was real. We all knew what had happened to Emmett Till, whose death in 1955 cast a shadow over my youth and that of virtually all black kids in Richmond and no doubt across America. Fourteen years old and from Chicago, Emmett was visiting his family in Mississippi when, on a dare, according to reports, he whistled at a white woman. White men came for him at his uncle's house, took him away, murdered him, mutilated his body, and dumped it in a river. We assumed that the Ku Klux Klan was to blame. Virginia was not Mississippi, but the Klan was with us, too. It could happen to any of us.

My father respected the skilled, courageous leaders in the black community in Richmond, including lawyers such as Oliver Hill and Spottswood Robinson III, who had strong connections to the legal side of the movement; but protesting was for other people. He himself worked hard at his humble jobs, and tried to get along with everyone. He followed the unfolding saga of civil rights as best he could, and he recognized that freedom for blacks was at stake and that we had to fight for it. But he made sure that my brother and I never risked our lives against anyone, much less the police or the Klan. His semi-literacy undoubtedly was a factor in the distance he kept, but at some point a wary conservatism had also shaped him. This conservatism itself had been shaped by a mixture of religion, morality, economics, and personality, factors that determine our political and cultural consciousness in such a stealthy fashion that most of us are shaped and bent like a tree in the wind without ever being fully aware of its subtle pressures.

LATER IN 1985, after my arrest, I again took to the streets in a symbolic action to protest South Africa's racial policies. In the company of Harry Belafonte, Jesse Jackson, and other demonstrators, I marched on the United States mission to the United Nations.

On the whole, however, I preferred to work more quietly with TransAfrica Forum and TransAfrica, for which I sometimes spoke publicly. Perhaps my most charged moment as a speaker came on a mission with Randall Robinson in 1988, when we visited Dartmouth College in Hanover, New Hampshire, to aid the anti-apartheid struggle there. What made the visit memorable for me was not simply the extremely cold weather but my sadness that apartheid apparently had its supporters among the students. To dramatize the plight of black South Africans, some liberal and radical students had erected shanties on the campus. However, after agitation by the *Dartmouth Review,* a right-wing student journal supported nationally by older conservatives, the shanties had been demolished in the dead of night, presumably by supporters of the journal. (This on the campus of a college that once had identified itself with a commitment to the education of American Indians.) Outdoors, in freezing weather, Randall and I spoke briefly to assure the anti-apartheid students that they were not alone in their struggle. Seldom have I felt so embattled and outnumbered in the struggle against South Africa.

Meanwhile, as George Bush and Robert Dole fought bitterly elsewhere in New Hampshire for the Republican party nomination to succeed Ronald Reagan as president, neither would promise to go beyond President Reagan's policy of "constructive engagement" with the white South African leadership. Most of us in the anti-apartheid movement considered "constructive engagement" to be a euphemism for "status quo." One morning, in the leading hotel in Hanover, as I stood in a corner, I watched Dole stride purposefully through the lobby, surrounded by members of his entourage. The minority leader in the U.S. Senate, he was pursuing the presidency of the United States, the most powerful position in the world. I could only hope that, if he became president, he would face the leadership of South Africa with the same aggressiveness that he brought to pursuing the presidential prize.

It is important to me that I keep my faith in electoral politics. In the 1960s, so many people I knew, especially younger blacks, scorned them. But principled, inspired, skilled politicians, such as Robert Kennedy, can make a difference. Through Sargent Shriver, his brother-in-law, and Donald Dell, I met him twice, in Washington, D.C., and in California, in 1968, when we had a long talk about politics, America, and the world. Kennedy burned with a desire to do good. A week later he was dead. Later, I applauded the ambition of Bill Bradley to run for the Senate. At one point in the mid-1970s, looking ahead to my retirement, I myself even thought seriously about running for public office. When I was growing up in Virginia, most public offices, aside from the most elementary, were barred to blacks, as they were across the South. I never grew up thinking that one day I might be president of the United States. I did not think that any black could ever be elected governor of reactionary, segregated Virginia. In fact, my chances of becoming president of the United States probably seemed better than my chances of becoming governor. I never dreamed that one of the older boys who came to play at Brook Field on the courts my father tended could become governor of our state. But Doug Wilder did so.

In the mid-1970s, far from Richmond and transplanted as a New Yorker, I thought of running for the United States Congress from the Eighteenth Congressional District on the Upper East Side of Manhattan. Our congressman, Bill Green, was popular and effective, but he was a Republican and by no means invincible. Ours is the celebrated "silk stocking" district, so called because of its wealth. The district is heavily populated but, with a good pair of walking shoes, one can walk around it in about two hours. A large part of the district is Jewish, and the people who approached me to run were themselves Jewish. They wanted to put together a group to look into my feasibility as a candidate. I would have run as a Democrat. Years later, in 1988, I voted for George Bush, and I have voted for other Republicans from time to time; I refuse to be a "Yellow Dog Democrat," as the expression goes—someone who would rather vote for a yellow dog than a Republican. Still, though an independent, I consider myself a supporter of the Democratic party. I think I would have made a good congressman; but my thoughts of Congress ended with my heart attack in 1979.

FOR ALL THE strength of my opposition to apartheid, I deplored—and continue to deplore—all the violence that has taken place in South Africa, including not only the violence of the police, the African National Congress, and the Inkatha or Zulu group but also the intellectual violence that would allow, for example, the Dutch Reformed Church there to defend apartheid. Still, I am with Thoreau, Gandhi, and Martin Luther King, Jr., in their belief that violence achieves nothing but the destruction of the individual soul and the corruption of the state.

With mounting excitement, I read the news, as the 1980s drew to a close, that the famous winds of change in Africa, announced by Britain's prime minister Harold Macmillan more than a generation before, finally seemed to be blowing democracy into South Africa. Change was coming imperfectly, through the concessions and maneuverings of South Africa's prime minister F. W. de Klerk in response to the pressures exerted on apartheid; but it was coming. I treasured the many letters and telephone calls that came to me from my friends there, because they were often far more enlightening than the news reports. Although I refuse to be cynical or pessimistic about the possibilities of social change, I also had to resist making too much of what those same winds had actually brought thus far to South Africa. Thus, in September 1989, at the United Nations Plaza Hotel in New York, I made a plea to the board of the Association of Tennis

Professionals, which was on the verge of approving two tournaments in Johannesburg for the coming year, not to do so. Passionately at times, I stressed that the major black South African leader, Nelson Mandela, wanted the sports boycott maintained, that the organizers of the Olympic Games were skeptical about South African promises, and that other sporting bodies were insisting on more telling signs of the demise of apartheid. To my intense satisfaction, the ATP board decided not to include the tournaments.

Accompanying me on that mission, at my invitation, was Mark Mathabane. Fifteen years before, as a boy of fourteen or so, he had followed me around Ellis Park in Johannesburg and stunned me with his remark that I had been "the first truly free black man" he had ever seen. Now he himself was free (in so far as any of us is ever free), and the author of an acclaimed book, *Kaffir Boy*, about growing up in South Africa, as well as other books.

In *Kaffir Boy*, Mark wrote about what my example and my first visit to South Africa had meant to him. "The more I read about the world of tennis," he recalled, "and Arthur Ashe's role in it, the more I began to dream of its possibilities. What if I too were someday to attain the same fame and fortune as Arthur Ashe? Would whites respect me as they did him? Would I be as free as he? The dreams were tantalizing, but I knew they were only dreams. Nevertheless, I kept dreaming; after all, what harm could that do me?" Finally, at Ellis Park, he saw me play. "How could a black man play such excellent tennis," he wrote about my victory over a white opponent, "move about the court with such self-confidence, trash a white man and be cheered by white people?" Eventually with the help of Stan Smith and others, Mathabane came to the U.S. to attend college and find expression for his literary talents that easily might have been destroyed in South Africa.

I THANK GOD that I lived long enough to see Nelson Mandela come to the United States and be welcomed with a ticker tape parade through the canyons of Wall Street in New York. I was seldom more proud of America and my fellow Americans than when I saw the way we welcomed him as a hero. The success of the parade was a sure and gratifying sign that many people, black and white, rich and poor, recognize his sacrifice and applaud the almost superhuman way he preserved his dignity, his humor, and his unquenchable moral sense through the nearly three decades of his imprisonment.

To have spent twenty-seven years in jail for political reasons, to have been deprived of the whole mighty center of one's life, and then to emerge apparently without a trace of bitterness, alert and ready to lead one's country forward, may be the most extraordinary individual human achievement that I have witnessed in my lifetime. I marvel that he could come out of jail free of bitterness and yet uncompromising in his basic political beliefs; I marvel at his ability to combine an impeccable character, to which virtually everyone attests, with the political wisdom of a Solomon. In jail, I am told, his white guards came to have such respect for him that in some ways he was their warden and they the prisoners, more prisoners of apartheid.

He became one of my heroes long before I met him, so it was a special thrill when we first came together. When the ABC-TV journalist Ted Koppel held an internationally televised "town hall" meeting with Mandela at City College in New York—a sensational appearance by the South African—I sat with other guests in a special section near the stage. At the end of the program, I approached David Dinkins, the mayor of the city and an old friend, and asked him to introduce me to Mandela. I knew that Nelson loved sports, but I had no idea whether he would know who I was on sight.

I watched David go over to Mandela and whisper in his ear. I saw Nelson's head raise abruptly, and he broke into a beautiful smile.

"Arthur is here?" he asked, with obvious surprise and delight.

"He's right here," David said, turning to me.

"Oh my brother," Nelson said, looking straight at me. "Come here!"

He threw his arms around me and held me for a moment in a most affectionate embrace. He told me that in prison, he had read my three-volume work *A Hard Road to Glory*, about black American athletes. A mutual friend, Yusuf Surtee, a prominent Indian merchant in Johannesburg and a financial supporter of the African National Congress party, had given him the books as a present. I didn't want to delay Mandela's exit from the hall, so I moved him along up the aisle and into the lobby, talking with him all the way. I could scarcely believe he was there at my side, I was so thrilled.

Ironically, I had first heard of Mandela in the 1960s, from a white man, a tennis professional. In fact, he was a South African, Ray Moore, with whom I used to discuss the philosophy and ways of apartheid all the time.

"I think there is one man in South Africa capable of leading my country out of this mess," Moore told me one day.

"Is he white?" I asked Moore.

"No, he's not," Moore replied. "He is a black man, a lawyer imprisoned on Robben Island, in the Atlantic. His name is Nelson Mandela."

"Mandela? I've never heard of him."

"Well, you will," Moore insisted. "In fact, I think he will become president of South Africa one day."

After that, I looked for news of this black man who apparently possessed the personal magnetism, intellectual ability, and moral character that Moore described. The idea that a black man could be president of South Africa in the foreseeable future also seemed farfetched. But since Moore, while quite liberal by South African standards, was himself not a political radical, his assessment of Mandela was really quite intriguing.

I thank God that I lived long enough for one last visit to South Africa, in November 1991, which I made in a delegation of African Americans invited by Mandela himself. To go to South Africa, I was compelled to lie on my application for a visa and declare that I did not have an infectious disease. I try never to lie, but I lied. I had to see South Africa at least one more time, to talk directly to friends there and see some of the changes for myself.

In many ways, Johannesburg, where we spent three days, had not changed much since 1977; but in at least two ways it was drastically different. The apartheid signs—WHITES ONLY, NONWHITES ONLY—were gone, except in a few instances. And, more astonishing, the black people seemed transformed. The old subservience and obsequiousness had vanished, and the same people now seemed self-assured and even fearless. They were ready for the future.

We saw a great deal of Mandela on this visit. I never entered his home but saw where he lived—a walled compound, replete with armed guards, built by the African National Congress with security uppermost in mind. I had several stirring conversations with him, which formed the highlight of my visit. As I had done once in the past, I stayed at the home of a wealthy, liberal Jewish merchant—not the same merchant, but another friend of Yusuf Surtee.

I visited the Colored poet Don Mattera, the author of the poem smuggled to me at the airport at the end of one of my visits in the 1970s. Mattera had fallen into official disfavor and, overnight, had become a nonperson, forbidden to publish his work, travel abroad, speak in public, and attend certain functions. Now he was free again. I had a private lunch with a group of whites, who peppered me with questions about President Bush's attitude to the changes that were beginning to sweep their country. All of us were absolutely certain that, in the wake of his military triumphs in Kuwait and Iraq during the 1991 Gulf war, Bush's reelection was assured.

Not least of all because our visit would have been unthinkable even two years before, it was a glorious occasion for most of us Americans on the trip, whose aim was to see justice for blacks in South Africa, because the prize seemed almost within their grasp. On the airplane flying back to the United States via London, we were almost euphoric about the unexpected improvements that had come to pass in so short a time in South Africa. The end of apartheid seemed a miracle at hand. The musician and producer Quincy Jones, the politician Adam Clayton Powell IV, Randall Robinson, the radio station owner Bert Lee, Earl Graves of *Black Enterprise* magazine, and many of the rest of us talked enthusiastically about the prospect of raising money, lots of money, to boost the funding of TransAfrica. Hollywood was a major source of support, and Quincy promised to throw a gala party at his home in Los Angeles to attract prospective donors.

Then someone—Randall, I think—brought us back to reality.

"We are getting awfully excited," he said quietly, "and yet I keep thinking about one thing."

"What's that?"

"For all the changes we have seen, Nelson Mandela still cannot vote in his own country."

That simple fact made us sober. We became quiet and reflective as our airplane flew on through the darkness toward London.

*   *   *

THE NEXT TIME I saw Mandela, I had made my announcement to the world about having AIDS. A few months later, at his invitation, I visited him in his hotel suite in New York City, which he was visiting quietly. Our main topic now was AIDS, both as it affected me personally and as an international scourge. I was pleased to see that he knew a great deal about the subject and was free of the prejudices that prevent many political leaders from confronting it. He stressed to me how poor the medical facilities are for blacks in South Africa, and how much help his country needs to cope effectively with its health problems. I told him about my foundation to fight AIDS and the extent to which I hoped it would contribute to the fight in Africa.

Once again, I was struck by Mandela's courage and wisdom. He faces as difficult a road as any political leader in the world, but I have every confidence in him. To me, he stands with Václav Havel of Czechoslovakia and few other living men and women as my ideal of the political leader today. I hope Bill Clinton does half as well. Compared to Mandela's sacrifice, my own life, like that of most other people who talk about the need for sacrifice and change, has been one almost of self-indulgence. When I think of him, my own political efforts seem puny.

I am sure I will never know with full understanding why I held back from the fray when I did and why I plunged into the fray, in my own fashion, when I did. All I know is that I have tried at all times to do what I thought was right and appropriate, and that sometimes the effort to do right, and above all not to do wrong, led me into inaction. My only true regret, however, is that now that I see the world more clearly than ever, as I believe I do, I don't seem to have the time left to try to translate my vision into action as I would like.

All of us, as I have said, can learn from the example of Mandela. For African Americans, however, he may have a greater lesson. On the most basic level, that lesson is about the need to resist oppression. But his lesson is also something more complicated and challenging. Mandela's example leads us to ask certain questions, on which I believe our future may depend. Can we African Americans emerge from the prison house of our history with true dignity, as he did—that is, with a determination to remain free but also without bitterness or any other compromise in our moral principles? Can we prevent our outrage at the wrongs we have suffered in America from destroying our spirit, from depriving us of the high moral ground we once held? Can we avoid the temptation to sink utterly into despair, cynicism, and violence, and thus become abject prisoners of our past?

When I was a youngster growing up in Richmond, I could answer these questions boldly and in the affirmative, as our parents and teachers and elders had taught us we must do. Now I grope for a response, which is at least part of the reason I see race as a burden, a grave burden, one that outweighs all others in my life.

CHAPTER FIVE

The Burden of Race

I HAD SPENT more than an hour talking in my office at home with a reporter for *People* magazine. Her editor had sent her to do a story about me and how I was coping with AIDS. The reporter's questions had been probing and yet respectful of my right to privacy. Now, our interview over, I was escorting her to the door. As she slipped on her coat, she fell silent. I could see that she was groping for the right words to express her sympathy for me before she left.

"Mr. Ashe, I guess this must be the heaviest burden you have ever had to bear, isn't it?" she asked finally.

I thought for a moment, but only a moment. "No, it isn't. It's a burden, all right. But AIDS isn't the heaviest burden I have had to bear."

"Is there something worse? Your heart attack?"

I didn't want to detain her, but I let the door close with both of us still inside. "You're not going to believe this," I said to her, "but being black is the greatest burden I've had to bear."

"You can't mean that."

"No question about it. Race has always been my biggest burden. Having to live as a minority in America. Even now it continues to feel like an extra weight tied around me."

I can still recall the surprise and perhaps even the hurt on her face. I may even have surprised myself, because I simply had never thought of comparing the two conditions before. However, I stand by my remark. Race is for me a more onerous burden than AIDS. My disease is the result of biological factors over which we, thus far, have had no control. Racism, however, is entirely made by people, and therefore it hurts and inconveniences infinitely more.

Since our interview (skillfully presented as a first-person account by me) appeared in *People* in June 1992, many people have commented on my remark. A radio station in Chicago aimed primarily at blacks conducted a lively debate on its merits on the air. Most African Americans have little trouble understanding and accepting my statement, but other people have been baffled by it. Even Donald Dell, my close friend of more than thirty years, was puzzled. In fact, he was so troubled that he telephoned me in the middle of the night from Hamburg, Germany, to ask if I had been misquoted. No, I told him, I had been quoted correctly. Some people have asked me flatly, what could *you*, Arthur Ashe, possibly have to complain about? Do you want more money or fame than you already have? Isn't AIDS inevitably fatal? What can be worse than death?

The novelist Henry James suggested somewhere that it is a complex fate being an American. I think it is a far more complex fate being an African American. I also sometimes think that this indeed may be one of those fates that are worse than death.

I do not want to be misunderstood. I do not mean to appear fatalistic, self-pitying, cynical, or maudlin. Proud to be an American, I am also proud to be an African American. I delight in the accomplishments of fellow citizens of my color. When one considers the odds against which we have labored, we have achieved much. I believe in life and hope and love, and I turn my back on death until I must face my end in all its finality. I am an optimist, not a pessimist. Still, a pall of sadness hangs over my life and the lives of almost all African Americans because of what we as a people have experienced historically in America, and what we as individuals experience each and every day. Whether one is a welfare recipient trapped in some blighted "housing project" in the inner city or a former Wimbledon champion who is easily recognized on the streets and whose home is a luxurious apartment in one of the wealthiest districts of Manhattan, the sadness is still there.

In some respects, I am a prisoner of the past. A long time ago, I made peace with the state of Virginia and the South. While I, like other blacks, was once barred from free association with whites, I returned time and time again, under the new rule of desegregation, to work with whites in my hometown and across the South. But segregation had achieved by that time what it was intended to achieve: It left me a marked man, forever aware of a shadow of contempt that lays across my identity and my sense of self-esteem. Subtly the shadow falls on my reputation, the way I know I am perceived; the mere memory of it darkens my most sunny days. I believe that the same is true for almost every African American of the slightest sensitivity and intelligence. Again, I don't want to overstate the case. I think of myself, and others think of me, as supremely self-confident. I know objectively that it is almost impossible for someone to be as successful as I have been as an athlete and to lack self-assurance. Still, I also know that the shadow is always there; only death will free me, and blacks like me, from its pall.

The shadow fell across me recently on one of the brightest days, literally and metaphorically, of my life. On August 30, 1992, the day before the U.S. Open, the USTA and I together hosted an afternoon of tennis at the National Tennis Center in Flushing Meadows, New York. The event was a benefit for the Arthur Ashe Foundation for the Defeat of AIDS. Before the start, I was nervous. Would the invited stars (McEnroe, Graf, Navratilova, et al.) show up? Would they cooperate with us, or be difficult to manage? And, on the eve of a Grand Slam tournament, would fans pay to see light-hearted tennis? The answers were all a resounding yes (just over ten thousand fans turned out). With CBS televising the event live and Aetna having provided the air time, a profit was assured. The sun shone brightly, the humidity was mild, and the temperature hovered in the low 80s.

What could mar such a day? The shadow of race, and my sensitivity, or perhaps hypersensitivity, to its nuances. Sharing the main stadium box with Jeanne, Camera, and me, at my invitation, were Stan Smith, his wife Marjory, and their daughter Austin. The two little girls were happy to see one another. During Wimbledon in June, they had renewed their friendship when we all stayed near each other in London. Now Austin, seven years old, had brought Camera a present. She had come with twin dolls, one for herself, one for Camera. A thoughtful gesture on Austin's part, and on her parents' part, no doubt. The Smiths are fine, religious people. Then I noticed that Camera was playing with her doll above the railing of the box, in full view of the attentive network television cameras. The doll was the problem; or rather, the fact that the doll was conspicuously a blond. Camera owns dolls of all colors, nationalities, and ethnic varieties. But she was now on national television playing with a blond doll. Suddenly I heard voices in my head, the voices of irate listeners to a call-in show on some "black format" radio station. I imagined insistent, clamorous callers attacking Camera, Jeanne, and me:

"Can you believe the doll Arthur Ashe's daughter was holding up at the AIDS benefit? Wasn't that a shame?"

"Is that brother sick or what? Somebody ought to teach that poor child about her true black self!"

"What kind of role model is Arthur Ashe if he allows his daughter to be brainwashed in that way?"

"Doesn't the brother understand *that he is corrupting his child's mind with notions about the superiority of the white woman? I tell you, I thought we were long past that!"*

The voices became louder in my head. Despite the low humidity, I began to squirm in my seat. What should I do? Should I say, To hell with what some people might think? I know that Camera likes her blond dolls, black dolls, brown dolls, Asian dolls, Indian dolls just about equally; I know that for a fact, because I have watched her closely. I have searched for signs of racial partiality in her, indications that she may be dissatisfied with herself, with her own color. I have seen none. But I cannot dismiss the voices. I try always to live practically, and I do not wish to hear such comments on the radio. On the other hand, I do not want Austin's gift to be sullied by an ungracious response. Finally, I act.

"Jeanne," I whisper, "we have to do something."

"About what?" she whispers back.

"That doll. We have to get Camera to put that doll down."

Jeanne takes one look at Camera and the doll and she understands immediately. Quietly, cleverly, she makes the dolls disappear. Neither Camera nor Austin is aware of anything unusual happening. Smoothly, Jeanne has moved them on to some other distraction.

I am unaware if Margie Smith has noticed us, but I believe I owe her an explanation. I get up and go around to her seat. Softly I tell her why the dolls have disappeared. Margie is startled, dumbfounded.

"Gosh, Arthur, I never thought about that. I never *ever* thought about anything like that!"

"*You* don't have to think about it," I explain. "But it happens to us, in similar situations, all the time."

"All the time?" She is pensive now.

"All the time. It's perfectly understandable. And it certainly is not your fault. You were doing what comes naturally. But for us, the dolls make for a bit of a problem. All for the wrong reasons. It shouldn't be this way, but it is."

I return to my seat, but not to the elation I had felt before I saw that blond doll in Camera's hand. I feel myself becoming more and more angry. I am angry at the force that made me act, the force of racism in all its complexity, as it spreads into the world and creates defensiveness and intolerance among the very people harmed by racism. I am also angry with myself. I am angry with myself because I have just acted out of pure practicality, not out of morality. The moral act would have been to let Camera have her fun, because she was innocent of any wrongdoing. Instead, I had tampered with her innocence, her basic human right to act impulsively, to accept a gift from a friend in the same beautiful spirit in which it was given.

Deeply embarrassed now, I am ashamed at what I have done. I have made Camera adjust her behavior merely because of the likelihood that some people in the African American community would react to her innocence foolishly and perhaps even maliciously. I know I am not misreading the situation. I would have had telephone calls that very evening about the unsuitability of Camera's doll. Am I being a hypocrite? Yes, definitely, up to a point. I have allowed myself to give in to those people who say we must avoid even the slightest semblance of "Eurocentric" influence. But I also know what stands behind the entire situation. Racism ultimately created the state in which defensiveness and hypocrisy are our almost instinctive responses, and innocence and generosity are invitations to trouble.

This incident almost ruined the day for me. That night, when Jeanne and I talked about the excitement of the afternoon, and the money that would go to AIDS research and education because of the event, we nevertheless ended up talking mostly about the incident of the dolls. We also talked about perhaps its most ironic aspect. In 1954, when the Supreme Court ruled against school segregation in *Brown* v. *Board of Education,* some of the most persuasive testimony came from the psychologist Dr. Kenneth Clark concerning his research on black children and their pathetic preference for white dolls over black. In 1992, the dolls are still a problem.

Once again, the shadow of race had fallen on me.

I AM ALMOST always aware of race, alert to its power as an idea, sensitive to its nuances in the world. Like many other blacks, when I find myself in a new public situation, I will count. I always count. I count the number of black and brown faces present, especially to see how many, if any, are employed by the hosts. For example, when I had a heart attack in 1992 after taking part in a demonstration against the U.S. policy concerning refugees fleeing Haiti, I was not too distressed to count the darker faces in the emergency room at New York Hospital, where I have often been. I saw some Filipino nurses, and far fewer blacks. One black nurse sounded Haitian. I saw a black female resident in cardiology, a young doctor from Cornell Medical School.

As might be expected, the floors were cleaned mainly by blacks. Two of the cleaners, both Haitian women, confided to me that they had heard about my participation in the demonstration, and that they appreciated what I had done. What I didn't tell them, but certainly thought, was that I would have been just as happy to do it if the people were Swedish rather than Haitian, if the Swedes were similarly oppressed. I am sure race had something to do with my decision to take part, but I would like to think that the dominating factor was that I saw an injustice being done, and decided to do something, however small, about it.

In my world, as privileged as it can be at times, there is absolutely no escape from race. My AIDS condition should be a matter purely of science and medicine, but race casts a further shadow over it. AIDS surfaced in America as a disease of drug users and gay people—and people of color, specifically Haitians at first, then sub-Saharan Africans in general. In a time of bewilderment about the disease, Haitians came under a terrible and unjust scrutiny because of reports that they represented a special risk. Then came more and more reports that AIDS might have started in Africa.

Certainly the spread of the disease there has been connected to casual heterosexual practices and a resistance to contraception. But no credible and respected scientist, as far as I know, has talked about Africa and AIDS in terms of blame or shame. Still, to many black Americans and Africans, this connection represented only the latest stigmatization of Africa as a center of evil and misfortune.

The gravest allegation made in connection with AIDS is that it did not come into being naturally but was created in the laboratory. One possibility is that it came about as the result of an accident, with fateful consequences. The other scenario, advanced by more people than one would think, is that AIDS was deliberately developed in a laboratory for the purpose of genocide. How else to explain, some people have argued, why its main targets are people tagged as social outcasts, such as drug users and homosexuals, and the darker peoples of the world, especially people of African descent? The filmmaker Spike Lee, a highly influential man among young blacks especially, has associated himself publicly with this position.

I myself reject the likelihood of a deliberate, genocidal creation of AIDS by racist, homophobic, puritanical white scientists. However, for a person of African descent like me who actually has AIDS, the main practical aspect of the controversy concerns the use of a drug called Kemron. No therapy for AIDS is more saturated with political and racial associations. Kemron was developed at the Kenyan Medical Research Institute in Nairobi, Kenya, by Dr. Davy Koech and a clinician, Professor Arthur Obel. On July 25, 1990, the president of Kenya, Daniel Arap Moi, announced its development to the world. Present at this gathering of scientists, researchers, and other interested persons was a delegation of African Americans from the United States. Among the black Americans was Dr. Abdul Alim Muhammad, who was there on behalf of Louis Farrakhan's Nation of Islam (or Black Muslims, as they used to be known). Another black American physician present was Dr. Barbara Justice, who had brought fifty AIDS patients to Nairobi for treatment.

All the visitors had been drawn by reports of "miraculous" results in patients taking Kemron. Indeed, given the strong suggestion that a cure for AIDS had been developed, the wonder is that many more visitors had not attended the ceremony. Dr. Justice believes that "if these reports came from anywhere else, it would have caused a stampede." Doctors Koech, Muhammad, and Justice agree that racism and reactionary Western notions about Africa have prevented the Western media from reporting on Kemron, despite the involvement of the U.N.'s World Health Organization in its use.

I myself do not have to be convinced that Europeans are skeptical about scientific claims by Africans emerging out of Africa, or that many whites do not associate scientific discoveries with blacks. The image of Africa remains disfigured by notions of ignorance and superstition that were so carefully draped about the continent over the centuries. But I am not going to ingest a drug simply to show support for the notion that science can flourish in Africa. I need proof that the drug works. Accordingly, I sought such proof.

Probing the matter, I found out that Kemron basically resulted from observations about cattle made by some veterinarians from Texas who were working in Kenya. These doctors noticed that when cattle were infected with retroviruses, they developed runny noses exactly the way people get runny noses from a virus. Tested, the nasal discharge of the cattle was found to be rich in the substance known as alpha-interferon. When a drug was developed based on this information and given to cattle affected by the viruses, they recovered faster. When they received it before an infection broke out, they seemed to escape the symptoms of the disease.

Apparently, Dr. Koech approached HIV as he would approach any other virus, such as influenza. We have no cure for influenza, but we treat its symptoms when they appear. We get rid of the symptoms, then wait for the next appearance of these symptoms before we treat them again. He decided that, following the example of infected cattle, he should concentrate on the nose and mouth in applying alpha-interferon to humans; and he also worked to find the proper dosage (which turned out to be fairly low) for human application. He would treat its symptoms with the alpha-interferon drug he called Kemron. At one point, Dr. Koech reported that 97 percent of his patients showed a positive response to the drug. He even reported that 10 percent of his patients became HIV-negative following treatment—although this doesn't mean that they were cured.

When I first heard about Kemron, I was excited. Two black-owned newspapers in New York City, the *Amsterdam News* and the *City Sun*, as well as the black-owned radio station WLIB, which commands a dedicated following among many low-income blacks in the city, trumpeted the news about this breakthrough in AIDS research from Africa. Assailing the Western medical establishment for refusing to acknowledge the radical power of Kemron, some writers and speakers ventured to say that racism lay behind the skepticism about Kemron. (Incidentally, since alpha-interferon is a natural substance, it cannot be patented, and no drug company can have exclusive rights to its production and sale. This fact has featured prominently in some explanations of why Kemron has not been pursued more actively as an AIDS treatment in the United States and Europe.)

My AIDS physician, Dr. Henry Murray, is an open, considerate man. Too many doctors are remote or patronizing, but he encourages me to read about the disease and talk with him about the latest trends and medications. However, when I told him about this fantastic development from Africa, he was unimpressed.

"Oh, we know all about it, Arthur."

"Kemron? From Africa?"

"Oh yes, it's a form of alpha-interferon."

"Right, Hank," I said. "Shouldn't I think about trying it?"

"Well, the latest data I have seen doesn't support their claims."

"But the Kenyans have statistical evidence that Kemron works," I countered.

"Well, maybe it works for them," Dr. Murray said. "No one here has been able to duplicate their results, and many reputable people have tried. Perhaps later studies will show something positive."

This was too important a matter for me to drop without further inquiry. As it happened, I had been invited to Washington, D.C., to see the U.S. Secretary of Health and Human Services, Dr. Louis Sullivan. He graciously offered to help me in my inquiries. For our meeting, Dr. Sullivan invited Dr. Anthony Fauci, who runs the Office of AIDS Research, a section of the National Institutes of Health. Apart from Dr. William L. Roper, who runs the Centers for Disease Control in Atlanta, Dr. Fauci is probably the government's leading American expert on AIDS. Kemron was only one of the many topics we discussed.

"Believe me," Dr. Fauci said, "the issue of AIDS and Africa and Kemron is far too sensitive for us to brush off even if we wanted to, which we do not."

"But have you given Kemron a fair shot?"

"I would say so. We instituted eight separate clinical trials to see if the claims for efficacy were genuine or not. At this time, we have the results from seven of the trials and we are waiting on the last one."

"And?"

"We won't do anything until the last trial results are in. But I can tell you, right now it looks as if we will have to reject Kemron. We have no hard evidence yet that it does any good. But something may yet emerge."

We discussed the skepticism among many blacks, as well as some whites, about the medical profession and medical research, and about some of the factors that had led to that skepticism. The infamous Tuskegee experiment, in which several black men had been abused in the name of scientific research on syphilis, was one factor. There was also the widespread belief that some of our major pharmaceutical companies routinely try out their drugs on people in Third World countries and conduct clinical trials only in the United States.

I left enlightened but still puzzled. I don't think for a second that the Kenyans were deliberately faking their data; but if so, eventually they would be found out.

Some time later, I met Dr. Justice, who had been present at the presidential press conference in Kenya when the efficacy of Kemron had been proclaimed. I like her. Professional but warm, friendly, and caring in her manner, she doesn't always dress like most New York doctors. Instead, her colorful clothing often reflects her love of Africa. She is obviously driven by her desire to help her patients. When she talks about medicine, she does so passionately and yet with apparent objectivity. Just as obviously, she exudes race pride.

I told her what Dr. Sullivan and Dr. Fauci had said about Kemron. She laughed, if a little sadly.

"I can tell you, Arthur, my patients are helped," she insisted. "They aren't cured, but they are definitely helped. Kemron is nontoxic, which is wonderful. It doesn't destroy the patient in order to save him, like AZT. In combination with other therapies, it works." But her comment seemed a retreat from the word "cure" I had seen in earlier headlines.

As for the NIH clinical trials, Dr. Justice insisted that they had not been fair; the samples of Kemron used had not been identical to that used in Kenya. The cards were stacked against the drug, she declared, just as the cards are stacked against any treatment that doesn't originate with a major company in the United States.

Science, race pride, and compassion are not incompatible, but in this world they often seem that way. In October 1992, I met a young black man, a teenager, who illustrated this point. I was walking across the campus of the Niagara County (N.Y.) Community College, where I had gone to deliver a speech, when he stopped me. While I wouldn't say that he confronted me, he was definitely intense in his approach.

"Brother Arthur, have you seen this? You need to read this, brother."

A member of the Nation of Islam, he was carrying a copy of their newspaper, the *Final Call*, from October 7, 1991. The headline read: "AIDS Treatment Found in Africa." He wanted me to read the story, which was about Kemron. "This can help you, brother. White people are keeping the truth from you." The young man talked to me at some length. He was not particularly articulate, but he was earnest and genuinely wanted to help me.

Sorting out the various aspects of this matter is difficult, but it can be a matter of life and death for me. I have faith in Dr. Fauci and Dr. Sullivan. I admire and respect Dr. Justice. I liked that clean, earnest young man from the Nation of Islam and I was moved by his concern for me. I do not believe that AIDS is the result of a conspiracy by powerful whites against black people and other people of color and homosexuals. And I do not take Kemron. I do not take it for the same reason I have not tried a half-dozen other suggested treatments. I have simply decided that I will try drugs that have proven their efficacy by consensus, after scientific studies carried out by reputable authorities. In this matter, as in others, I cannot allow myself to be swayed by arguments based on theories of racial conspiracy and racial genocide.

*   *   *

AS A CELEBRITY, I encounter few examples of overt racism directed specifically at me. Perhaps I encounter more than I acknowledge, because I never want to dignify ignorant or malicious people by assuming they are fully aware of what they do. I am well known because of my years as a tennis player and my exposure on television as a commentator, and few people try to humiliate a celebrity. (Rarely, of course, I come across someone who takes a special pleasure in doing precisely that.)

I remember vividly, however, growing up under segregation. I remember the mandatory all-black schools, and the white line behind which I had to ride on buses. I remember the kindly white bus driver who politely but firmly made me move to the back of the bus after I had sunk blissfully into the most cherished seat for a young boy: down front, right across from the driver. I remember the kindly white tennis official, Sam Woods, who would not allow me to play in municipal tournaments in Richmond, and all the other not-so-kind officials who barred my way so that I finally played in only one official tennis tournament while I was a junior in Virginia. I remember that the University of Virginia, the state school founded by Thomas Jefferson, was forbidden to me because of the color of my skin.

In St. Louis, where I lived during my senior year in high school, I played freely with a cadre of brilliant white players, all about my age. But there were private clubs where they were welcome but I was not, and one tennis court from which I was literally and ignominiously chased. I also sensed the limits of hospitality and friendship between me and most of the white boys I played with. Sipping a cold Coca-Cola after practice was fine, and an occasional visit to the home of one or another; beyond that point, a wall rose between us, to keep us apart. In Los Angeles, where I attended UCLA, the barrier against interracial dating fell, but an exclusive club called Balboa Bay still barred me from its grounds; and the mother of the first white girl I dared to date recoiled in horror when she saw me on television and discovered that I was black, a detail that her daughter had failed to mention in singing my praises.

After I became better known following my selection for the Davis Cup team and my entry into the top ten of American players, both in 1963, I faced racial discrimination less and less. By this time, too, I was on my way to becoming a master at the game that all African Americans must learn if they wish to preserve their sanity: how to live with reasonable freedom and dignity and yet also avoid insult, disappointment, and conflict rooted in racism. I learned not so much to turn the other cheek as to present, wherever possible, no cheek at all. I learned to give no opportunity for a bigot to pounce on and exploit. I learned in moments of humiliation to walk away with what was left of my dignity, rather than lose it all in an explosion of rage. I learned to raise my eyes to the high moral ground, and to stake my future on it. I revered Martin Luther King, Jr., because, on the question of race, no African American commanded that ground as splendidly as he did, with surpassing eloquence and (despite his human failings, which disturbed me) consistency of argument.

Although I ceased to experience racial discrimination on a daily basis, race remained a burden for me, the most oppressive burden of my life. In fact, race is a double burden. Coping with racism is onerous; but so is coping with the myriad effects of that racism on blacks in general, the ways in which the harsh conditions under which most of us live have led to patterns of behavior that are themselves destructive. And yet I am no tragic mulatto, caught poignantly or forlornly between the races, as are many Coloreds in South Africa or mulattos in the Caribbean. Any person, black or white, who refuses to surrender himself or herself to racism is bound to know that feeling intimately. One is on the margin or between two groups if one chooses to be rational rather than emotional, judicious rather than passionate, inclusive rather than sectarian. In this racial divide, I often find myself critical of both whites and blacks. In the end, I am not for black or white, nor even for the United States of America, but for the whole of humanity. I can't define myself finally as an African American, or an American. My humanity comes first. I have felt that way since I have known myself, and I hope to die that way.

As for the very existence of African Americans in the United States, I truly believe that many people wish that we would go away, vanish, cease to exist; doubtless even many blacks have that feeling, and wish that they could lose their color in a tide of whiteness. On the ladder of minorities in our nation, we blacks are at the bottom. Jewish Americans are first among minorities (Jews are not a minority according to the Department of Labor, but by virtue of their numbers); then Asian Americans; then Hispanic Americans; then blacks. This was always the case; it will probably always be the case. I remember how in the segregated South poor whites could be kept in check by rich whites simply by reminding them that they were not blacks, that even in their poverty they were higher in the pecking order than black Harvard professors or black millionaires.

The need for us to be at the bottom seems integral to the identity of the nation. At every turn, our character and competence are questioned. Usually, the challenge is deviously expressed. However, certain foreigners, such as the Japanese, have openly questioned our abilities and our integrity. In sport, our capacity to lead and manage teams is doubted, as by the former broadcaster Jimmy "the Greek" Snyder and the baseball executive Al Campanis. People in positions of power and influence, who are in charge of making important decisions, do not believe we can do the job; sometimes it hardly matters what the job is. Our reputations, our abilities are constantly being impugned.

Because I am often the only black, or one of very few blacks, in certain organizations and social settings, I am also alert to the phenomenon that I and others call racial "tipping." In many white circles, blacks are acceptable as an element only if they comprise a certain small percentage of the people involved. Beyond that number, the presence of blacks threatens whites, the organization or group begins to lose whatever cachet it formerly enjoyed, and a sense of doom taints the atmosphere. Tipping is probably most potent in the area of housing; at a certain point, usually long before any real problems arise, white flight begins. But tipping enters more subtly into a host of other areas. We African Americans are perceived as acceptable in a token amount, toxic beyond it. This is a devastating commentary on the majority's perception of our nature.

In the past, some blacks undoubtedly liked being the only African American admitted into certain circles, in that it heightened their sense of accomplishment and prestige. I take no satisfaction in such exclusivity. I take no pride in the fact that twenty-five years after winning the U.S. Open, I am still the only black American man to have won a Grand Slam event. (However, I resent the suggestion I have heard that I should have done more to encourage younger black players; I think I have done much, and conscientiously.) I take no pride in being the first and only black member of a certain country club to which I belong. Wherever I go, I want to see other blacks present, whether on the tennis court, in the board room, or in the most prestigious club-house.

Nevertheless, in the last ten years or so, what has increasingly dominated my thinking about race in the United States is not what whites think about blacks and do to us, but what we blacks think about and do to ourselves. Perhaps this has always been my concern, but I don't think so. In most ways, we have never had as much power as we have commanded in the last twenty years. Under segregation, we African Americans lacked, to a great extent, the capacity to act in any substantial way to affect our future, to control not only our destiny but, in a way, our daily lives. Hemmed in by segregation, physically threat-ened by police and the Ku Klux Klan (which were sometimes the same, no doubt), we were a dependent, intimidated people. Apart from civil insurrections, we seemed to be beneath the notice of most whites. Overt racism erected walls about our community that few of us could scale or were allowed to scale. We developed certain solid institutions in response to segregation, notably the black church and our black schools and colleges; but as a community we were more acted upon than acting. Our middle class conducted its life with a constant aware-ness of the pressure of the white world. This awareness gave a quality of mimicry to black life but also stimulated the community to serve itself.

The cornerstone of identity in the African American world was the knowledge that we as a people had been historically wronged by the larger culture that dominated us. We believed that we were morally superior to that culture because it was only a misfortune to be a slave but a shame and a sin to be an owner of slaves. Here and there in the Bible, a verse might seem to support slavery, but the overwhelming weight of Judeo-Christian morality opposed the ownership and exploi-tation of human beings, whether in slavery or in the neo-slavery of segregation. We were the meek who would one day inherit our share of the earth.

Now, as we approach the close of the twentieth century, I believe that we have lost much, perhaps most, of that moral high ground.

One can argue in legal terms about reparations for slavery or segregation, or about the merits or demerits of affirmative action; but broad, deep moral arguments about racism in America have become harder to make. We African Americans cannot argue easily from a basis of morality because we are now, unlike as short a time as one generation ago, a moral example to far fewer people, even among ourselves. Many of us have abandoned God. I don't mean to criticize the masses of our hardworking, churchgoing people. I refer especially to younger, talented people, who have had certain opportunities and should be preparing to become our leaders. I remember reading that Martin Luther King, Jr., had said that he thought black Americans might eventually prove to be the agents or vehicles through which America redeems itself as a nation—that is, if America would look into its heart and admit that it had been founded on the forcible theft of land from the Indians and on the exploitation of Indians and Africans, and then redeem itself morally by addressing and solving the problem of race and racism. Such an option for redemption hardly exists any longer.

Now the moral fabric of African American culture, like that of America as a whole, is sadly compromised. Our churches are not nearly as influential as they once were. Our family life is disintegrating. Our respect for our elders, for the weaker among us, has dwindled. Our educational standards and expectations are low and falling fast. Our ability to generate jobs, always a problem, is even more so. Our crime rate is soaring, both in terms of the number of crimes and in terms of the heinousness of those crimes. In April 1992, the month I made my announcement that I had AIDS, *Newsweek* documented our crisis. The mortality rate of black children, 17.7 per 1,000 births, is more than twice that of white children. Among Americans with AIDS, blacks number 28.8 percent; 52 percent of afflicted women are African American, as are 53 percent of afflicted children. Nearly half of U.S. murder victims are black. Homicide is the leading cause of death among black males between the ages of fifteen and thirty-four. One in every four black men between twenty and twenty-nine years old is on probation, on parole, or in prison. One-fifth of all black males from fifteen to thirty-four have a criminal record, according to one study. Black children are "three times more likely than whites to live in a single-parent household." Of all black American children, 43.2 percent live in poverty as defined by the government. Most blacks seem to agree that the quality of our lives is worse now than ten years ago. It is almost certainly worse than in the 1960s.

What happened to black America since 1954? That was the year when the black community and the nation were electrified by the news that segregated education was to end, that the U.S. Supreme Court had declared it unconstitutional in the decision *Brown v. Board of Education.* First, I think it is accurate to say, we passed through a period of elation and optimism. I myself remember the day when word swept through our grammar school that we children would thereafter be going to school with whites; we would have all the rights and opportunities that whites had. The truth was somewhat different. In the 1960s and early 1970s, a small but important group of blacks was able to take advantage of the Civil Rights Act of 1964 and the Voting Rights Act of 1965. This group proceeded to move out of the old neighborhoods and leave the poorer, less educated strata to fend for themselves without the leadership and guidance that more fortunate blacks had often provided.

The national economy started to change. Blacks, who had been dependent on high-paying blue-collar manufacturing jobs, were often made obsolete as workers when the economy became more oriented toward information. Masses of immigrants, ready to work harder for less, entered the U.S. by crossing its borders legally and illegally at every available location. In places like Miami and Los Angeles, immigrants from Cuba and Central America devastated the internal black American economy by securing first the lowest-paid jobs, then moving upward until they had evicted black Americans almost entirely from the workplace. Single-parent families headed by women began to proliferate. The public schools began to deteriorate, as increasing numbers of students entered school without first having been prepared at home to accept the rigors of education. The cost of attending college soared. Crime exploded.

Behind all these ominous trends is, unquestionably, the cumulative impact of racism on African American culture. The cruel denial of jobs in sector after sector of the economy, the imposition of job ceilings that keep blacks down among the lowest levels of the company structure, the exclusion of blacks from the social settings that stimulate leadership in a variety of areas—these unquestionably account for most of the decline of the African American community. The decline is real. However, I do not view the decline as irreversible. We are no more prone to crime, immorality, and other forms of delinquency than any other social group. But I estimate that it would take at least a generation, perhaps more, before African American culture can regain the moral authority it once possessed. Then we would have, as we still did when I was a child, a sense of the integrity of the family, including mother and father; a sense of the value and power of education; a sense of the deep importance of religion and moral instruction; a sense of pride in ourselves as achieving, thinking human beings; a sense of our place in the community of peoples, regardless of race; a sense of our superiority to those who would deny us our rights because of the color of our skin.

Something fundamental has changed in African American culture, and for the worse. It hit me hardest when I was sitting at home one recent afternoon, watching CNN in the aftermath of the revolt in Los Angeles. Two members of the most notorious youth gangs, the Crips and the Bloods, were being interviewed about the possibility of an end to their years of bloody strife. On the subject of the police, Crips and Bloods were united. They hated the police. With a bitterness no doubt born of years of insult and injury, they denounced the police as interlopers in the community, outsiders who despised the residents and brutalized them routinely. The alienation of the two men was unmistakable.

What shocked me finally, however, was not their hatred of the police, which one might expect, but their attitude to the beating of the white truck driver Reginald Denny during the riots. Denny, driving his truck, had found himself in the wrong place at the wrong time. With a television camera in a helicopter broadcasting the event, several young black men pulled him from his truck and beat him savagely and without mercy. Although some people had tried to blame Denny for the attack by saying that he had provoked it by making racial slurs against blacks, Denny's only crime probably was that his skin was white. Naïvely, I expected the Crips and the Bloods, despite their hatred of the police, to concede that the beating of Denny was unjustifiable, that it had been wrong. Their response was exactly the opposite. Denny meant nothing to them. His innocence meant nothing to them. The principle of right and wrong meant nothing to them. Society despised them; they would despise society and its ideals.

Watching the television screen and listening to these two young black men, I felt sick. That's not us, I thought. That's just not us. It was as if spirits from another planet had come to earth and invaded black bodies. We were once a people of dignity and morality; we wanted the world to be fair to us, and we tried, on the whole, to be fair to the world. Now I was looking at the new order, which is based squarely on revenge, not justice, with morality discarded. Instead of settling on what is right, or just, or moral, the idea is to get even. You get even, although doing so is almost always a short-term proposition that ultimately leaves you further behind than where you started. Reginald Denny has not only recovered, but is talking humanely and idealistically about forgiveness. As I write, the young men accused of beating him are in custody, awaiting trial, and recalcitrant.

Not long afterward, I saw the television journalist Ed Bradley questioning a group of youngsters about morality, about the determination of what is right and what is wrong. In my boyhood, right and wrong were clear and unequivocal; but to the boys present, everything was shaded, compromised. Is it right to steal? Sometimes. Often? In practice, yes. Is there a moral aspect to sex? Not really. You get what you can from a woman. Do you have an obligation to a child you father? No; that's the mother's problem, not mine. Is it all right to cheat in school? Yes; just don't get caught. Getting caught is stupid. And so on.

What went wrong within black America? We might as well ask what went wrong with America as a whole. What happened to blacks is, to be sure, only a heightened degree of the national weakening of morality and standards. As for black America, I don't know of any single answer to that question, only several possible answers. However, the cruel irony of African American history is that although we are not nearly equal to whites in terms of opportunities and freedoms, we have declined as a group exactly at the time we achieved the highest degree of freedom we have ever had, and secured the largest number of rights we have ever had. It is almost as if the new rights and freedoms *caused* the decline, which of course is not true. At least, not completely.

I know that the deterioration occurred in my adult lifetime. Thus, I must bear part of the responsibility for the way in which African American culture has declined. Not I myself personally, but my generation collectively; if we wish to take most of the credit for what is creditable, then we must shoulder most of the blame for the amount that is discreditable. I see 1965 as the major watershed in modern African American history. That year dwarfs 1954 and *Brown* v. *Board of Education*. In 1965, when I was twenty-two years old, Stokely Carmichael (now Kwame Toure) promulgated the "doctrine" of Black Power and inaugurated the Black Power movement. He did so in one brilliant harangue in Greenwood, Mississippi, from which, in my opinion, black America has never adequately recovered. Carmichael was a leader of the Student Nonviolent Coordinating Committee (SNCC), a youth-oriented offshoot of Martin Luther King, Jr.'s Southern Christian Leadership Conference (SCLC).

In promulgating Black Power, Carmichael wittingly or unwittingly (the former is much more likely) turned his back on the moral emphasis and genuine nonviolence of King's leadership and moved toward a radically secular philosophy of racial emancipation. In retrospect, 1965 was the beginning of the end of the dominance of morality in African American culture. Instead, the amoral quest for naked and vengeful power would rule thereafter. No one should have to wonder where Black Power came from. It came out of the evil record of slavery and segregation, from the willful attempt by whites to keep blacks in a state of subservience through the denial to them of decent, just treatment in a society allegedly built on law. I am completely in support of the idea that blacks should garner as much power and wealth as we legitimately can. Nevertheless, I believe that Black Power, as promulgated, may have created many more problems than it ever solved, because legitimacy was deliberately excluded as a criterion.

I met Stokely Carmichael at least twice during the 1960s. In 1968, the year of the speech that got me in trouble with my army superiors, he also spoke at the Church of the Redeemer in Washington, D.C., at the invitation of the Reverend Jefferson Rogers. Something of Stokely's militancy may have rubbed off on me and moved me to deliver my own remarks, although they were tepid compared to his

language. Viscerally, emotionally, I admired Carmichael. His raw courage inspired me. Then, gradually, he and other young leaders at the
time like H. Rap Brown and Huey Newton (of the Black Panthers)
lost me. They lost me because they seemed to abandon principle in
their thinking and their actions. What started as a movement toward
liberation ended too often as a regime of dogmatism, coercion, hatred,
violence, and what would later be called sexism. I saw a chilling
similarity between the segregation that ruled my youth and the proposed new order under Black Power. For the first seventeen years of
my life, white people in Virginia had told me what I could do, where
I could go to church, in which taxi I could ride, where I had to sit on
the bus, in which stores I could try on a coat. Then, in my second
seventeen years, militant black people were trying to tell me, once
again, exactly what to think and do. I rebelled.

In many respects, Black Power was an improvement over the
old ways. Undoubtedly, an emphasis on morality led many blacks
toward passivity, obsequiousness, and even self-hatred. Black Power
promised a long overdue emphasis on gaining self-determination,
self-definition, and wealth. Looking back, however, I see the simple
truth that the old emphasis on morality was far more consistent
with the acquisition of money and power than the doctrine of Black
Power ever was. Defined by an excess of racial romanticism and
chauvinism, Black Power as often as not drove a wedge between
young black Americans and the very thinking and behavior that
would enable them to achieve positions of power. The main tool
for the acquisition of wealth and power is knowledge and self-discipline. In this way, young blacks could take advantage of the new
freedom afforded by the civil-rights acts and the changing mores of
the nation. But Black Power almost completely discredited the acquisition of knowledge and the rigor of self-discipline.

The discrediting of formal education as it existed in the United
States was perhaps the most disastrous result of Black Power. Unquestionably, our formal education had ignored black history and culture.
But when the idea of a black student learning Russian or Polish,
medieval history or quantum physics, became anathema in the more
militant circles, as it did, a disaster was in the making. Such an
education, it was said, amounted to a betrayal of our racial heritage.

The only legitimate areas of knowledge were those that could be defined through their connection to Africa. The assumption seemed to be that Africa itself did not need experts on Russia, Poland, medieval European history, or quantum physics, in addition to experts on Africa. If the discrediting of education started with the curriculum, it did not stop there. White teachers and professors became suspect or worse. The discipleship of student to professor, which is the principal method by which deep learning is passed on, so that experts nurture experts, became nearly impossible; how could a proud young black man subject himself to a white figure of authority? Finally, in increasingly wide circles among teenage blacks, learning itself became discredited. To study hard, to aim for good grades, has become to "act white," which is supposed to be the gravest charge one can level at a young black man or woman today. However, since the best students in the United States increasingly are Asian, perhaps "act Asian" should be the charge; in which case the element of color disappears.

I LEARNED MUCH about the changing face of blacks and education during the lively "Proposition 48" and "Proposition 42" debates of the 1980s. Eventually implemented in 1984 by the National Collegiate Athletic Association (NCAA), the governing body of college sports in the United States, "Prop 48" sought to raise the high-school academic requirements for students entering college who wished to compete in intercollegiate athletics. Incoming freshmen who did not meet these academic requirements could be given scholarships but could not play for their schools during their first year. "Prop 42," passed later, sought to deny athletic scholarships to such students. Behind the proposals were not only a spate of recent scandals in which former college athletes with degrees proved to be semi-literate but also a deepening sense that many athletic departments had subverted the true mission of their colleges and universities in the name of athletic success. The issue became charged with racial tones because a disproportionately high percentage of college athletes in the major American sports—football, basketball, baseball, and track—are black.

The black presence in many colleges and universities is close to a sham. In 1983, an article by sociologist Harry Edwards in the *Atlantic*

Monthly documented the sorry situation. Although entrance requirements were often pathetically low, 25 to 35 percent of young black
high-school athletes could not meet them. In college, as many as 65 to
75 percent of blacks with athletic scholarships never graduated. Of
those who graduated, perhaps 75 percent did so with degrees in
physical education or some other major or concentration designed to
reflect their athletic prowess but with limited use after school. (In 1993,
ten years after Edwards's article, a report revealed that one school,
North Carolina State University, long famous as a power in collegiate
basketball, had not graduated a single basketball player since 1985.)

Prop 48 allowed a freshman to play for one of the 277 Division
1 or top athletic schools only if the student had made a 2.0 grade point
average (a C average) in high school and only if his or her courses
included English, mathematics, the social sciences, and the physical
sciences. It also required the athlete to have a combined score of 700
(out of a possible 1600) on the Scholastic Aptitude Test (SAT) or 15
(out of a possible 36) on the rival American College Test (ACT). The
SAT and ACT tests are mandatory steps at most American colleges.
Previously, students required only a C average, without regard to the
courses taken, and many of the courses were scandalously devoid of
intellectual content.

These new requirements should present no challenge whatsoever
even to the average student. In recent years, however, fewer than 50
percent of black students taking the SAT had scored as high as 700;
on the ACT, only 28 percent reached 15. Meanwhile, more than 75
percent of whites achieved 700 or 15 on the tests. (If you scored 700
on the SAT and tallied 15 on the ACT, then 90 percent of students
taking the test outscored you in verbal achievement, and about 65
percent outscored you in math.)

Although these proposals would affect athletes of all races, some
black college presidents, charging racism, led the opposition to them
and threatened to withdraw their schools from the NCAA. Among
white institutions, presidents were generally for the changes, while
athletic directors generally were not; in black schools, however, opposition was often led by presidents. The president of Southern University
in Louisiana, for example, called the proposal "patently racist." The
proposal was caused, he said, by the fact that "the black athlete has

been too good. If it is followed to its logical conclusion, we say to our youngsters, 'Let the white boy win once in a while.' This has set the black athlete back twenty-five or thirty years. The message is that white schools no longer want black athletes." Another official pointed out, without embarrassment, that the new entrance standards for athletes would be higher than the general entrance standards for most black colleges and even some white schools. The National Association for the Advancement of Colored People (NAACP), Jesse Jackson through his Operation PUSH group, the National Baptist Convention, and other black organizations also opposed the change.

I was one hundred percent behind the proposed higher standards. Lobbying behind the scenes, I also wrote at least one letter to *The New York Times* calling for college presidents to stand up for education; the *Times* also published my essay "Coddling Black Athletes," in which I urged that "we should either get serious about academic standards or cut out the hypocrisy and pay college athletes as professionals." I published another essay in *Ebony* in which I talked about having visited black high schools where "the obsession with sports borders on pathology." I agreed completely with what the respected football coach Joe Paterno of Pennsylvania State University said in his provocative declaration at the 1983 NCAA convention: "For fifteen years we have had a race problem. We have raped a generation and a half of young black athletes. We have taken kids and sold them on bouncing a ball and running with a football and that being able to do certain things athletically was going to be an end in itself. We cannot afford to do that to another generation."

I found myself opposing two nationally known black basketball coaches: John Chaney of Temple University and John Thompson of perennially ranked Georgetown University. Chaney called the NCAA "that racist organization." As a highly publicized protest against the attempted passage of Prop 42, Thompson left the coach's bench during at least two basketball games involving his team. Both of these men are genuinely interested in education, but the positions they took seemed on the wrong side of all the key issues involved in the devaluation of education among blacks in the United States. In a long, sometimes acerbic telephone conversation, Thompson explained to me in detail his objections. First, whatever the benefits to our society in general, blacks would suffer from the changes because fewer would meet the requirements and be allowed into college. Once again, he argued, when America decided on some rise in standards, blacks paid the lion's share of the price for this change.

Thompson's second objection was that the proposition endorsed standardized tests (SAT and ACT) that were culturally biased; in addition, they are hardly infallible at predicting later success, including academic success. "Cultural bias" is the phrase of choice for nationalistic blacks when their philosophy collides with the basic demands of education. If whites do better, then the tests must be culturally biased. No one raises this question when the children of poor immigrants from Southeast Asia outclass native-born Americans in scholastics. My own position is different from Thompson's. Can one attribute a low test score to socioeconomic bias? Perhaps. Can one invoke cultural bias to explain a 700 SAT score? Ridiculous!

To Thompson's first objection, that black athletes would be barred by the new standards, I asserted my belief that any loss in numbers would be short-term. In response to the new standards, black youngsters would simply rise to the challenge and meet them. To the objection of cultural bias, I responded that Thompson could hardly come up with a credible alternative set of requirements that would yield a higher number of qualified entering black students. Did he really want an essay test, instead of the multiple-choice format of the SAT and ACT tests? Then, I told him—only half in jest—*no* black kid would get in, since the quality of writing among black students in general had become notoriously poor. As for John Chaney's mantra that black kids "deserve a chance"—of course they do, I responded. Everyone deserves a chance. What Chaney's plaintive cry reflects, however, is the obsession with entitlement that is rampant among young blacks. The idea that society owes them special favors for average efforts has taken root with a vengeance.

In my essay "Coddling Black Athletes," I wrote:

We need to address the deep-seated cynicism of coddled, black public-school athletes, many of whom are carried through school with inflated grades and peer group status that borders on deification. High school coaches need to be held accountable for the academic preparation of their would-be Michael Jordans.

The critics of Proposition 42 seriously underestimate the psychic value that black athletes place on their athletic success and how that could be used to motivate them academically. The screening process for superior athletes starts earlier—when they are 11 or 12—and is more efficacious than for any other group of Americans. Social status is conferred at once. And they learn early that they don't get the idolatry, attention, and, ultimately, Division 1 scholarships for their intellectual promise.

Proposition 42—or something like it—would motivate high school coaches and their best players to take education seriously. Most important, that dedication to academic concerns among athletes would set a tone in the schools that would very likely inspire nonathletes to study harder.

The ethos of entitlement must be countered. I remember a distressing visit to Stamford High School in Connecticut, at the invitation of coaches there, to meet their varsity athletes at the time that "Prop 48" was being hotly debated. I asked the kids—many of them black, and most of them male—if they thought it fair that persons who performed weakly in academics should be given athletic scholarships. The response of every black male was that he was entitled to the scholarship, even if someone more qualified academically would be deprived of one. Not one suggested that athletes should be held to the same standards as nonathletes in competing for scholarships. They argued that they had spent endless time in training, that blacks had been discriminated against, and so on; it finally came down, however, to their sense of entitlement. On display was the increasingly dominant African American adolescent ethos of entitlement, of "You owe me," which I consider monstrous. One can be sure that an adolescent with such an attitude will make no particular effort at scholastics. Why should he? His teacher (black *or* white) owes him a passing grade.

I can understand the argument that blacks should have been paid reparations for slavery and segregation. By an act of Congress, Japanese Americans interned during World War II received $20,000 per family for that injustice. Germany is still paying reparations to Jews through its relationship with the state of Israel. No one has paid black Americans anything. In 1666, my state, Virginia, codified the conversion of black indentured servants, with limited terms of servitude, into slaves. The Emancipation Proclamation came in 1863. In my time, no one has seriously pursued the idea of making awards to blacks for those centuries of slavery and segregation. We may indeed be entitled to something. But our sense of entitlement has been taken too far. One of the major tasks of my teachers as I grew up was to make sure that no black kid gave up the struggle to do better because of despair in the face of segregation. We were taught that segregation counted for nothing against our duty to ourselves to work hard and do well. Our future, if we stayed in the South, was circumscribed by the "Sacred Six" list of jobs for blacks, serving blacks. By choosing one of these careers—physician, dentist, lawyer, teacher, minister, or mortician—one could even have a measure of prestige and prosperity. We nevertheless worked hard. Should we now give up because of an oppressive sense that we have not been compensated for historic wrongs done to us? Absolutely not.

The cult of entitlement is not limited to the poor. One Christmas not long ago, I was in the company of a close friend of mine, a successful doctor, and his son Bobby, who was himself a recent graduate of an elite private college and a renowned law school. African Americans all, we were guests in the sumptuous home of a nationally known television personality, also a black American. Our talk turned to affirmative action.

"Bobby," I asked my friend's son, "would you have accepted entrance into the law school under the rule of affirmative action, if your grades were not good enough for normal admission?"

"Yes, I would have," he replied.

"Why? Affirmative action wasn't meant for you, surely. You were born and brought up in luxury, with the best teachers and private schools from kindergarten on up. You've lived a charmed life."

"As a black, I belong to a group that has been historically abused and discriminated against. I'm entitled to redress."

"Is that your best argument?"

"Also, we need a greater ethnic diversity among lawyers, even if we don't need more lawyers. And law-school entrance requirements are probably slanted to favor whites."

"So you would accept affirmative action?"

"Yes, I would. Don't you think I should?"

"No, Bobby. Philosophically, intellectually, I think affirmative action is just about indefensible."

"Well, Arthur, all my friends think like me."

"Yes, I know. We have a problem there. A serious problem."

If American society had the strength to do what should be done to ensure that justice prevails for all, then affirmative action would be exposed for what it is: an insult to the people it is intended to help. What I and others want is an equal chance, under one set of rules, as on a tennis court. To be sure, while rules are different for different people, devices like affirmative action are needed to prevent explosions of anger. Practically, affirmative action is probably necessary. But I would not want to know that I received a job simply because I am black. Affirmative action tends to undermine the spirit of individual initiative. Such is human nature; why struggle to succeed when you can have something for nothing?

THE PROBLEM OF leadership continues to plague black America. The very fact that we speak of "leaders" and "role models" as much as we do tells of our lack of power and organization. No reasonably coherent body of people would think in terms of "leaders" and "role models." Jewish Americans, for example, do not have leaders and role models, as we define them, even though certain highly influential people are Jewish. But we depend on all sorts of blacks to be leaders and role models for the community. We even think of athletes and entertainers in this way; we see basketball players and pop singers as possible role models, when nothing could be further, in most cases, from their capacities.

We blacks look for leadership in men and women of such youth and inexperience, as well as poverty of education and character, that it is no wonder that we sometimes seem rudderless. One major reason for the ineffective record of Black Power was that the major exponents were young people—almost all of them young men—who had few

qualifications for leadership beyond bravery. Vision, learning, experience, the wisdom that age often brings were all generally lacking. We
are also afflicted, it seems to me, with the Messiah complex, which is
another sign that we as a people are wandering in the wilderness. I often
think that if the blacks of Memphis had organized themselves prop-
erly, they would not have felt the need to send for Martin Luther King,
Jr.—the Messiah—to help them with a local crisis involving garbage
collectors. Then he would not have been killed, like a Messiah, doing
what others should have done for themselves.

I must also confess, although I know I may offend some people,
that I did not fully share their passion for Malcolm X. I was fascinated
by his autobiography, but until his conversion following his pilgrimage
to Mecca, I found him in other ways hard to accept. Having lived
under white-imposed segregation, I was not about to deliver myself to
the black-imposed segregation central to the Nation of Islam. I
thought that his teachings on race (derived from the Nation of Islam),
about blacks as the superior people and whites as mutant devils produced by the mad scientist Yacub, were preposterous. I admired
Malcolm's bravery and his determination to educate himself. I admired
and still admire the self-help ethic of the Nation of Islam, and the
emphasis on cleanliness and self-discipline. Sometimes I bought copies
of the newspaper *Muhammad Speaks*, simply to find out what was going
on, or what the Muslims thought was going on. But the "white devil"
rhetoric made little sense to me. Nor was I completely impressed and
convinced by the story of Malcolm's conversion. "Malcolm," I wanted
to ask him, "do you mean to say that you had to go all the way to the
Middle East and actually *see* some blond, blue-eyed Moslems before
you would believe that some existed? I've met a few on my travels. I
could have saved you the trip."

The current passion for Malcolm has less to do with the actual
Malcolm, admirable as he was in certain ways, and much more to do
with both the hunger among our young people for guidance and their
capacity to grasp at straws, to fantasize about power and authority. We
leave whole worthy sections of Malcolm's character and creed un-
touched, such as his thirst for knowledge and his prolonged effort to
educate himself; his self-discipline; his ability to grow. I think the Spike
Lee motion picture, whatever one may think of it as cinematic art, gives

a fairly rounded portrait of the man; and yet, in the world, Malcolm lives mainly as an embodiment of black rage at and defiance of whites, and Martin Luther King, Jr., seems to have few followers or admirers among those who admire Malcolm. It is as if King spoke only to whites, Malcolm only to blacks.

In any event, Malcolm was more than a cut above certain leaders today who talk militantly but who, compared to Malcolm, seem to have few genuine ideas or ideals, or the courage for which he was justly famous. In this category I would place New Yorkers such as the Reverend Al Sharpton and Professor Leonard Jeffries. Such men may mean well but need to be challenged. In my opinion, the key to such leaders is their instinct to build and maintain a power base that is usually small but also distinct and their very own. I am well aware that for such people, I hardly count. "I don't give a damn," I imagine them saying, "what Arthur Ashe or anyone else like him thinks. I must guard my power base." To maintain that power base, the "leader" has to talk and act in a militant way, no matter what he actually thinks. Sharpton, in running in 1992 for the U.S. Senate (a distressing thought, were it not for the various white demagogues who have sat in the U.S. Senate, some no more qualified than Sharpton), has attempted to broaden his base; but his record is not encouraging, especially escapades such as his defense of the unhappy Tawana Brawley, who helped to polarize the state of New York along racial lines with an unlikely story of abduction and rape by white men. Jeffries, the chair for nineteen years of the Department of Black Studies at City College of the City University of New York, represents to me the almost complete subversion of an intellect by race. His blanket, pseudo-scientific attacks on whites, and Jews in particular, are indefensible—and he himself has hardly defended them, since he has published virtually nothing of his own in his years as a professor at the college.

Whenever I visited my father in Virginia, we would usually watch the news on television together. Quite often, after listening to some black leader speak, Daddy would shake his head. "Now that don't make any sense to me," he would say. "Arthur, does that make any sense to you?" Often it didn't; yet I had to assure my father that, semi-literate though he was, he hadn't taken leave of his senses.

Worried about the quality of black leadership, a small group of well-to-do blacks, of which I was a member, some years ago met regularly in such resort settings as Hilton Head, South Carolina, and Miami. Each time, we paid the expenses of one prominent black politician to visit and talk with us. Among those who came were the former mayor of Atlanta Andrew Young, and Douglas Wilder when he was lieutenant-governor of Virginia. We wanted to stimulate an exchange of opinions among the leaders, because we found that many did not speak to one another but instead strove to protect their individual turfs. It was a tiny gesture, but I hope it helped.

Although Sharpton and others like him in the African American world gain the headlines, I am grateful for those other blacks who quietly prepare themselves to occupy positions of authority and to represent all of us in a morally responsible way. I refer to talented, farsighted blacks such as Andrew Young, the former U.S. ambassador to the United Nations; Douglas Wilder, the governor of Virginia; John Lewis, the former civil-rights worker, now a congressman from Georgia; Maxine Waters, the California congresswoman whose district includes many people tragically affected by the recent Los Angeles disturbances; Kurt Schmoke, the mayor of Baltimore; Maynard Jackson, the mayor of Atlanta; Willie Brown, the speaker of the California Assembly; Sharpe James, the mayor of Newark; and David Dinkins, the mayor of New York. Some, like my friend David, may have made a few political mistakes; basically, however, they are all persons of integrity and ability.

In many ways I am philosophically closest to Young; our temperaments also seem almost to mesh. An ordained minister, Young is a reconciler rather than a divider of persons; he is pragmatic in a way that apparently involves no compromise of principle. True pragmatism, I believe, takes into account the moral consequences of an action. If the action leads to immorality, then one has not been genuinely pragmatic, merely opportunistic. And yet one must be able to act. Speaking about the need to make decisions, Doug Wilder said to me once, "You have to be willing to pull the trigger. First you have to think that you are right, that what you are doing is morally defensible, that it is good for the people you wish to help. Then you have to be willing to pull the trigger. You have to act."

The black electorate must also act. The habit of electing and reelecting demagogues and characters with dubious records, such as Marion Barry in Washington, D.C., is unfortunate. On this score, I thought John Lewis's recent election in Georgia something of a watershed in African American political history—a small watershed, perhaps, but one nevertheless. Lewis defeated the favorite, Julian Bond, who was his opposite in almost every way. Light-skinned, handsome, and aristocratic in his bearing, Bond comes from a distinguished family; he is highly educated, politically sophisticated, and has a long personal history of activism. In 1968, at the national convention of the Democratic party, he was even nominated for the vice-presidency of the United States, before someone discovered that he was too young to qualify for the job. His honesty was unquestioned. Lewis was none of these things, except for his honesty and his record of activism; as a civil-rights worker, he had been beaten repeatedly. But he was perceived as morally above reproach, one of the masses and yet no demagogue; in addition, he was clearly responsive to the needs of both blacks and whites. Against the odds, he won the election. Much as I admire Bond, I thought the largely black electorate showed wisdom in making its choice. We have not always chosen wisely.

I think of myself as being in some respects a "race man," an expression that black Americans use to describe someone committed to his people and vigilant about racial injustice. Still, I am appalled by the level of irrationality in our community and especially by the complicity of some newspapers and radio stations in encouraging this excess. Irrationality certainly also exists among whites, but it seems to be fostered more readily within our community by people who should know better. Our suspicion of whites and hostility to them routinely go beyond the dictates of reason. When I read certain newspapers aimed at blacks, however, I sometimes wonder whether race is not abused to some extent as a subject by these weeklies, so inflammatory and irrational they can be. In the past presidential election, for example, certain papers repeatedly mauled Jesse Jackson for allegedly having "sold out" to Bill Clinton. In the first place, Jackson had been lukewarm in support of Clinton; in the second, only a short-sighted African American could fail to see that to win the election Clinton had to steer his campaign down the middle, to recapture many of the white Democrats who had defected to the Republicans. To the editors of such newspapers, however, this logic meant little; the opportunity to be divisive was there, and some seized it.

The same is true of the call-in radio shows on WLIB, a radio station that probably reaches more blacks in New York City than any other station. Many of my black middle-class friends refuse to listen to WLIB, or claim not to. They insist that what is spoken there is often unsubstantiated, reckless, and even racist. The comments of many of the callers, and even some of the hosts, indeed often seem irresponsible. Nevertheless, I know I have never turned off the station in anger or disgust. No matter how absurd the comments, I believe that whatever little effectiveness I have depends in large part on knowing what our people think. In addition, all is not confusion and discord, as some of my friends insist. In fact, I agree with much of what is said on the station, either by callers or the hosts, on the subject of race. Above all, I sense the hurt and sorrow behind the wild accusations. These are people who suffer and have suffered. A radio station like WLIB is one of the few vents for their seething emotions, their frustrated thoughts and dreams. Still, I will not support racism or extremism, no matter what the source.

I look for responsible, intelligent African American political leaders. At one time, I had high hopes for the Reverend Jesse Jackson. In 1984, when he made his first run for the presidency, I even founded an organization called Athletes for Jesse Jackson. (To tell the truth, few athletes were for anyone but themselves, and fewer were for Jackson after dealing with his staff. One athlete, the football player Butch Woolfolk, had so much trouble getting a simple reimbursement for his expenses on a trip for Jackson that I finally gave him the money myself.) I was determined to support him all the way. The first iota of doubt came when Jackson began to claim that Martin Luther King, Jr., had died in his arms; people who were at the Memphis motel when King was shot told me that such a thing never happened. I began to wonder about someone who would exaggerate his relationship to King in order to enhance his stature as a leader. I also began to think that Jesse liked the limelight a little too much; I was irked by the fact that he almost never spoke to me in public without looking around to see to whom else he might want to talk. I was not flattered by this lack of focus.

When Jackson formed the Rainbow Coalition, several of us were asked to contribute $5,000 each. I was prepared to send the money, but I doubted that it would be wisely spent. What was Jesse Jackson actually going to do? What was his mission? After the 1988 election, I began to drift away. When he moved to Washington from Chicago, I assumed he would run for the mayoralty of the District of Columbia. To my disappointment, he didn't. All I saw was an ineffectual maneuvering to stay out in front, to remain *the* black leader in America without having any executive experience whatsoever, without once testing his ideas and abilities in the crucible of public office. I thought he was determined to monopolize the attention of the media so that no other black leader, such as Kurt Schmoke or Maynard Jackson, could ever rival his fame. Rather than develop a plan, he seemed restlessly to seek one photo opportunity after another.

Accordingly, his reputation has suffered in many circles. Talented, intelligent, and shrewd, he needs to decide on a few areas of involvement and focus on these, rather than try to be Minister Plenipotentiary from black America to the world. Like most of us, I still admire and like him; but he must settle down if he is ever going to be effective. If he does settle down, he could be an even greater force for social progress than he already is.

WHILE I THINK that the concept of the "role model" is an indication of our instability as a people, I know that it is a valid concept in our culture, where failure is so much a part of our lives that anyone who succeeds is scrutinized for his or her secrets to success. Whether I like it or not, it seems clear that blacks who succeed have a special obligation to try to live exemplary lives. When someone like the entertainer Eddie Murphy appears to flaunt his children born out of wedlock, it probably appears to impressionable young people that the way to success is to turn one's back on institutions such as marriage. In a special *Newsweek* investigation of the black male published a few years ago, many young men openly declared that they felt a strong obligation to have as many children as possible, but no obligation whatsoever to these children or their mothers. Behavior by celebrities that reinforces such thinking is unfortunate. When Vice President Dan

Quayle spoke out against unmarried single women having children, he did so by criticizing the television comedy series "Murphy Brown." I believed that he was right in pointing to the potential negative impact of television images of fatherless children (although we must always respect the freedom of expression); he simply picked a poor example in attacking the fictional character Murphy Brown.

I am also appalled by the number of celebrities who become involved in crimes of one sort or another, but especially crimes involving sex. Of these, athletes are probably among the prime offenders, with Mike Tyson the most celebrated—although not necessarily the most delinquent. Statistics indicate that a high percentage of sexual crimes reported on American campuses involve college athletes. That a disproportionate number of these are blacks distresses me. I remember a sorrowful conversation some years ago with Julius Erving, once a basketball superstar but a man who even then set high standards of behavior for himself and met them. Erving had been so shocked at some words uttered by a promising young basketball player, Quintin Dailey, that we talked at length on the telephone about it. Responding to questions about the charge that he had sexually assaulted certain women, Dailey seemed to brush off the matter. "That's all over now," he reportedly said. "All I'm concerned about is getting back to basketball." Julius and I both wondered how he apparently could turn his back on the severity of what had befallen those women and ignore the seriousness of the allegations against him. But we were dealing with a new generation, and the old morals and sense of discretion apparently no longer apply.

I do not think that every black athlete or entertainer has an obligation to thrust himself or herself into positions of leadership. However, our situation is increasingly desperate, and I admire those athletes and entertainers who consciously try to give something back to the people, if only by exemplary behavior. I admire former stars such as Julius Erving in basketball, or Lynn Swann in football, for what they have made of themselves. I am less happy with the demureness of someone like Michael Jordan, who is as popular as he is rich. While I would defend Jordan's right to stay out of politics in general, I think that he made a mistake in declining to give any open support to Harvey Gantt, the respected black politician who ran for the U.S. Senate in

1990 from Jordan's home state of North Carolina. For me, the main point is not that Gantt and Jordan are both black; rather, it is that Gantt's opponent, Jesse Helms, has a long history of supporting segregation, and the contest was close. For blacks across America, that Senate contest was the most important in decades. Instead, Jordan stuck to his apolitical position. "I don't really know Gantt," he said, in response to criticism of his silence. "Well, Michael," I would have told him, "pick up the telephone and call him!" A few appearances with Gantt might well have made the difference. Instead, Helms returned to the Senate.

FEW ASPECTS OF race relations in America have disturbed me as much as the enmity in certain quarters between blacks and Jews. The entire climate of black–Jewish relations has become stormy. Recently in New York City, with its large Jewish and black populations, a center of trouble has been the Crown Heights section of Brooklyn, where Hasidic Jews of a particular sect live surrounded by blacks. This sect, law-abiding but exclusive and zealous, is hardly representative of Jewish culture as a whole. And many blacks who live near them are from the Caribbean, of hardworking immigrant stock but often without a fully informed understanding of Jews or of American race relations. Some prominent blacks have either expressed or silently encouraged anti-Jewish sentiment of varying degrees of seriousness. Jews and African Americans have had to deal with the bigotry preached against Jews by Louis Farrakhan in the name of the Nation of Islam, which has a documented history of hostility to Jewish culture, although its leaders often protest this charge.

I have no reason to feel anything but affection and respect for Jews as a people in the United States. A long time ago I came to the personal realization that of all the people who have helped me become a success in life, a disproportionately large percentage of them have been Jews. And as far as I know, I never sought them out to ask their help. They took the initiative, and continue to do so. Whether or not they are assuaging certain guilty feelings is, to me, irrelevant.

When I was growing up in Richmond, Jews occupied a prominent and favored place in my life, and in my father's life. Before and after he found his main job with the Department of Recreation of the city of Richmond, my father worked for a number of wealthy Richmond Jews. He worked for the Schwarzchilds, who owned a chain of jewelry stores in Virginia, and the Thalhimers, who owned a chain of department stores. My father also worked for Daniel Schiller, the treasurer of Thalhimer's, who lived within walking distance of Westwood, the black enclave in western Richmond. Apart from the people my father worked under at the Department of Recreation, almost all the white people with whom he regularly associated were Jewish. He found them fair and honorable. In my own life, the dominant Jewish figure was Mr. Paul, who owned a store by that name at the corner of Oak Road and Brook Street, near our house. It was years before I realized that he was Jewish. I see now that he was probably the poorest Jew I knew as a child, and he was not poor.

Among blacks in Richmond, as among people elsewhere, certain anti-Jewish phrases were current, although in a mild way for the most part. For example, to "Jew you down" meant to get the better of you in a deal. Almost certainly the speaker was no anti-Semite but rather an unthinking person using expressions he or she had picked up somewhere. My father saw clearly that even great wealth did not save the Jews of Richmond from bigotry. He liked to tell the story of driving William Thalhimer to see a man about a piece of land that Thalhimer wanted to buy. The man hated to sell the land to anyone, but he hated above all selling it to a Jew. As Daddy listened, the man insulted Thalhimer in every way he could. Thalhimer said nothing. The deal was concluded. Driving back, my father asked Thalhimer why he had meekly taken those insults from an inferior.

"Arthur," Thalhimer said, "I came out here to purchase that piece of land. I got the piece of land. It belongs to me now, not to him. That man can go on cursing me as long as he likes. I have the land."

That incident had a major impact on my father. It deepened his pragmatic sense; it made him see the world in a different way. It made him a better provider for his family.

I became aware of Jews in a more complex way on the tennis team at UCLA. Among my closest friends were Allen Fox and Larry Nagler, seniors in my first year. One day, Nagler, my doubles partner, invited me to his house in Los Angeles. Lox and bagels, which I had never eaten before, were served. Suddenly I realized that Nagler, my doubles partner, was Jewish, and that his close friend Allen Fox was also Jewish. It was a revelation to me. I had thought of them simply as white. In those days, to be Jewish in the top ranks of tennis was to encounter a certain amount of prejudice. In 1951, ten years before, when Dick Savitt won Wimbledon, his right to a place on the Davis Cup team was challenged in some circles because he was Jewish.

Once I understood that Nagler and Fox were Jewish, a new dimension opened up among us. I discovered that both assumed that everyone thought of them as Jewish, and that some people therefore did not like them. Their reaction struck me as quite similar to the double consciousness that blacks live with all the time—seeing oneself through one's own eyes but also constantly through the eyes of the dominant group, in their case Christian whites. Fox, whose undergraduate major was physics, later earned a doctorate in psychology. He was an atheist then, as I remember it; Nagler was religious. We had far-reaching discussions about religion, race, and politics—the kind of debates and discussions that make college life so wonderful and cement relationships. They laid the foundation for my gratifying relationship as an adult with Jews and Jewish American culture.

I began then to understand the complex ways in which Jews see their place in American culture, where they enjoy a place of privilege because they are white and often gifted but also experience something of the bigotry visited on them historically by Christian peoples. I think that any objective analysis of their relationship to blacks would have to conclude that Jews have done more than any other ethnic or religious group to help us. They have been in the vanguard of the civil-rights struggle not simply out of self-interest in combating bigotry but also because they were being faithful to their belief system. That is why I find it painful to read assertions by people like Leonard Jeffries that "the truth needs to come out" about Jewish–African American relations. Then I discover that Jeffries offers few documents or studies, notes and statistics, or references, only sweeping generalizations based mainly, from what I understand, on his history as an unproductive scholar at City College, an institution that has graduated a number of Nobel Prize winners, most or all of them Jewish.

We in black America are far too addicted to theories of conspiracy, which again indicates our lack of power and confidence. Yes, many motion pictures, produced by individual Jews, cast blacks in menial roles; but was that part of a *conspiracy* to defame blacks? I don't think so. When people say "Jews," I ask, "*Which* Jew?" Similarly, I hope that when people say "blacks," someone asks, "*Which* black?" We cannot reduce the relationship between African Americans and Jews to personalities. Jesse Jackson's "Hymietown" remark (he used this term to mean New York City in a conversation made public by a black reporter) is a part of *his* biography, not ours collectively. Similarly, I refuse to make too much of the occasion when Jackson flew to Brussels to the International Jewish Congress and delivered a conciliatory speech. That speech is an episode in the story of Jackson and Jews; it is at best a footnote in the saga of black–Jewish relations in the United States.

Whatever wrong that individual Jews may have done to blacks, I find no justification whatsoever for the blanket attack on Jews as a people that a few so-called leaders of our people have launched and encouraged. Most black Americans understand this point; however well Leonard Jeffries plays in parts of Harlem, among blacks I know in Virginia he and his charges matter not at all. These attacks on Jews are part of the strategy of leadership that has emerged among our demagogues in the decades since 1954. They follow what is apparently the number-one rule: attack your friends and allies, rather than your enemies. Your friends and allies will not resist nearly as much as your enemies, and are more likely to make concessions to you. I have noticed how few of these so-called leaders ever attack outright bigots or the strongholds of bigotry. The venom is reserved for attacking friendly whites—that is, when the main target isn't other blacks. Some critics will no doubt profess to see irony in my statement, but we as blacks lash out at one another and try to drag one another down even more readily than we lash out at our allies. When black demagogues make scapegoats of Jews, we must resist it for what it is: further evidence of the self-hatred and the intellectual and spiritual confusion that racism breeds.

In important ways, black America is isolated from the rest of America and conflicted within itself. So many of the supposedly progressive decisions taken in the last two generations have backfired. They usually backfire because principles of universality and morality have been set aside in favor of the goal of quick power, usually of a limited kind. Take, for example, the tendency now to redraw voting districts in ingenious, sometimes tortured ways, in order to allow one ethnic minority or another to send one of its own to the state legislature or U.S. Congress. While it is indeed desirable to have all sorts of politicians representing the people, the creation of such "safe" districts for ethnic groups virtually exempts elected officials from the need to concern themselves with consensus or to synthesize a coalition. In New York, we have seen many whites essentially disenfranchised in this way by the allegedly democratic process; and the beneficiaries are usually lily-white interests and the Republican party.

The people of the United States need leadership from the top and at every level below the top. In 1992, the unwillingness or inability of George Bush to lead the nation in its troubles cost him the presidency. In 1988, unimpressed by his Democratic opponent, Dukakis, I voted for Bush. He seemed a decent, experienced administrator, although I was appalled by the infamous campaign commercial in which a furloughed black felon named Willie Horton was used cynically to frighten white voters into Bush's camp. But especially after his triumph in the Gulf war against Iraq, when his approval rating in the polls reached 90 percent of Americans, Bush allowed himself to be convinced by callow advisers that he did not need to do anything more to win reelection. "With such an approval rating," one of them allegedly said, "George Bush can sleepwalk and win reelection." Thereafter he showed no vision, no aggressive leadership in facing our national problems—economic, racial, or moral. He lost me, and he lost the country.

Believing as I do in the politics of inclusion and in the party of hope rather than the party of memory, I moved fairly early to support Bill Clinton. I contributed money to his campaign, and I wrote him a long letter about the issue of national health care. One evening at home, I received a warm telephone call from him and we chatted for a few minutes and promised to try to see each other. At a fund-raising dinner, I sat next to him for a while and was favorably impressed by his dynamism and his intricate knowledge of health-care issues, on which I consider myself an expert. I was also pleased by his evident ease around people of color; he belongs to the first generation of whites to grow up in this country appreciating something of the full complexity of African American culture. Unlike earlier generations, his generation has known blacks at virtually all levels of society, from high school to college and beyond. I do not look for miracles from President Clinton, but I am confident that he will work to further the cause of justice and opportunity for all. I am depressed a little only by the fact that, for the first time, the president of the United States is younger than I am.

I AM ONLY too well aware of the extent to which I dwell on the question of morality, and of how much I make it a part of my thinking on race. I hope I am not a hypocrite or a humbug. Have I become more and more concerned with morality and God as I find myself closer to death? Perhaps. But I don't think my poor health is the reason. I think I am simply being faithful to the way I was brought up, and that I would feel this concern even if I expected to live to be a hundred years old.

I am aware of the distance between me as I live, on the one hand, and the masses of black people as they live, on the other. Money and fame can be insuperable barriers to understanding, even among members of a family. But have I lost the *right* to criticize other blacks, as well as the *ability* to do so with penetration and insight? Again, I hope not. Although the world has changed and I have changed since my boyhood, I have always tried to keep up as best I can with the changes. I have never wanted to live far away from people who look like me and my family; I have always drawn strength from being close to home.

I hope that my fellow African Americans know that my criticism comes from a deep, familial love of us, a wish for us to be happier and more prosperous in the world. I feel this love alive in me despite my criticism of some of our ways and despite my insistence that in my essence I am a human being first and foremost, and not someone to be defined mainly by the color of his skin.

In 1981, I dedicated my book *Off the Court* to "that nameless slave girl off the H.M.S. *Doddington*, and her daughter Lucy, her granddaughter Peggy, her great-granddaughter Peggy, and her great-great-grandson Hammett, all of whom were born, lived, and died as slaves." She was one of my ancestors. My roots are deep in the black past, all the way through slavery to Africa. I would not wish it otherwise. That is why I feel so keen a sense of hurt when I see black Americans morally and spiritually, as well as economically and politically, adrift in the world.

I wish more of us would understand that our increasing isolation, no matter how much it seems to express pride and self-affirmation, is not the answer to our problems. Rather, the answer is a revival of our ancient commitment to God, who rules over all the peoples of the world and exalts no one over any other, and to the moral and spiritual values for which we were once legendary in America. We must reach out our hand in friendship and dignity both to those who would befriend us and those who would be our enemy. We must believe in the power of education. We must respect just laws. We must love ourselves, our old and our young, our women as well as our men.

I see nothing inconsistent between being proud of oneself and one's ancestors and, at the same time, seeing oneself as first and foremost a member of the commonwealth of humanity, the common-wealth of all races and creeds. My potential is more than can be expressed within the bounds of my race or ethnic identity. My human-ity, in common with all of God's children, gives the greatest flight to the full range of my possibilities. If I had one last wish, I would ask that all Americans could see themselves that way, past the barbed-wire fences of race and color. We are the weaker for these divisions, and the stronger when we transcend them.

CHAPTER 6

The Striving and Achieving

MY DAVIS CUP campaigns, my protests against apartheid in South Africa, and my skirmishes over academic requirements for athletes were doubtless the most highly publicized episodes of my life in the 1980s after my retirement. However, most of my time was spent much more quietly. This was the notorious "real world" that sometimes had seemed so far away while, as a professional athlete, I flew around the world in pursuit of my tennis career. This real world proved, though in a different way, as challenging as those more publicized episodes. As I ventured into the other areas I had judged crucial to me as I faced retirement—public speaking, teaching, writing, business, and voluntary public service—I quickly discovered that the mundane exerted its own peculiar pressures. Success here, too, had its price; success called for diligence, attentiveness, and not a little humility. I believe that I had some success, but I also had my share of failures as I got on with the patient, unspectacular striving and achieving that, in the end, might bring me as great a sense of satisfaction as any victory on the tennis court ever did.

To me, a nine-to-five job was out of the question. Thanks to my earnings and investments, I did not have to look for a traditional salaried job, and my temperament would not allow me to slip easily into such a harness. I had the freedom to work as hard as I wanted, when and if I wished. I could indulge my passion for reading; Jeanne and I could continue to travel, which we loved. At this time, and for twelve years altogether, we also had a second home near the sixteenth green at one of the Doral Resort and Country Club golf courses in

Florida. There, in the sun, I worked at my tennis responsibilities for the resort, and on my golf game for myself. With my heart condition, golf had superseded tennis as my main sport; with every year I had become more and more entranced by the fairways and the greens.

As much as I enjoyed this leisurely life, however, I found myself continually looking for a chance to do something more purposeful and consequential. My public lectures, in particular, kept me aware of issues and ideas that had relatively little to do with the comfortable life I was leading in Florida or New York. By choice, I was not represented by a professional speakers' bureau; I wanted to pick my own engagements, without special regard to the size of the fees. (I stuck to this policy for twelve years after my retirement, until my AIDS announcement created too great a demand for me to handle on my own.) As for my talks, I tried to speak out of my own experience, practically; I avoided hectoring young people, but sought to teach them something important about life as I had learned from it. On the whole, I found speaking quite satisfying. And I was seldom more satisfied than when I found myself on a college or university campus, addressing a gathering of young people.

Although the mood of the campuses had changed from the 1960s, when peace, love, folk songs, and marijuana seemed to reign, I was happy to find that idealism still burned brightly among the students, as well as a genuine affection for ideas. Loving books myself, I knew that I would enjoy being a teacher. But what could I teach in a college? Not tennis. I knew that I would soon tire of being a college coach (no doubt, my Davis Cup experience had something to do with this insight). If I could choose, I would teach history, or politics. Unfortunately, my only degree was in neither field.

Nevertheless, I began to receive invitations to offer college courses. To my surprise and pleasure, I also began to receive honorary doctorates, including one from Princeton in 1982. As for teaching, the most attractive offer was probably from Henry Louis Gates, Jr., then a junior professor at Yale. In 1983, I lectured at Yale when I was selected for the Kiphuth Fellowship (named after a man who coached swimming there from 1917 to 1959), which is given annually to someone "of rare character" in sport, physiology, literature, or the arts. A gathering of some five hundred students, faculty, and staff heard me speak on

"Collegiate Athletics: A Reappraisal." Strolling with Gates and some of his students among Yale's venerable Colonial and Gothic Revival buildings, I felt comfortable. Completing high school with virtually a straight-A average, I had been assured by one mentor with excellent connections that Harvard was ready to admit me, doubtless with an eye on its tennis team. I chose instead to go to UCLA. Although I never regretted this decision, the chance to teach in the Ivy League was tempting.

However, I turned down Yale and chose instead to teach at a college that, in just about every way, is Yale's polar opposite: Florida Memorial College (FMC), a historically black school of some twelve hundred students in Miami. The college was not far from the Doral. The invitation had come from my old friend the Reverend Jeff Rogers, director of the Center for Community Change there. In 1968, Rogers had invited me to give the speech in Washington, D.C., for which I had been quietly reprimanded by my Army superiors. We had stayed in touch, and after moving to FMC, he was instrumental in having me appointed to the college's board of trustees.

Excited at the prospect, I proposed to teach an honors seminar on "The Black Athlete in Contemporary Society." Two aspects of the course stirred me. First, I would be working with black college students in a historically black college for the first time in my life; this was my major reason for declining Yale's offer, although I hoped to teach a course there eventually. And second, we would be exploring a fascinating subject, delving into the corpus of scholarship on blacks and sport. I soon had two surprises. One concerned the volume and the quality of material on this subject that meant so much to me. The other had to do with the performance of many of the students in my class.

For the first two or three meetings, my dozen students seemed bright and alert enough. Then I received their first papers, and the first shock. Three students, all women, handed in well-researched, finely written papers. Almost all the others, in varying degrees, upset me so profoundly that my hands shook with disbelief and anger the first time I read their prose. Their command of English was so abysmal, their sense of organization so weak, their mastery of logic and argumentation so pathetic that I could not believe that these young students would ever graduate from college. As I sat at the dining-room table that evening, reading the papers, my mood shifted from anger into depression.

"Jeanne, please listen to this," I said. I read a sentence or two. "Can you believe that someone in college wrote this?"

"Oh my," Jeanne replied. "He has a problem."

"And listen to this one." I read another.

"Sorry, Arthur," Jeanne said, "*you* have a problem."

Indeed I had. The last thing I wanted was to be perceived as a snob come down from New York City eager to heap scorn on the students, or for blacks to think that I had been socializing with rich white people for so long that I had lost touch with reality. Maybe I have, I told myself.

As soon as I could, I went to see Jeff Rogers. I knew I could be frank with him. He listened to my complaints patiently, and was philosophical.

"Arthur, I know what you are saying is true. I've seen some of those papers, too. But you have to understand what these kids have been through, what their families have been through, just for them to get to this point. This is not UCLA."

"But I am *not* just UCLA," I said. "I grew up in Richmond, under segregation. I went to all-black Maggie Walker High School. And I went to an all-black high school in St. Louis, too. Nobody wrote like this. Besides, my seminar is supposed to be for honors students. Are these honors students?"

"How do you know that no one wrote like that at Maggie Walker, Arthur?"

"I just know it. There were some awfully bright kids in class with me."

In our little group, we went on to be professionals of many kinds, doctors and lawyers and serious musicians. My classmate Isaiah Jackson, for example, studied Russian at Harvard, then turned to music. He became a symphony orchestra conductor, and is now one of the most acclaimed younger conductors in the United States. I myself more than held my own at UCLA.

"And what about the kids in the other classes?" Rogers asked. "What about the other schools in Richmond? In any case, you went to school in another age altogether, Arthur. And perhaps you were all put together because you were bright, the children of the strivers."

Jeff may have had a point there. I hadn't thought about it before, but I could see now what he was talking about. My schooling indeed had taken place a long time in the past. But had education and its results changed so much?

"All I know, Arthur, is that we at this college, or those of us here who care about students, have to look out for all the young men and women out there. We have to look out for the bright and the dumb, the honest and the crooked, the brave ones and the punks. Here at FMC, sure, we give the benefit of the doubt to some of the kids we admit. But somebody has to give them the benefit of the doubt, after what they have been through in this country. You know the white man isn't going to do that. Certainly not here in Florida, not anywhere in the United States, really. So we have to be prepared to do it, Arthur. We have to work with the kids, help them to see that there's a better way to do things. That's our job. And it's not always pleasant."

I went away feeling more chastened than uplifted, almost as if I had now committed myself to remedial instruction. But when some of the students drifted in late to class, or stayed away altogether without an excuse, or made feeble, trifling excuses to explain why they hadn't read this book or finished that paper, I felt my indignation rise again. Then, I didn't want to hear about the effects of history and the legacy of slavery and segregation. At some point, each individual is responsible for his or her fate. At some point, one cannot blame history. Does the legacy of slavery explain why Mr. Jones eased into class ten minutes late this morning? Why Mr. Smith yawned in my face and claimed that he had not known about the assignment? Or why Miss Johnson, who obviously comes from a family with means, asked me to explain what *exactly* I was looking for in the essay I had assigned? Or why those three other young women, out of the same general background, executed their assignments on time, and so well?

Sticking by my rules about grading, I watched one student after another drop the course. The rest of us plodded on. Even those who dropped it were polite, but on the whole I was rather disheartened. To a reporter from *Ebony* magazine in Chicago, I put on a bright face. "I don't think it's the teaching *per se* that excites me," I reported, "but the teaching of black students. There are lots of things that black students need to know and have impressed upon them." However, that semester was one of the more discouraging seasons of my life. Its main virtue was to make me even more determined to try to make a difference in the area of education, in particular. Certainly it was the major reason for the uncompromising position I took on the question of higher academic standards for athletes governed by the NCAA.

On the other hand, my discouragement did not diminish my high regard for the historically black colleges, which I believe must be preserved. I grew up in Richmond with one of them, Virginia Union University, across the street from my home, and another, Hampton Institute (now Hampton University), not far away. Such colleges are curators of our culture just as, whether we like to admit it or not, Harvard is a curator of Anglo-Saxon culture in the United States. Harvard may appoint a Chinese president, but it is emphatically an Anglo-Saxon university, a fact about which it need not apologize. Notre Dame and Fordham have a special place in Roman Catholic culture, Brandeis and Yeshiva in Jewish American culture. We as African Americans have Howard, Tuskegee, and Spelman, and should help them.

To this end, I am a veteran supporter of the United Negro College Fund, which is the leading tax-exempt charitable fund in the African American community. I support the UNCF because of the high value I place on these colleges and because the fund is both nonpolitical and highly efficient. Nevertheless, I also believe that if any of the historically black colleges cannot maintain a certain level of excellence or financial stability, it should take steps to change its private status and ethnic identity if that is essential to its survival, or close.

The other shock that came in connection with my course at Florida Memorial College resonated for at least the next five years of my life. It led me to devote much of that time to the serious study of the subject of African Americans in sports, and to publish my findings in three books on the subject.

In preparing my course syllabus, I quickly discovered, to my surprise and chagrin, that virtually nothing had been written by scholars, black or white, on the history of black involvement in sports in America. Hunting in the New York Public Library on Forty-second Street, I found only two books: Edwin B. Henderson's *The Negro in*

Sports, published in 1938, with a revised edition in 1948; and A. S. "Doc" Young's *Negro Firsts in Sport*. I was baffled by this poverty of information. After all, in major sports such as boxing, baseball, football, basketball, and track, African Americans comprised a disproportionately high percentage of the leading athletes. When one dug deeper, a rich history of black involvement in these and other sports began to appear. I became convinced that I had stumbled onto a story that had to be told. After all, these were my people in two senses: as black Americans and as athletes.

Burning with a sense of obligation, I decided to forgo the chance of an advance from a publisher and to spend my own money to hire a team to research and write a comprehensive study of the subject. Eventually I spent about $300,000. I hired a personal assistant, Derilene McLeod, to help with typing, filing, and general organization. She turned out to be an inspired choice; falling in love with the project, she kept it on course over the years. As researchers, I hired first Sandra Jamison, a skilled librarian, then Rodney Howard, who brought a sophisticated academic background to the project as well as boundless enthusiasm, which we needed. Francis Harris compiled much of the material in its extensive reference sections. Kip Branch, a professor at Wilson College in Chambersburg, Pennsylvania, polished my prose.

In 1988, dedicated to Jeanne and Camera, *A Hard Road to Glory: A History of the African-American Athlete* appeared in three volumes. Together, the volumes cover the subject from 1619 to around 1985.

A Hard Road to Glory was an emotional experience for me because it dealt so intimately, at almost every stage, with both the triumph and tragedy, the elation and suffering, of blacks as they met not only the physical challenges of their sport but also the gratuitous challenges of racism. No sport was exempt from this painful double history, so that compiling the record was a fairly relentless exposure to disappointment.

One fact, seldom recalled, sums up the bittersweet history we were bent on recovering. The Kentucky Derby is the most celebrated horse race in America. On May 17, 1875, when the first Kentucky Derby was run, all but one of the fifteen jockeys were black. Then, when the law required that jockeys had to be licensed, one by one black jockeys were excluded by the Jockey Club; systematically, whites drove them out of the sport. Starting in 1912, and in nearly every year since, no African American has ridden in the Derby. Racism destroyed a tradition so effectively that most people, black or white, probably assume that blacks had never been a part of the Run for the Roses.

I found a similar story in other sports. I myself had never heard of Josh Gibson, possibly the most brilliant long-ball hitter in baseball history; or Marshall Taylor, the world champion cyclist in 1899; or George Poage, the first African American to win an Olympic medal. Yet these individuals had been better known than most of the black political leaders of their day. I learned much about the remarkable heavyweight boxer Jack Johnson, and about the historic impact of his victories and his personality on the society of his time. In some ways, he was an anticipation of Muhammad Ali, "cheeky," as the English say, in the way he flaunted his three white wives and his wealth in the days before World War I, when blacks in America lived truly in the lion's mouth.

Sadly, we found few primary sources for all this history. Instead, we improvised. Leafing through old issues of college yearbooks, we searched for photographs of black players. We hunted through the dusty files of black newspapers. We pressed individuals about their parents and their parents' parents. Through the black media, we appealed to the public for further information. We begged people to search for medals and other mementos that their families might have saved, as we tried to reconstruct the past. In this highly personal way, we recovered our history.

Talking to various historians, I discovered why this subject had been neglected: academic snobbery and timidity. People, especially men, are passionately interested in sport; yet sports history is often considered beneath the notice of serious historians. Most publishers were also unwilling to subsidize such basic research by awarding a substantial advance to a scholar. Eventually, however, I more than covered my investment, which suggests that many people want to know this story. Proud as I am of various other accomplishments and successes, I take a special pride in being regarded, since the publication of the three volumes that make up *A Hard Road to Glory*, as an authority on the subject of African Americans in sport.

* * *

"MONEY MAKES ME happy." Who would make such a crass remark? I did, in my book *Portrait in Motion*, written with Frank Deford. But the truth is that I'm glad I have enough money to live comfortably, and I enjoyed adding to my bank account as I earned money on the tennis court and in various business deals when I was a professional. I was not born poor, but my father was hardly rich. I long ago decided that, on the whole, I much prefer having money to not having it. In that sense, it makes me happy.

On the other hand, I also learned a long time ago what money can and cannot do for me. From what we get, we can make a living; what we give, however, makes a life.

Along the way, as I went about the business of making money and then trying to keep it so that I could retire one day with peace of mind, I learned some wrenching lessons about the interplay between dollars and common sense. I will not pretend that my experience can provide lessons to everyone, or even to many people. In some respects the world of sport has changed, and my experience means little. Moreover, not many people earn large sums of money in the first place, much less for hitting or kicking a ball. Still, I would like to share what I have learned.

I came along too early in the open era of tennis to collect any of the huge prizes awarded in the 1980s and 1990s. Some of these prizes are extraordinary. For example, in December 1992 the Grand Slam tournament in Germany awarded two million dollars to the winner (Michael Stich of Germany) and one million dollars to the runner-up (Michael Chang of the United States). However, I earned a fair amount in my time. Even more important, I have kept much of it. I have done so because of prudent management and a relatively modest way of life compared to my income.

The fields of sport and entertainment are creating many instant millionaires in America and Europe today, and especially many black millionaires. I wonder about all this money being made by young people, and how it is being spent. If I were asked, on the basis of my own experience, to advise these men and women about money (and the advice may hold for people who have much less money), I would say the following: First, decide on a plan. Set financial goals and priorities for yourself. Second, get the best minds you can afford to help you with legal and financial matters. These experts tend to *make* money for you with their expertise, rather than *take* money from you with their large fees. Third, in recruiting such people, do not be prejudiced or sentimental about such matters as gender, skin color, facial features, or social class. Good lawyers and financial experts come in all colors, genders, and backgrounds. Fourth, read before signing any contracts, but then stick to the agreements you sign. Resist the urge to try to wriggle out of financial arrangements and obligations. A wise person decides slowly but abides by these decisions. Fifth, be prudent in your generosity. In fact, although charity is important, dispense with generosity if you must; deal first with your primary responsibilities.

For some athletes and entertainers, generosity is their gravest problem. Among boxers, for example, Joe Louis and Sugar Ray Robinson were legendary for their charity toward all, which they often expressed in hundred-dollar tips. At one point, Louis owed the U.S. government four million dollars in income tax, which the government forgave (it had no hope of ever collecting this money). If I remember correctly, Joe eked out a living near the end of his life as a greeter in a Las Vegas casino. Sugar Ray Robinson also made a fortune but died a relatively poor man. The problem continues, and often it begins with individuals who regard a professional athlete in the family as a cash cow. Late in 1992, *Sports Illustrated* ran an instructive story about the gifted basketball player Dominique Wilkins. An open, trusting man, Wilkins had been supporting at least six members of his family, who allegedly did little or nothing to help themselves. When Wilkins finally married, and his wife put a sudden stop to the bleeding, everyone involved was hurt. But that is the kind of tough decision someone has to make.

I do not mean that one should avoid helping family members. I have helped to put two cousins through graduate school; that is money well spent. One should also help friends in need, but carefully. Even with the care I take, I can still think of half a dozen people who allowed the issue of repayment of a small loan to disrupt our friendship. For a thousand dollars each, two different friends compromised my respect for them. Over the years, I have had to write off several bad loans to friends. Most professional athletes and entertainers suffer in this way, but black athletes probably suffer more than others. Certainly it is an old problem. I remember being startled to read about a black boxer who complained bitterly about people who "put the touch on you," as he phrased it. This was George Dixon, the first black man to be a world boxing champion, in the 1890s.

In at least one way, I am in a peculiar category among athletes in the United States. My generation was probably the last in which young athletes made large amounts of money and were also college graduates. Just as the open era transformed my sport, so did free agency transform the other sports and reduce the incentive for a superior athlete to finish college, or even to take it seriously. This trend has affected both blacks and whites, but blacks have been hit harder. It seems fair to say that many either have never finished their degree requirements or, frankly, were such poor students that they would not have been admitted to college but for their athletic skill and the unscrupulousness of many schools. Often, even with rich contracts, these athletes are on their way to being paupers. Not only are they naïve in handling legal and financial matters; they often lack the one quality that might save them: the ability to interact in a prudent, respectful way with their lawyers and financial managers. Many young athletes are probably doomed, tragically, to return to the poverty from which sport almost saved them.

From the start of my professional career, when I left the Army in 1969, I have been fortunate to have as my lawyer and manager Donald Dell. Over the years, certain people, especially blacks, have ventured to criticize me for relying so heavily on Dell.

"You call yourself a role model for young blacks," one friend snapped at me not long ago, "but you have a white man handling your money?"

"I don't call myself a role model," I replied. "And I don't have a white man handling my money. I have Donald Dell, who happens to be white."

"There's no difference, Arthur. None at all."

"Yes, there is!"

"I'm surprised," he went on, "that you don't have a white wife!"

"Well, if I had one, it would be my business and my business alone, wouldn't it? And she would be my wife, first and foremost, who happened to be white."

Some blacks and some whites also insist that I could do much better with a different manager, no matter what his race. They say that Donald is not astute enough, by which they probably mean not greedy enough. I tend to chuckle when I hear such criticism, because I am quite satisfied with the way my finances have worked out over the years. I am tempted to chuckle even louder when I see how poorly some of these same critics of Dell's are doing financially.

I am quite sensitive to the fact that blacks must try to support other blacks, including black professionals, because we are shut out from so many fields by racism. Try, for example, to find an African American real-estate agent among the prominent real-estate firms in Manhattan, or a black waiter or waitress in a leading Manhattan restaurant. But one cannot let skin color alone determine the choice of an expert. In my case, when I started earning large sums of money, I knew of only one black agent in the sporting world. (He had been a classmate of mine at UCLA.) By the time I turned professional in 1969, I was committed to Dell. I had known Donald's parents since I was a teenager, when his brother Dickie and I competed in the same tournaments; and I played under Donald as captain on our Davis Cup team in 1968 and 1969.

I did not start off with a total commitment to Donald as a lawyer and manager. Trust has to be earned, and should come only after the passage of time. Eventually that trust in Donald became like granite. Perhaps someone else could have gotten more for me in this deal or that; but more money is not the deciding factor for me in choosing a lawyer or manager, and it shouldn't be for anyone. My whole career has been built, I now see, on seeking and following good advice, and on working with other people rather than striking out on my own into territory others knew better. In starting out, I invested, literally and metaphorically, in a community effort with other tennis players who were as uncertain as I was in 1968 where professional tennis was going. All that we were sure about was that we had one another, and wanted to help shape the future of the sport.

In 1969, I rejected an offer of $400,000 over five years to turn myself over to the management of one of the major entrepreneurs then emerging in tennis. At that time, $400,000 was an extraordinary amount for a professional athlete in the United States, and especially to someone coming out of the Army with precious little cash in his bank account. Still, I refused the money and threw in my lot with a group of other players to help form an organization called Players Enterprises Incorporated (PEI). I laugh to think of today's tennis players cooperating in this way; but we made it work, at least long enough for us to affect the growth of open tennis. All the money we earned as prizes or for playing exhibitions went to PEI. In turn, it paid our expenses and also a salary based on the size of our individual contributions to the pool. The company also made it easy for us to stage exhibition matches, which earned us more money; and, as employees of a company, we saved on taxes. Perhaps most prudent of all, PEI also set up retirement and trust funds that would take care of us once we left the professional game.

Dell and his partner at the time in ProServ, Frank Craighill, provided legal advice to PEI. Then, when ProServ expanded into other areas of sports management, I became one of its top clients. My trust in Donald solidified. Between 1976 and 1986, for example, he and I worked without a formal agreement between us. In 1986, changes in the federal tax law mandated a written agreement between clients and financial managers. I think the law is a good one, but the piece of paper we co-signed is much less important to me than the feeling of trust we share. I did not have to immerse myself in the minutiae of money management, but allowed Donald and his colleagues to help me meet my goals. To facilitate matters, I assigned a limited power of attorney to certain officials at ProServ. (Except in rare circumstances, no one should assign a *general* power of attorney to anyone.)

From early in our arrangement, I was put on a budget. I would enthusiastically recommend a budget for anyone, especially professional athletes. Based on my estimated income for the coming year, I was assigned a certain amount of money, and the rest of my money was off limits to me, unless I insisted. This is an invaluable arrangement, to which the most sensible professional athletes adhere. Michael Jordan, for example, lives on a budget, although his annual income exceeds my total net worth, and perhaps even the net worth of several small nations. (Michael's agent is the highly respected David Falk, who used to be my lawyer when he worked at ProServ.) I try never to exceed my budget, and one way I do so is by remembering certain realities of purchasing. If you buy a car that sports a sticker price of $40,000 (and I wouldn't), you really pay at least $60,000 for the vehicle, depending on your tax bracket. That is the amount of money you must earn so that, after federal and other income taxes and other fees and expenses, you can buy the car. In every practical sense, the price tag should be $60,000.

Between 1970 and 1986, I did not even own a car—that is, except for a certain Rolls-Royce, a 1924 Silver Ghost, I spotted one morning in Australia and fell in love with. I told myself that it was a sound investment. Well, it wasn't, not for me. I brought it back to the U.S. but never drove it. I finally sold it (at a slight loss) to a friend in Richmond.

I spend very little on clothing. I own only four sport coats, five suits, and five pairs of shoes. They are all items of fairly high quality, but it makes sense to pay more for high quality. I am frugal, as are most professional and ex-professional tennis players. (As players, we receive so many things free, including tennis clothing, shoes, and racquets, that we tend to choke at paying for anything.) However, I rarely hesitate to pay for an experience, whether it is a concert or a vacation to an exotic land. And I try not to impose my own frugality on my wife and daughter, for I see it more as a habit than a virtue.

Perhaps I have left the impression that I am a model of prudence in handling money. Let me dispel that notion, at least a little. From bitter experience, I know that my ability to make money on my own as an entrepreneur or a venture capitalist is limited. My college degree in business and the advice and management of ProServ have not prevented me from making a mess now and then of some idea. I was adventurous on the tennis court, and I have some of that fire in me where money is concerned; sometimes I haven't been able to keep the fire under control.

My first major business venture on my own, outside of tennis, had a magical appeal to me: it involved Africa. I have never been excessively romantic about the Motherland, but Africa is where most of my ancestors came from and I longed for a chance to build a lasting bridge of my own to the continent. In 1979, in partnership with a friend from Richmond who not only held an M.B.A. but also shared my enthusiasm for Africa, I started a trading company, International Commercial

Resources. To the chagrin of Dell and my other advisers, almost all of its capital came directly from my pocket.

We were cautious, very cautious. We began our adventure by negotiating with the government of Liberia, which seemed the safest, most stable place in Africa for an American to do business. Its connections to the United States run deep; in 1821, sponsored by the American Colonization Society, a boatload of freed slaves from the United States reached the area to begin a systematic process of repatriation of Africans who had been slaves or the descendants of slaves in America. In 1847, Liberia formally established itself as an independent state but kept its special ties to the United States. Many of those ties persist today: for example, its official currency is the U.S. dollar.

Our main dealings were with an efficient and apparently principled government administrator, Charles Taylor, who was himself a confidant of the president of Liberia at that time, William R. Tolbert. In an agreement reached with the government, our company was hired to supply the nation with various essential goods and services. We signed our agreement, and I settled back to receive a decent return on my investment. I never saw a penny of the money again. In 1980, Tolbert's government was overthrown in a violent coup led by a master sergeant, Samuel K. Doe, and Tolbert was murdered, along with several members of his family. By the end of the decade, Liberia was immersed in such bloody strife that half the population fled the country in terror and at least 20,000 people died. The leader of one of two armed factions opposing Samuel Doe was none other than our contact, Charles Taylor. In 1990, Doe himself was killed. In 1992, Taylor's forces were accused of murdering six American nuns living near Monrovia, the capital. Liberia, an economist friend told me, is now close to being a "pre-Somalia" state.

I lost a six-figure sum on that venture. The key to business speculation, I am told, is to risk only the money you can lose without batting an eye. ProServ was not worried, but, believe me, I batted an eye.

My Liberian disaster did not extinguish the fire of entrepreneurship in me. However, my next independent business venture was far more modest. With my good friend Doug Stein, I stepped into the clothing import business in gingerly fashion. Doug and I decided to found a company, STASH—a combination of Stein and Ashe—to sell clothes wholesale. He had friends in the rag business (as the clothing industry is called in New York); and I also had friends in the rag business, including connections to certain major department stores. We could not miss. However, no doubt spooked by my Liberian fiasco, I panicked at the first sign of trouble. This time I lost only a thousand dollars. After Liberia, it actually felt like a profit.

My last memorable business venture was sentimental, like my Liberian gamble, and even more costly. It involved family—my brother, Johnnie Ashe, a warrant officer in the U.S. Marines, with experience in construction. We decided to build an apartment complex in Jacksonville, North Carolina, that would serve Marines in the Parris Island–Camp Lejeune complex. I would put up much of the money in cash and personally guarantee bank loans to cover other costs. Cautiously, we made the decision to build the complex in various stages. My brother put his experience as a Marine engineer to good use and oversaw the construction of the first stage, then the second. I flew down to the site frequently, and came to enjoy the sound of hammering and sawing. To me, it sounded like money—the money I was about to make. However, the project meant more than money to us; it was a brotherly venture. Accordingly, we named the complex Cordell Village, after our late mother, Mattie Cordell Cunningham Ashe.

When Cordell Village reached the size of sixty-five apartment units, some strains in the business began to show. Our rents were falling short of expenses, and we put off our plans to expand. My brother and I were struggling to stay afloat, hoping against hope to succeed, when without any warning Iraq's Saddam Hussein invaded Kuwait. At first, I saw no connection between Saddam and my investment in Cordell Village. Soon, however, the link was clear. When President Bush ordered the buildup of forces in the Persian Gulf in August 1990, we, the owners of Cordell Village, were on our way to ruin. Overnight, half of the apartments at Cordell Village emptied as our resident Marines headed for the sands of Saudi Arabia and Kuwait.

In autumn 1990, not a moment too soon, we sold the complex to the people who had been managing it for us. They were happy with the deal; I was ecstatic to be getting out, because my financial loss was huge and growing steadily. It easily exceeded my Liberian disaster. Once again, my managers at ProServ took my failure calmly. But once again, I batted an eye.

I suppose the word must be out that I fancy myself as an entrepreneurial type, because hardly a week passes without a new business offer coming my way. Most involve tennis. I listen politely and refuse almost all. Surprisingly few are unethical, and these I reject out of hand. The last thing I would want to do is to contribute to the current crisis in business ethics in the United States. I remember my shock when I learned that a benefactor had given $20 million to the Harvard Business School to start a program in business ethics—not to increase productivity, or to improve worker knowledge, but for ethics. That is a selfless gift, but also a sad commentary on the state of affairs.

Although I still believe that I have the makings of a captain of industry, my record has been much better when I have worked for other people, including as a consultant. I am proud of the length of my association with my key employers, and I like to think that I have returned in kind their faith in me. For twenty-two years I have been with Head USA, the manufacturer of ski and tennis equipment and clothing; Head stuck with me even after losing a few accounts in the South because of my race. Since 1970, also, I have been with the Doral Resort and Country Club, the largest resort in southern Florida. I cannot forget that the Doral made me its director of tennis only nine years after the Admiral Hotel nearby refused to house me during the Orange Bowl tournament in Miami, although all the other junior players—who were white—stayed there. For more than sixteen years, I have been a consultant or columnist with *Tennis* magazine. My relationships as a columnist with the Washington *Post* and a consultant with Le Coq Sportif, the sports-clothing manufacturer, also go back many years. The longevity and human quality of these connections mean far more to me than the money they bring.

WITHOUT QUESTION, MY single most fascinating and satisfying involvement outside of my family since my retirement has been as a board member of the Aetna Life and Casualty Company, where I have served for the past ten years. Membership on a board probably seems like a fairly humdrum business connection, but it is not. Tennis led me to Aetna, but my work with Aetna has taken me far away from the life of a tennis professional. From the inside, I have looked into the heart of a major American commercial enterprise, but one of a special kind, involved in the crucial matters of health, welfare, and finance. More than a hundred years old, and with 45,000 employees, Aetna is one of the giants of the American corporate world. Its assets total just under a hundred billion dollars; its income in 1991 was around nineteen billion. Aetna is the largest diversified financial-services firm in the United States.

At some point in the 1970s, Aetna took over sponsorship of the World Cup, a tennis competition that pitted the United States against Australia, when the Australians were still a major power. The first Aetna-sponsored Cup tie in the Hartford area was memorable for me most of all because, after eighteen straight losses to Rod Laver, I finally beat him. But at least one other feature of the competition as sponsored by Aetna made the tournament worthwhile. Each year, before the first match, a private dinner brought the players together with Aetna's top executives. For four or five consecutive years, I sat at dinner next to Aetna's president, William "Bill" Bailey. Not once did he and I talk about tennis. Instead, we explored social and political matters, including the issue of health care.

In the late 1970s, I became a consultant to Aetna. Previously, I had served as a consultant to Philip Morris, the tobacco company, along with my fellow tennis players Roy Emerson, Manuel Santana, and Rafael Osuna. Philip Morris's president, Joseph Cullman III, became a second father to me, an invaluable mentor; and to this day, I remain close to him. I remember that almost from the start of my consultant-ship I had been troubled by the link between tobacco and lung disease; yet, unquestionably, tobacco had helped tennis when tennis needed help. The first sponsor of the U.S. Open in 1968, when I won it, was Marlboro cigarettes. Virginia Slims played an even more decisive role in the rise of professional women's tennis. This link between smoking and disease troubled some of us among the players, but it did not become a major issue until later.

I had also served as a consultant to the U.S. Army, after the Army suffered through some unpleasant incidents of racial friction among servicemen, in West Germany in particular. With Aetna, my task was somewhat different. I assisted Bill Bailey and his colleagues with minority recruitment, and especially the recruitment of employees who might become mid-level management and rise even higher within the company. At that point in the history of American race relations after the civil-rights struggle of the 1950s and '60s, many firms were competing to secure the most promising black American prospects in business. Aetna was eager to do well here, and I tried to help as best I could.

Evidently, Aetna was satisfied with my effort. One day in July 1982, I was with the Davis Cup team in St. Louis, where we were playing Sweden. It was the day McEnroe and Wilander played their unforgettable match lasting more than six hours. I had returned exhausted to my hotel, ready to fall asleep, when I found a note to call Bill Bailey in Hartford. I returned his call at once.

"Arthur, there is a matter of some urgency I need to talk to you about."

"Can we talk about it now, Bill?"

"No, I don't think so. When you are back in New York, in the city, I'll come down at your convenience and we'll meet at your apartment and we'll have a talk."

"At my apartment?"

"Yes, that would be best, I think."

"Can't you give me a hint what you want to talk to me about, Bill?"

"Sorry, Arthur," he replied. "I can't. It has to be face to face."

My first reaction was one of panic—a relatively mild attack, but panic nevertheless. What had I done wrong? What gaffe had I committed? What terrible rumor or report had Bailey heard about me that he wanted confirmed or denied? I was completely on the wrong track. When Bailey finally settled down in an armchair in the living room of our apartment on East Seventy-second Street, he did not complain about a gaffe or question me about a rumor.

"Arthur," he said, "we want you on the board of directors of Aetna."

I was flabbergasted. As the nature of his offer finally sank in, I became more and more elated at the prospect. I was happy for two reasons above all. First, the company had nothing to do with sports. Second, although it would take me into the corporate world, it also had everything to do with serving the basic needs of the masses of people. For me—as I sought to find ways of maturing and expanding the range of my activities and usefulness, my striving and achieving—this was almost the ideal assignment. I stood for election to the board. As Bailey assured me would probably happen, I was duly elected a director; and I have served on the board ever since.

At our first meeting at the headquarters in Hartford, I had fresh reasons to marvel at the fact that I had been asked. At the age of thirty-nine, I was by far the youngest member of the board. And virtually everyone else was a superstar of American business. I sat in the company of Warren Anderson, the president of Union Carbide; David Roderick, chairman of the board of U.S. Steel; Randolph Blatz, chairman of the board of Insilco; William Donaldson, founder of the asset-management firm Donaldson Lufkin Jenrette; Bayliss Manning, the former dean of the Stanford University Law School and a partner at the prestigious law firm of Paul, Weiss, Rifkind, Wharton & Garrison; Barbara Franklin, who served as the second Secretary of Commerce in the Bush administration, and her husband, Wallace Barnes, who heads a $500 million company called the Barnes Group; and Jack Donahue of Pittsburgh, the owner of Federated Investors and the largest single stockholder in Aetna.

This was extraordinary company for an aging jock. The quality of the board was impressive. Make no mistake—I hardly felt an iota of social insecurity. These were powerful, affluent people; but I had met and socialized with many powerful, affluent people in my long career. Moreover, as a professional player I had traveled all over the world, which also put me at ease in elite company. No, I felt little insecurity on the social side. But did I have enough business acumen to make a contribution to this group? *That* was another matter. Bailey set me straight: "Everybody asks what they think of as stupid questions at first. Just ask your questions, like everyone else, and they'll be answered, and that will be that." Since I have never been one to feign knowledge I do not have, I at once felt much more comfortable on that score.

But had I been brought in merely for window dressing? Only the most obtuse, self-deceiving black Americans fail to ask this question when they find themselves invited into an otherwise white circle. I knew that I was not the first African American board member at Aetna, but I also knew that I was only the second, and had been asked to serve on the board after the first, Hobart Taylor, had died. Was I merely a token of Aetna's interest in social and cultural diversity? I wanted to be more than a token; I wanted to be an essential member of the board. Fortunately, I was soon satisfied that the board needed me, or someone like me; someone who was not a chief executive officer, with a gaping chasm between his or her lofty administrative position and the mass of poor or even middle-class people; someone who brought a different cultural history to discussions; someone who was acutely sensitive to the problems hovering over the health and financial services at the heart of Aetna, for minorities and others as well.

I had never served on the board of directors of a business before, let alone a business with such vast resources. At first, I was impressed by the staggering sums of money we voted on—money transferred from one part of the company to another, or appropriated for a special reason, such as the opening of a new subsidiary in Mexico or Malaysia. However, the novelty of big money quickly passed. I had to come to terms with some of the contradictions involved in the board's duties. We vote on every important aspect of the company but do not manage Aetna, which has its own managers. We vote on all major decisions affecting the company, but these decisions have been thoroughly screened by the time they reach us; almost all of our votes are unanimous. Are we then simply a debating society and a rubber stamp? No. We serve the stockholders and must answer to them at the annual meetings. In the long term, the company is in our hands.

At almost every board meeting, as polite and as civilized as we are, we feel the sharp tension between abstract ideals and our obligation to perform for the stockholders. We face the phenomenon of redlining, for example, practiced by many banks and insurance companies. The lender draws a red line on a map. He or she lends to people on one side, but not to people on the other. Those on the other side of the red line are frequently people of color. The lender speaks of the need for prudent investment. The people cry for justice.

As an African American, I feel an obligation to speak up for the people across the red line. My special task, however, is to speak so that we come closer to a solution that will satisfy both the lender and the people. Therefore, the task is also to avoid at all times hypocrisy, demagoguery, and insult. In this respect, too, my experience as a board member has been gratifying. I do not have to convince the CEOs and the superlawyers around me that justice must be for all. From a practical as well as an ethical point of view, they know that justice must be for all. They know better than most that sound business decisions must result in more than an instant windfall of dollars. The long-term consequences of our decisions will also translate into dollars—or a lack of dollars—in the future. If you prick a CEO, he bleeds, too. I will never forget Warren Anderson's personal agony as he faced the tragic consequences of the accident at the Union Carbide plant in Bhopal, India, in 1984, when more than 3,000 people were killed.

Probably far more than the color of my skin, my personal assault by heart disease and AIDS has helped me to find my identity as a board member. While I am surely not the first board member to fall seriously ill, my first heart attack, at the age of thirty-six, undoubtedly raised my interest in health insurance and life insurance to an acute pitch. If my interest started to flag, my second heart operation, in 1983, the year after I joined the board, definitely brought me back into line.

Ironically, I had just attended an Aetna board meeting in Hartford in April 1983 when this second round of heart trouble began. After the meeting, I was in a limousine with other board members, on our way to catch the company helicopter for a swift ride back to New York City, when a pain in my chest became so uncomfortable that I knew I could not get on that aircraft. When we had arrived near the helicopter, I got out of the car without raising an alarm, then spoke casually to everyone else after they had gotten out. "Sorry, guys," I said. "I just realized I forgot to do something. I have to take care of it. Go on without me." Then I turned to the driver. "Please take me to Hartford hospital. Right now." Two months later, in New York City, I underwent my double-bypass operation.

My discovery that I had AIDS complicated my concern with health care in ways that I could never have anticipated. Once I found out I was infected, I informed the chairman of Aetna, Jim Lynn, and later passed the word to his successor, Ron Compton. I also revealed it in confidence to Bayliss Manning, the senior member of the board in length of service, and my mentor there. I would have resigned if they had suggested it, but all were eager for me to continue to serve as long as I could.

More than thinking of myself as a spokesman for racial minorities and the poor in the inner sanctum of this mighty life-insurance company, I perhaps more acutely believe that I represent the army of the sick in America and around the world. In a way, I also represent all male gays, all hemophiliacs, and all intravenous drug users who might become infected with HIV. And perhaps I also represent the dying.

Without becoming morbid or unduly sentimental, I try to respond practically to these feelings. I accept my board membership on a giant insurance company as a trust. Thus in 1992, I was distressed to read in *The Village Voice*, a newspaper I read regularly and respect, an article attacking Aetna and me, by name. The writer accused Aetna of cruelly denying insurance policies to people who are either HIV-positive or suffering from AIDS. I was accused of colluding with the company despite my own condition. The truth is that I would never have remained on the Aetna board if it had such a policy; but I have certainly voted in support of prudent and sensible changes in connection with individual life-insurance policies. At a certain point, Aetna decided to stop selling *individual* health-insurance policies to anyone. No individual is exempt from this decision. We did so for a simple, sufficient reason: we were losing money on individual policies. To make a profit, we would have had to raise premiums sharply. We insure groups of people. We absolutely do not require these groups to test its members or its prospective members for AIDS. And most groups do not require tests for basic individual coverage, only for excessive amounts of coverage.

I am proud of Aetna and of my association with the company. In Hartford, the company has enjoyed for many years the reputation of being an excellent employer and a conscientious citizen. In fact, many people there used to talk about "Mother Aetna," who takes care of her children and is a concerned neighbor. It has also developed the reputation of being a fair employer of minorities, including blacks.

In the absence of a national health-care program, which I hope will come one day to the United States, Aetna and companies like it stand between many people and the destitution caused by the runaway cost of medical treatments. That fact is very important to me.

MY LAST IMPORTANT area of work since my retirement has been in the world of social programs and foundations—that is, those programs and foundations I have started or helped to start. The first was the Ashe-Bollettieri Cities program, or ABC. Then came, with a somewhat different focus, an organization called Athletes Career Connection (ACC). Still later I formed the Safe Passage Foundation. And most recently, I established a foundation in my own name to fight AIDS. These are my main ventures into the world of public service.

As the name suggests, I started ABC with Nick Bollettieri, who is probably the most famous tennis instructor in the world and the head of the Bollettieri Tennis Academy in Bradenton, Florida. Nick has a gift for working with the young. At the academy and elsewhere, he has nurtured and trained some of the finest players in tennis, including Jimmy Arias, Andre Agassi, Jim Courier, Monica Seles, and Aaron Krickstein. I myself have known Nick since I was fifteen years old. Originally from Pelham, which borders the Bronx in New York, Nick likes to stress that despite his fame he is basically an average guy from a neighborhood where Italians, Jews, Irish, and blacks lived together in harmony. If so, he is above average in almost all other ways. A master salesman, promoter, and teacher, he is a man of high energy and practical enthusiasms.

ABC had its germination one day at Roland Garros Stadium in Paris in 1987, when Nick and I sat together watching one of his charges play a match at the French Open. Between points, we were talking about the deteriorating conditions in American cities, about violent crime and drug abuse and rampant juvenile delinquency, when Nick turned to me almost explosively.

"Arthur," he blurted out, "we've got to help those kids! We've got to do something for those kids!"

"What do you think we can do?" I asked.

"Well, let's think about it. I know we can do something!"

We thought about it over several weeks, and slowly came up with a plan. In 1988, we launched the ABC program. Ironically, we launched it the same week that I discovered I had AIDS.

Our idea was to use tennis as a way to gain and hold the attention of young people in the inner cities and other poor environments so that we could then teach them about matters more important than tennis. To start our program, we deliberately chose some tough neighborhoods, the kind of places as far removed as possible from the genteel world of tennis. We decided on our venture into Newark as the centerpiece and prototype of our efforts. Administratively, ABC was first run from Nick's academy in Bradenton, which helped keep our expenses down—or, perhaps more accurately, quietly passed many of those expenses on to Nick. To do so, we had to have the support of Bob Kain, in charge of tennis at International Management Group, the biggest sports-management company in the world, which owns the Bollettieri Tennis Academy. Kain gave his blessing. As long as we broke even financially, or kept our losses to a minimum, the arrangement could continue.

Eventually we began to see that ABC did not fit in well at the Bollettieri Academy. Working together, Nick and I brought several of our students down to Florida to stay at the academy for various lengths of time. Undoubtedly most of these students benefited from the facilities and the coaching, but in the end we had to concede that the joint effort could not continue. Money was the main problem. To maintain the program, we needed to secure funding from the governments of the cities we served. These cities understood our usefulness, by and large; unfortunately, extracting money owed to us from the City Hall bureaucracies sometimes took many months. At one point, to my embarrassment, ABC (or these city governments) owed the Bollettieri Academy as much as $300,000.

I knew full well that this situation could not continue. Gradually and understandably, the Bollettieri Academy and Nick himself withdrew from ABC, which has changed its way of operating. I was sorry to see Nick go, because he had tried hard to make the connection work. To facilitate the change, I started another organization, the Safe Passage Foundation, which would preside over ABC and another one of my program efforts, Athletes Career Connection, which had been running for some time. Here we worked initially with a consortium of seven colleges and universities (Seton Hall, Fordham, Spelman, Morehouse, American, Howard, and Pennsylvania) to try to redress the terrible attrition rate among black college athletes. I started ACC right after I discovered that only one in four black athletes in football and basketball at Division One schools (the top sporting echelon in the United States) ever graduates from college. This statistic appalled me. My aim was to stimulate the athletes to take their studies seriously and to consider in a realistic way the full range of career options open to them after college.

Athletes Career Connection did well for a while, then foundered during the recession that started across the United States around 1990. Sad to say, as colleges slashed their budgets, a program such as ours was often the first to go.

I intend the Safe Passage Foundation, as the name implies, to continue my efforts to help poor young people, especially poor young black people, make the transition from youth to adulthood without a crippling loss of faith in society and in themselves. Safe Passage can hardly solve the problems of poverty, racism, juvenile delinquency, cynicism, sexual promiscuity, crime, and drug addiction that plague the youth of this country. But, as Nick Bollettieri insisted, we have an obligation to try to do something to counter this social and spiritual plague. Too many people have simply given up.

That is why I am deeply grateful when, for example, veteran tennis champions like Bjorn Borg and Guillermo Vilas play an exhibition match as they did in Mahwah, New Jersey, in the summer of 1992 to raise money for Safe Passage; or when an enlightened, progressive mayor such as Sharpe James in Newark, New Jersey, allows us space in City Hall itself, rent-free, to run our program there. We have almost a thousand Safe Passage kids in the Newark area, from a "tiny tots" tennis program to one for high-school juniors and seniors. We use tennis to attract the kids, but we make sure that we spend about one-third of our time talking about other, more serious matters. I always try to lift the sights of the youngsters to new heights. Trying to be the next Michael Jordan is fine, I tell them; but why not also aim for the goal of owning the team that employs the next Michael Jordan?

Late in 1992, the giant international food company Nestlé became the first major sponsor of the Safe Passage Foundation when it awarded us a grant of $100,000. Although some of my energy must also go to support the Arthur Ashe Foundation for the Defeat of AIDS, I intend to keep working to administer and find support for Safe Passage. Through tennis, lives are being changed and spirits reclaimed. I have seen it work in Newark and I know it can work anywhere, as long as we can find selfless adults of goodwill who recognize the dangers facing us and the fact that our young people need our help desperately.

* * *

SINCE MY RETIREMENT, I have not become a senator like Bill Bradley, or a Supreme Court justice like Byron White. In part, I have had to curtail my activities and ambitions because of my illnesses. However, I have tried to keep on with my striving because this is the only hope I have of ever achieving anything worthwhile and lasting.

In doing so, I am not driven by an obsession to scratch my name indelibly on the pages of history. The years pass, and the world forgets the efforts of virtually all individual men and women of goodwill. And yet those efforts are not necessarily in vain because they are forgotten. They may bear fruit in myriad unrecognized ways, small but potent— in one life helped here, in a single future brightened there. I know I could never forgive myself if I elected to live without humane purpose, without trying to help the poor and unfortunate, without recognizing that perhaps the purest joy in life comes with trying to help others.

CHAPTER SEVEN

The Beast in the Jungle

"JEANNE," I SAID. "Something is wrong with me."

It was a beautiful late-summer morning in 1988. I was standing in front of her, in our suite at the Sagamore Resort on Lake George in upper New York state. Camera, who was a year and a half old, was with us. We had just come back from breakfast.

I had wanted to call home and monitor the messages on my telephone answering machine. I raised my hand up to the telephone on the wall and started dialing my number. Or rather, I tried to dial it. My fingers made an attempt to respond to my will, but they struggled in vain to do what I asked. I was trying to put my index finger on the buttons, but the finger wasn't working very well. Perplexed, I looked at my hand and tried again.

"What is it, Arthur?" Jeanne asked.

"My fingers. I can't get them to work well."

"Maybe they are numb because you slept on them?"

"Yes," I said. "That must be it. But no, they aren't numb. I can feel them, definitely. I just don't seem to be able to use them."

"I'll dial for you," Jeanne said. And she did, without giving a hint of alarm.

At this point, in fact, neither of us was alarmed. Mainly because we had both been through some fairly harrowing times with doctors and illnesses, an unresponsive finger did not seem like much to be concerned about.

A month or so before, I had gone to the Sagamore for an Aetna board meeting. We on the board had been seeking some fresh approaches to certain problems, and decided that a change of scenery, away from the company headquarters in Hartford, might inspire us to think creatively. That meeting, everyone agreed, had been a success. Clearly, the quality of the resort and its superb location in the famous Finger Lakes region in upstate New York had something to do with our results. A month later, when Jeanne and I impulsively concluded that we needed to get away from our Westchester County home in the village of Mount Kisco, north of New York City, for two or three days, we thought at once of the Sagamore. We would relax there, then return home in time for the start of the most important American tennis tournament of the year, the United States Open. We needed to be rested, because the two-week tournament is typically a happy madhouse.

Then we decided to invite Donald Dell and his wife, Carole, to come along with us upstate. Donald and Carole, who were visiting from Potomac, Maryland, where they live and where Donald's management firm, ProServ, had its main offices, would also be going to the U.S. Open.

We were having a good time together, until this strange numbness in my hand. I quickly dismissed the idea that what was happening to my fingers could have been caused by sleeping on my hand. Had I suffered a small stroke? That was a distinct possibility. Should I leave the hotel early and head home to my internist? We decided to stay. Frankly, I expected to go to sleep that night and awake to find my fingers back to normal.

However, by the time we checked out of the Sagamore, my right hand was hanging from the wrist, almost completely limp. Now I was somewhat alarmed. Nevertheless, when I telephoned my doctor, I did not suggest an emergency. Something seemed to be wrong with my hand; would he look at it? He asked me to come in the next day, Friday, August 26.

In the morning, a television crew came to our house to interview Jeanne and me for the "CBS This Morning" show with Harry Smith. In those days, one feature of the show each Friday was a visit to someone's home. Our house in Mount Kisco, built before the Civil War, was somewhat special. Thinking about my hand, Jeanne and I had considered for a moment canceling the interview, but finally we decided against it. My appointment with the internist would come soon enough.

The television interview was pleasant in most respects but also something of an ordeal. No matter how hard I tried, I could not move a digit up, down, or sideways. My right hand, now completely limp, literally hung dead from my wrist. As I answered questions and talked about the house, I tried to act as nonchalant as I could; I certainly told no one from CBS that something was wrong. The truth is that I had to prop up my right hand with my left. I still have no idea how I got through the interview without anyone on the crew taking notice. I answered the questions with as much charm as I could muster, but my mind was elsewhere.

Around noon, I drove some eight minutes from our house to the offices of Dr. William Russell at the Mount Kisco Medical Group. I knew the way very well. The group offices were almost across the street from the Northern Westchester Hospital Center, where I served on the board of directors. I had confidence in Dr. Russell, an able internist whom we had consulted professionally in the past. He inspired confidence. Dr. Russell is the picture of the genial suburban family practitioner, someone almost out of Norman Rockwell's America of a bygone age, but with the latest medical and scientific technology and information close at hand. Mature in years and manner, he is gentle, attentive, reassuring. Whenever I consulted him, he would ask not only about me but about Jeanne and Camera; often he asked about them first, before inquiring about *my* health. I liked that. He didn't fumble for their names, but instead showed a genuine concern for their well-being. And he loved to play and watch tennis.

As I entered the office, I sensed such an unusual degree of excitement in the air that I wondered whether or not I was projecting my own nervousness onto the scene. As it turned out, Dr. Russell and his colleagues and staff in the medical group were on the verge of moving out of their old quarters into a new, sparkling facility across the street. But nothing interfered with the courtesy and orderliness of my reception, and I was soon ushered into Dr. Russell's office.

The sight of my hand, as limp as a flag on a still day, made him sit up. Listening to my complaints, he looked closely at the offending hand. He hefted it, pulled on my fingers, flopped it about.

"Have you been feeling dizzy at all?" he asked.

"No. Not at all."

"Shortness of breath? Any trouble breathing?"

"No. I feel fine."

"A fever of any kind?"

"No."

"Did anything strike your hand? Did you use it in some forceful way?"

"No. Nothing like that happened at all. It simply went dead."

"Well," Dr. Russell said, "I think there is only one way to go, and we have to do it right now. Something is interfering with the signals from your brain to the hand. The interference is almost certainly in the area of the brain, because I can't think of any other likely reason for your hand to stop working."

"What's next, then?"

"I am going to arrange for you to have a CAT scan of your brain right away. I don't want to alarm you unduly, but that's the main way to proceed right now. And I do mean right now."

The last time I heard a doctor speak to me with such a sense of urgency was July 31, 1979, when Dr. Lee Wallace, playing tennis on a court near my own, suspected that I was having a heart attack and insisted that I go straightaway from the tennis court to New York Hospital.

Dr. Russell made a telephone call or two. When I went across the street to the CT facility, the attendants were waiting for me. By this time I was more nervous than when I arrived at Dr. Russell's. I had seen CAT-scanning machines before; they look like a set of timpani drums turned upside down. Keeping as still as I could, I waited while the machine's X-ray mechanism did its business of photographing the brain at various angles. The entire procedure took about twenty minutes.

When I joined Dr. Russell and a radiologist in an adjoining room, there, up on the light box, were the CT images of my brain, very much like smaller, more familiar X-ray pictures of my chest or my knee.

"Hmm," Dr. Russell said. At least, that's what I remember him saying, as a look of genuine concern settled over his face. Stunned might be too strong a term, but he was obviously taken aback. I looked quickly at him, then looked again at the pictures. He was as professional as any doctor could be, but I could tell that he did not at all like what he was seeing. Doctors are trained to be dispassionate, since they see sick people all the time. However, trained or not, it is not always easy to react stoically to bad news.

I peered at the images, looking for clues to what had rattled him. I did not think I knew what to look for. I had never seen CAT-scan images of my brain before. Then I saw that the two hemispheres of my brain, which should have been nearly identical, were not. The right side of the brain was clear. The left side showed an irregularly round shape—a splotch. If the rounded brain looked like the moon, then the splotch looked like one of those arid lakes or seas on the moon. This splotch, I thought, looks exactly like the Sea of Rains. What was it doing on my brain?

As we sat and stared, I could feel Dr. Russell becoming more nervous, more uncomfortable.

"What is that?" I asked, pointing at the splotch.

"Look," he said. He spoke slowly, choosing his words carefully. "I don't want to steer you wrong. I'm not a neurologist or a neurosurgeon." The radiologist with us wasn't sure, either; we clearly needed some more opinions.

"Could you find someone at New York Hospital?" My heart surgeries had both been at St. Luke's–Roosevelt Hospital on the Upper West Side in Manhattan; but my cardiologist, Dr. Stephen Scheidt, was attached to New York Hospital, on the Upper East Side.

"Of course."

The drive back home, although it took only eight minutes, was pretty awful. Up until the moment of seeing the CAT scan, I had not felt extreme anxiety. What had triggered my anxiety now was not the CAT scan itself but the jolting effect of the image on Dr. Russell. Obviously he thought that I had something serious to fear.

Was it a stroke? A small one now, but the precursor of a massive one? A massive stroke that might leave me unable to care for myself? Was it a tumor of the brain? Cancer of the brain—inoperable? Would I face months of extreme pain and then certain death? Or would an aneurysm snuff out my life in a split second, as it had snuffed out Grace

Kelly's life as she drove her car with her daughter Stephanie in the beautiful hills of Monaco?

I knew a little about the brain from what I had learned in high school and in a course on physiological psychology I had taken at UCLA. Even the medical terms were somewhat familiar to me. Of course, while my knowledge of medicine was not negligible, most of it was limited to the subject of the heart. The brain was new territory.

In our kitchen, Jeanne listened to me explain what had happened. I talk about her now as my "co-patient," and she has been exactly that for a long time.

Around three-thirty that afternoon, carrying the CAT-scan images and trying to remain calm, I entered the office of Dr. John Caronna, a neurologist at New York Hospital. A woman, one of his colleagues, gave me a sort of rudimentary preliminary examination.

"Stand up, please," she instructed me. "Hold your arms out. Follow this object with your eyes." She needed to make sure what was functioning and what was not. My hand was definitely not functioning, but the rest of me seemed fine.

I watched as Dr. Caronna looked closely at the pictures of my brain. Thinking about it now, I realize that the splotch on the left side of my brain was by no means an entire mystery to him. He already had his preliminary diagnosis, or at least his informed suspicions. However, like Dr. Russell, he was cautious.

"Something is in there. We can see that. But what? I don't think we can know for certain without a biopsy."

"You mean a brain operation?"

"Yes," he replied. "We need to look at the tissue, examine it. I think we have to talk to a neurosurgeon. He can explain your options."

Now it was his turn to make telephone calls. Soon we were joined by a neurosurgeon, Dr. Russell Patterson, and Dr. Stephen Scheidt, my cardiologist. They looked at the images. They, too, were cautious.

"Mr. Ashe," Dr. Patterson assured me, "we don't have to do anything right away. Obviously something is going on, probably an infection of some sort. We can simply wait and see what happens next."

I laughed, a nervous laugh. Right, I thought to myself, we can wait, and watch the entire arm go dead. Then the rest of me. "What's the other option?"

"On the other hand, we could go in right now. As soon as possible. That way, we would know exactly what we are dealing with. And we can get as much of the infected tissue out as we can."

"Let's go in," I said.

I did not hesitate in making that decision. Nevertheless, the next day I had an MRI at St. Agnes Diagnostic Center in White Plains, Westchester. Then I sought a second opinion, based on the CAT scan and the MRI, at Brunswick Hospital in Amityville, Long Island. The new experts told me nothing different; all agreed that surgery was necessary.

This would be the fourth operation of my life. The first, in 1977, had been comparatively minor, on my heel. The second had been major—my quadruple-bypass in December 1979, after my heart attack the previous July. The third had been my corrective double-bypass in June 1983. Now, new ground: brain surgery.

My thoughts about the U.S. Open tournament vanished from my mind. Although I had work to do there and columns to write for the Washington *Post*, none of that mattered now; they would be put on hold. On Wednesday, August 31, I checked into New York Hospital for a fresh battery of tests, including a spinal tap and a blood test. On Friday, the results came back. Jeanne, Doug Stein, and Eddie Mandeville were with me when I heard the bad news. In fact, they gave it to me. I was HIV-positive.

None of the physicians at the hospital had wanted the grim task of informing me, so they passed the word to Eddie Mandeville, who had been visiting me every day and, as a physician, had become entirely familiar with my case. Eddie told Doug, who is also a doctor, and the two of them waited for Jeanne to arrive that day at the hospital before letting her know.

"What does this mean about Jeanne?" I asked. She reached out quickly, put her left arm around my shoulders, and squeezed my hand hard. "You and me, babe," she said. "You and me." She herself had yet to be tested for HIV.

We immediately traced the infection back to the two units of transfused blood after my second heart-bypass operation, in 1983. The most recent medical data had indicated that the HIV virus could stay dormant for years after infecting one, then surface in the form of an opportunistic infection. A brain operation would ascertain if I had such an infection.

On Thursday, September 8, Dr. Patterson performed the operation, which lasted about forty-five minutes. Brain operations are delicate but typically do not last long. When I regained consciousness after the operation, I felt far better than after my heart surgeries. Postoperative pain can be quite substantial, and I was certainly groggy. But compared to the way I felt after my second heart operation, I was fine. Although my head was heavily bandaged, and I was receiving fluids intravenously, I felt very little discomfort.

The first report I received was encouraging. I did not have a brain tumor but rather an infection of some kind. The operation was a success, in that Dr. Patterson had removed all traces of the infection. Part of this matter was sent at once to the laboratory for a biopsy.

The following day, the results came back. Jeanne was with me in my hospital room when Dr. Patterson informed us that the infection was toxoplasmosis. When he gave us the news, I remember Jeanne taking my hand and squeezing it hard and long, as if she would never let it go, just as she had done when I heard the news of my HIV infection. Toxoplasmosis, which used to occur infrequently, had become notorious as one of the specific diseases that—in conjunction with the presence of HIV—marked the condition known as Acquired Immune Deficiency Syndrome, or AIDS. Not only was I HIV-positive; I had full-blown AIDS.

"Aha," I said; or so Jeanne tells me.

In facing past crises that amounted, like this one, to a *fait accompli*, my left-brain–dominated mind immediately summoned up two words to help me cope with the new reality: "That's that." The two findings of "HIV-positive" and "AIDS" were new facts of my life that I could not evade. There was nothing I could possibly do about either one except to treat them according to the most expert medical science available to me. Neither would go away, and I had to make the best of the situation. If that attitude and those feelings sound almost inhuman, at best stoical, I can respond only that this is my way of dealing with adversity. I wasn't frightened or nervous. The public hysteria over AIDS was probably then at its zenith, but I would not become hysterical.

At the hospital, in our moments alone, Jeanne and I wondered if God had chosen us to undergo publicly all these medical challenges. But there were perfectly sane and credible explanations for my medical condition. Heart disease is certainly hereditary, and both my parents had suffered from it. As for my AIDS, I was simply unlucky to have had a couple of units of transfused blood that may have been donated in 1983 by some gay or bisexual man, or some intravenous drug user who perhaps had needed the money badly. I will never know for sure, and this is not an issue I dwell on.

Pulling ourselves together after the shock, Jeanne and I talked about who should be told, and when. Of course, we were sure that half of the hospital staff already knew these results. And being a public figure made me further vulnerable; I knew that at some hospitals employees were secretly being paid by news organizations to provide them with morsels of gossip. But if the story could be kept out of the newspapers and magazines, and off of radio and television, then who should we tell? Almost certainly we would not tell my father; I did not think his heart could take news like that. We considered it an absolute blessing that Camera, only twenty-one months old, hardly needed to be told anything about my condition. Her need to know would come much later.

QUICKLY I BECAME an expert on toxoplasmosis. Ironically, as terrible as the disease sounds, it is not normally a cause for alarm. Many people carry the parasite *(Toxoplasma gondii)* that causes toxoplasmosis, but very few of them are bothered by the condition itself. One common way to become infected is domestically, through exposure to cat feces in kitty litter; another is by eating raw or undercooked meat. The result is often only mild fever and pains, which just as often disappear without medication, or even without being treated. The parasite can be attacked effectively with a wide range of antibiotics. However, in rare instances toxoplasmosis can cause serious problems, including encephalitis. Doctors often warn pregnant women not to handle kitty litter, because when toxoplasmosis is passed on to babies it can cause severe neurological impairment.

In some ways, as bizarre as it may seem, I was almost fortunate in the particular opportunistic infection that had attacked my body, considering some of the others. The most devastating of the AIDS-defining or AIDS-related illnesses has been a peculiarly deadly form of pneumonia commonly known as PCP, so called because it is caused by the protozoan *Pneumocystis carinii*. More than half of all AIDS sufferers find themselves infected with PCP, which has killed more AIDS patients than any other opportunistic infection.

Among the other AIDS diseases are: meningitis; the cancer known as Kaposi's sarcoma (KS); the aptly named "wasting disease"; diarrhea; candidiasis, commonly called thrush; lymphoma; dementia; and tuberculosis. To have any one of these diseases, however, does not mean that one is exempt from having any of the others. Quite the contrary.

A parasite had attacked my brain, and the resulting abscess had been removed. But the brain would hereafter be vulnerable because HIV can lead to a wide range of brain infections, including one leading to dementia. At least half of all patients suffering with AIDS experience a degree of dementia, with symptoms ranging from moderate memory loss to deep depression, massive disorientation, radical motor disability, and even a kind of psychologically induced total paralysis. In the last stages of AIDS, no matter what has been the major opportunistic infection, dementia often asserts itself in a frightening way.

My toxoplasmosis could return. In fact, it was probably bound to return sooner or later. Toxoplasmosis affects between 20 and 30 percent of all AIDS patients. The good news was that because it could be treated effectively with antibiotics, I probably would not have to undergo surgery for that particular reason again. But the general condition of full-blown AIDS remained, and both toxoplasmosis and the other opportunistic infections remained deadly threats.

"Deadly" was a literal expression. I remember several years ago hearing the Surgeon-General of the United States, C. Everett Koop, say with his trademark bluntness: "If you contract AIDS, you will die." How long I had to live, I did not know. But from the day I found out that I had AIDS, I have had to live with the knowledge that my days are numbered.

NO ONE IN my hospital room that day had to ask the question I knew would be on many people's minds, perhaps on most people's minds.

But the rest of the world would ask: How had Arthur Ashe become infected?

To almost all Americans, AIDS meant one of two conditions: intravenous drug use or homosexuality. They had good reason to think so. Of the 210,000 reported cases of Americans, male and female, afflicted with AIDS by February 1992, 60 percent were men who had been sexually active with another man; about 23 percent had been intravenous illicit drug users; at least 6 percent more had been both homosexual and drug abusers; another 6 percent or so had been heterosexual; 2 percent had contracted the disease from blood transfusions; and 1 percent were persons with hemophilia or other blood-coagulant disorders.

The link between individual behavior and infection is crucial to AIDS. Indeed, AIDS was "discovered" in North America in 1980, when doctors in New York and Los Angeles noticed that an unusually high number of young male homosexuals had contracted *Pneumocystis carinii* pneumonia without the usual precondition, an immune system depressed by prescribed medicine. At about the same time, a normally quite rare disease, Kaposi's sarcoma, also began to spread; and once more the victims were young male homosexuals. Later that year, Dr. Michael Gottlieb at UCLA, a federally funded clinical investigator, was the first to notify the Centers for Disease Control about the puzzling outbreak of infections.

By the middle of the following year, the evidence was conclusive and alarming that a new disease was with us, and that it was becoming a nationwide epidemic. The search then began for its cause. After much hard work, HIV was isolated and identified in 1983. An individual tested positive for HIV when a blood test determined the presence in the blood of antibodies fighting the attack by the human immunodeficiency virus, or HIV. Then AIDS was finally defined as a combination in any person of HIV and one or more of over two dozen opportunistic diseases. The search for a cure continued—and continues.

How one contracts AIDS apparently has a lot to do with how one will be infected. Kaposi's sarcoma, for example, the reddish-purple, blotchy skin cancer that is for some patients the most humiliating of all the infections—because of the disfiguring lesions that make the disease so visible—means that the AIDS virus had probably been acquired through oral–anal sexual contact, more often among gay or bisexual men. Hemophiliacs, however, rarely fall prey to Kaposi's sarcoma. (I probably will not be touched by it; small comfort.) And if a man with AIDS has been an intravenous drug user, he could easily die sooner than if he acquired AIDS through homosexual intercourse. The steady, illicit use of drugs typically undermines the immune system; AIDS is only a heightened version of this systemic weakening.

So how, the public would want to know, did Arthur Ashe contract AIDS? Had I been quietly shooting up heroin over the years? Or was I a closet homosexual or bisexual, hiding behind a marriage but pursuing and bedding men on the sly?

Perhaps because I had been a famous athlete, I suspect that few speculators would think that I was an intravenous drug user. I knew that this is not very sound logic, but logic is not the main point here. In any event, I was not and have never been a drug user. Like most young people in the Woodstock generation, I had tried marijuana. But I regard the use of cocaine as insanity, and heroin as an abomination.

I also know that I can look anyone in the eye and say two things about my sex life: in almost sixteen years of marriage, I have never been unfaithful to my wife; and I have never had a homosexual experience. Many people might not believe me, but I cannot do anything about their skepticism, or their idle malice. And it is not for me to worry about their doubts or their malice.

The facts of the case are simple. Recovering from double-bypass heart surgery in 1983, I felt miserable even though I had experienced post-operative pain before. I can remember a conversation I had with a doctor in which I complained about feeling unbelievably low, and he laid out my options for me.

"You can wait it out, Arthur, and you'll feel better after a while," he said. "Or we can give you a couple of units of blood. That would be no problem at all."

"I would like the blood," I replied. I don't think I hesitated for a moment. Why feel miserable when a palliative is at hand? Surely there was nothing to be feared from the blood bank of a major American hospital, one of the most respected medical facilities in New York City. In fact, less than a month later, in July 1983, Margaret Heckler,

President Reagan's Secretary of Health and Human Services, confidently made an announcement to the people of the United States: "The nation's blood supply is safe." Her words are etched in my memory.

This was ignorance—and perhaps arrogance—speaking. Unfortunately for me and about 13,000 other recipients of blood transfusions before March 1985, the nation's blood supply was not safe. That is the number of people who (according to the Centers for Disease Control, or CDC) either developed AIDS or probably became HIV-positive from blood transfusions but had not yet developed AIDS by April 1992. According to the CDC, a total of 6,694 persons had contracted AIDS from blood transfusions, and an estimated 6,000 had become HIV-positive without contracting AIDS to that point. The day after my announcement, I read these figures in *New York Newsday*.

In March 1985, too late for those unlucky 13,000, government officials finally had a test in place for all blood banks to be able to detect the presence of HIV, as well as other diseases, including hepatitis, which was already targeted. Did this mean that the nation's blood supply was now, finally, totally safe? No. Between March 1985 and March 1992, according to the CDC, twenty Americans became infected by AIDS through a blood transfusion. To be sure, this was a dramatic and gratifying reduction in the rate of infection. But because a donor might be infected with HIV for several months without any clinical evidence of infection, the nation's blood supply is not 100 percent safe. Unless some method of purifying HIV-contaminated blood is found—and no such method is even remotely in the offing—the blood supply will never be completely safe.

THE NEWS THAT I had AIDS hit me hard but did not knock me down. I had read of people committing suicide because of despair caused by infection with HIV. Indeed, in the preceding year, 1987, men suffering from AIDS were 10.5 times more likely to commit suicide than non-HIV-infected people who were otherwise similar to them.

In 1988, the AIDS suicide rate fell, but only to 7.4 times the expected rate. In 1990, it was 6 times the expected rate. The drop continued, but the far greater likelihood of suicide among AIDS patients persists, according to a 1992 issue of the *Journal of the American Medical Association*. (Incidentally, most of the HIV-infected men who kill themselves use prescription drugs to do so, instead of the guns that most male suicides use.) The main reason for the decline in this suicide rate, according to the report, was the general improvement in treatment, including the development of drugs that gave AIDS patients more hope. By 1992, however, the suicide rate was starting to rise again, as many of the therapies for AIDS, including those I was dependent on, began to show their limitations.

For me, suicide is out of the question. Despair is a state of mind to which I refuse to surrender. I resist moods of despondency because I know how they feed upon themselves and upon the despondent. I fight vigorously at the first sign of depression. I know that some depression can be physically induced, generated by the body rather than the mind. Such depression is obviously hard to contain. But depression caused by brooding on circumstances, especially circumstances one cannot avoid or over which one has no control, is another matter. I refuse to surrender myself to such a depression and have never suffered from it in my life.

Here is an area in which there are very close parallels between ordinary life and world-class athletic competition. The most important factor determining success in athletic competition is often the ability to control mood swings that result from unfavorable changes in the score. A close look at any athletic competition, and especially at facial expressions and body language, reveals that many individuals or even entire teams go into momentary lapses of confidence that often prove disastrous within a game or match. The ever-threatening danger, which I know well from experience, is that a momentary lapse will begin to deepen almost of its own accord. Once it is set in motion, it seems to gather enough momentum on its own to run its course. A few falling pebbles build into an avalanche. The initiative goes to one's opponent, who seems to be impossibly "hot" or "on a roll"; soon, victory is utterly out of one's reach. I've seen it happen to others on the tennis court; it has sometimes happened to me. In life-threatening situations, such as the one in which I now found myself, I knew that I had to do everything possible to keep this avalanche of deadly emotion from starting. One simply must not despair, even for a moment.

I cannot say that even the news that I have AIDS devastated me, or drove me into bitter reflection and depression even for a short time. I do not remember any night, from that first moment until now, when the thought of my AIDS condition and its fatality kept me from sleeping soundly. The physical discomfort may keep me up now and then, but not the psychological or philosophical discomfort.

I have been able to stay calm in part because my heart condition is a sufficient source of danger, were I to be terrified by illness. My first heart attack, in 1979, could have ended my life in a few chest-ravaging seconds. Both of my heart operations were major surgeries, with the risks attendant on all major surgery. And surely no brain operation is routine. Mainly because I have been through these battles with death, I have lost much of my fear of it.

I was not always that way. I had been a sickly child, but for most of the first thirty-six years of my life, until 1979, I nurtured a sense of myself as indestructible, if not actually immortal. This feeling persisted even after my heel surgery in 1977. For nine years since my first heart attack, however, I had been living with a powerful sense of my own mortality. And I have had many other signs, in the deaths of others, that have led me to think of my own end as something that could be imminent. So AIDS did not devastate me. AIDS was little more than something new to deal with, something new to understand and respond to, something to accept as a challenge, as if I might defeat it.

One can ready oneself for death. I see death as more of a dynamic than a static event. The actual physical manifestation of the absence of life is simply the ultimate step of a process that leads inevitably to that stage. In the interim, before the absolute end, one can do much to make life as meaningful as possible.

What would have devastated me was to discover that I had infected my wife, Jeanne, and my daughter, Camera. I do not think it would make any difference, on this score, whether I had contracted AIDS "innocently" from a blood transfusion or in one of the ways that most of society disapproves of, such as homosexual contacts or drug addiction. The overwhelming sense of guilt and shame would be the same in either case, if I had infected another human being.

A friend of mine has ventured the opinion that much as I love

Jeanne, I am truly crazy about Camera. Well, Jeanne loves me, but I think she, too, is truly crazy about Camera. The thought that this beautiful child, not yet two years old, who has brought more pure joy into our lives than we had ever known before we laid eyes on her, could be infected with this horrible disease, because of me, was almost too much even to think about.

Both Jeanne and Camera were quickly tested. Both, thank God, were found to be free of any trace of HIV. Their testing has continued, and they remain free of infection.

BEFORE I COULD sort out some of the ideas exploding in my head about AIDS, I had to deal physically with a post-operative problem. Because I am allergic to penicillin, I was given a different antibiotic, one that is sulfur-derived, after I came out of surgery. For some reason, the sulfur crystallized in my system and I developed kidney stones, which were responsible for the most excruciating attack of pain I have ever felt in my life.

Then, just as I was about to celebrate the end of that ordeal, I had a violent reaction to the sulfur derivative. I developed a quite severe case of a condition called Stevens-Johnson Syndrome, which left my entire body looking exactly as if I were ready for the burn unit at New York Hospital. For five days I could neither talk nor eat, because my mouth had become painfully sore.

As soon as I recovered, I turned my attention to the main matter at hand—using all the resources of medical science to hold AIDS at bay. Just as I was girding myself for the battle, I was struck in the face, or so the blow felt. In October 1988, a month after my biopsy and the discovery that I had AIDS, the prestigious magazine *Scientific American* devoted its entire issue to AIDS. One article in particular transfixed me. In it, the author asserted that 90 percent of AIDS patients die within three years of being diagnosed. But my doctors and I had no idea how long I had been suffering with AIDS before my biopsy revealed the presence of toxoplasmosis. How long had the parasite been creating its abscess in my brain?

I couldn't bring myself to ask my AIDS specialist, Dr. Murray, how much longer I had to live. I asked him something else. "Will you

With my mother, 1943

My mother, Mattie Cordell
Cunningham Ashe, around 1946,
Richmond, Virginia
The Browns' Studio

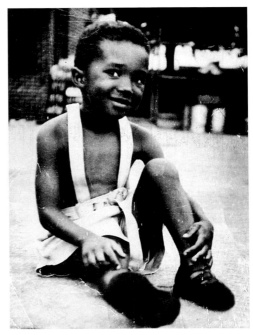

About two years old, around 1945,
Richmond

With my tennis trophies at home, 1955

With my schoolmates Ralph Williams (top left), Fredi Savage (seated left), and Elaine Terry at Maggie Walker High School, Richmond, around 1958   *Scott L. Henderson*

Talking tennis at Brook Field Park with my friends Aubrey
Taylor (left) and Roy Smith, around 1960   *Scott L. Henderson*

With my brother, Johnnie, and my father, Arthur Ashe, Sr., in
1963 at the NCAA tournament in Princeton, New Jersey

Returning home from Los Angeles
to Richmond, around 1964
Scott L. Henderson

At my party for Margie and Stan
Smith before the U.S. Open, 1974
Jessica Burstein

At commencement exercises,
Princeton University, 1982, when I
received an honorary doctorate
John W. H. Simpson

As Davis Cup
captain with John
McEnroe and Jimmy
Connors in
Bucharest, Rumania,
1984   *Russ Adams*

With Billie Jean King, preparing
to cover Wimbledon for
television, 1984   *HBO Photo*

With John McEnroe,
U.S. vs. Sweden, Davis
Cup, 1984   *Russ Adams*

With Donald Dell
(left), John McEnroe,
Sr., Gloria Kramer
(Mrs. Jack Kramer),
and President Ronald
Reagan on the White
House lawn, 1981
The White House

With my father (far
left) and my step-
mother, Lorene Kim-
brough Ashe, and
Virginia Governor
L. Douglas Wilder at
the governor's birthday
celebration, January 23,
1988   *Office of the
Governor of Virginia*

At the White House
with President George
Bush, Arnold
Schwarzenegger, and
Dr. Louis Sullivan
(right), Secretary of
Health and Human
Services, 1990
The White House

With Jeanne and
Andrew Young at a
dinner in Atlanta,
Georgia, 1991
Jean Young

Arrested outside the White
House, September 9, 1992
AP/Wide World Photos

With Nelson Mandela
at his hotel in New
York City, the summer
of 1992
Jeanne Moutoussamy-Ashe

My old college roommate and friend, Charlie Pasarell (left), and Donald Dell at the Arthur Ashe Tennis Center, Philadelphia, 1989
Jeanne Moutoussamy-Ashe

With Pam Shriver (left) and Steffi Graf at the National Tennis Center, Flushing Meadows, New York, August 30, 1992   *Art Seitz*

At my AIDS announcement press conference in New York City, April 8, 1992
Angel Franco, New York Times Pictures

At my long-time friend and mentor Joseph Cullman's eightieth birthday
celebration at the Museum of Natural History, New York City, the day
after my AIDS announcement, April 9, 1992. Standing: Joan and Joe
Cullman. Seated: Carole Dell

On our wedding day, February 20, 1977, United Nations
Chapel, New York City *Jill Krementz*

A family gathering for Camera's christening, April 11, 1987, Mount Kisco, New York   *Jeanne Moutoussamy-Ashe*

With Jeanne after our wedding, 1977. From left: her brother John; her father, John Sr.; her sister-in-law Penelope, now Mrs. Gainer; her brother Claude; and her mother, Elizabeth Moutoussamy
Jill Krementz

New Year's Eve, 1990. Seated with me: Jeanne and Eddie Mandeville. Standing: Harriette Mandeville, Danny Parker, and Christine Parker
Alvin Schragis

With my father at St. Luke's–Roosevelt Hospital, New York City, before my first bypass operation, December 1979   *Jeanne Moutoussamy-Ashe*

Camera's sixth birthday, New York City, December 21, 1992
Jeanne Moutoussamy-Ashe

In the yard of our home
in Mount Kisco,
New York, 1989
Jeanne Moutoussamy-Ashe

At the Westchester
County Fair,
New York, 1989
Jeanne Moutoussamy-Ashe

With Camera's
godfather, Doug Stein
(far left), and Eddie
Mandeville on Super
Bowl Sunday,
January 31, 1993
Harriette Mandeville

On the beach, Eleuthera,
the Bahamas, 1990
Club Med Photo

Eleuthera, the Bahamas, 1990
Jeanne Moutoussamy-Ashe

With Dr. Henry F. Murray
at New York Hospital,
January 4, 1993, discussing
my PCP diagnosis
Jeanne Moutoussamy-Ashe

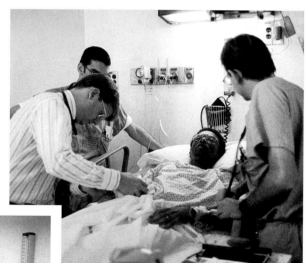

In the coronary-care section, New
York Hospital, September 1992
Jeanne Moutoussamy-Ashe

Mayor Dinkins visits me in the
coronary-care section, New York
Hospital, late summer 1992
Jeanne Moutoussamy-Ashe

Working on *Days of Grace* in New York Hospital, January 1993
Jeanne Moutoussamy-Ashe

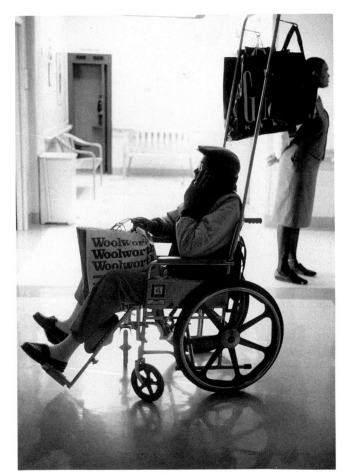

Discharged from
New York Hospital,
January 18, 1993
Jeanne Moutoussamy-Ashe

With Camera at the covered Centre Court at Wimbledon, June 1989
Jeanne Moutoussamy-Ashe

At work, October 1992   *Jeanne Moutoussamy-Ashe*

be able to tell me when I have about three months left?" I estimated that I would need at least three months to put my affairs in ideal order in the event of my death.

"I think you will know as much as I know," he countered. "After all, both of us will be keeping a close watch on your cell count. Beyond that, we both may be in the dark. We'll do our best, Arthur."

I took the *Scientific American* article seriously. As I approached the summer of 1991, or three years after my biopsy, my sense of anxious expectation mounted. Could I make it to Camera's fifth birthday party, in December 1991? I made it. What about my wedding anniversary, on February 20, 1992? I arranged for dinner reservations and Jeanne and I dined and celebrated. And then came Wimbledon, in June. I was there.

As with other people suffering from a combination of medical problems, I became a professional patient. The most important people in my life outside of my family were Dr. Scheidt, my cardiologist, and Dr. Murray, an infectious-diseases specialist and my AIDS doctor. In fact, I am surrounded by doctors. In the last dozen years, in addition to sundry internists, my cardiologist, and my infectious-disease doctor, I have been treated by a neurologist, a neurosurgeon, a cardiothoracic surgeon, a dermatologist, and a dentist whose other patients are only too keenly aware that he attends to at least one person suffering from AIDS. (My dentist lost almost half of his patients when word got out that he was treating me; fortunately, many later returned.) In addition, as I have mentioned, my close friends Doug Stein and Eddie Mandeville are doctors; and Jeanne's best friend is an obstetrician-gynecologist whose practice consists almost entirely of indigent women who are HIV-positive.

I was fortunate to have Dr. Murray as my AIDS physician. From the start, he has treated me with utmost respect as a patient. In the enterprise of medicating Arthur Ashe for AIDS, he wanted me to be an active partner. He encouraged me to read about the disease and all the new medications, and to feel free to say anything I wanted at our sessions together. He never tired of answering my questions, and I had many of them. I know full well that all doctors are not as open-minded. As a board member of the Commonwealth Fund, which specializes in problems involving health, the cities, and the elderly, I have seen studies of patients' complaints about physicians that list at the absolute top the doctors' chronic unwillingness to listen to them.

Independent of each other, Dr. Murray and Dr. Scheidt are vital to me. They have had to coordinate their different treatments to be careful that the side effects of certain therapies in one area do not jeopardize my health in another. Although I am aware that the doctor–patient relationship requires some professional distance, I think of these physicians as my friends.

As a patient, I try to do my part as diligently as possible, and especially to take all prescriptions scrupulously, as ordered. For my heart condition, I was taking five medicines every day. I was taking Mevacor, in a bullet-shaped capsule, which reduces cholesterol mainly by influencing the liver not to produce the substance. Another drug was Procardia, a football-shaped pill that is a vasodilator, relaxing and thus dilating the arteries and facilitating blood flow. The third drug was Tenormin, in tablet form, a beta-blocker, which decreases the heart's need for oxygen. Tenormin, which makes the heart beat slower and softer, is sometimes prescribed to reduce a person's anxiety level, to calm the patient down. For some athletic competitions, such as the Winter Biathlon, which combines skiing and shooting, it is a banned substance.

As many older men now do, I started taking an aspirin every other day, as a blood thinner and anti-coagulant. I also took nitroglycerin pills and paste, then later wore a time-release nitroglycerin patch on my chest. Nitroglycerin also dilates the arteries. I take daily a large number of natural vitamins. A supply of amyl nitrate, which is a sort of super-vasodilator, sits in my medicine chest for emergencies; in case of a heart attack, it could save my life.

As for AIDS, the most significant decision facing me and Dr. Murray was whether to take AZT (azidothymidine). Since 1988, AZT has been the outstanding therapy for AIDS. Desperate for an effective medication, doctors had introduced AZT into AIDS therapy only the previous year. To the thousands of persons swept by the first tragic tidal wave of mortality caused by AIDS, AZT was a miracle drug. So urgent was the need for this therapy that the Food and Drug Administration approved its use without requiring the completion of the exacting clinical trials to which all drugs are normally subjected.

AZT never underwent a complete "double-blind" study. I soon heard a story that many patients in the government tests—almost all of them gay men—banded together to disrupt the process in the name of life—their own lives. AZT was being administered to them on a clinical-trial basis, along with placebos. The patients, desperate for a cure, somehow learned to tell the placebos from the AZT pills. They threw out the placebos, divided the AZT pills among themselves, and kept their subterfuge a secret from the scientists and administrators. Nevertheless, the testing was abandoned and the drug rushed into service because it clearly slowed the replication of the virus.

But AZT was controversial in other ways. A gift from heaven to many desperate people, it was poison to others. Developed for use in cancer chemotherapy to destroy cells then in the process of actively dividing, AZT was only later applied to AIDS. Some scientists believe that AZT, which relentlessly kills cells but cannot distinguish between infected and uninfected cells, is as harmful as AIDS itself. After all, HIV is actively present in only 1 of every 10,000 T-cells, which are vital to the immune system; but AZT kills them all. Dr. Peter Duesberg, the once eminent and now controversial professor of molecular and cell biology at the University of California, who bitterly disputes the notion that HIV causes AIDS, has called AZT "AIDS by prescription."

Dr. Duesberg argues that the use of recreational drugs, not sex, led to AIDS. It is well known that many gay men used—and many of them continue to use—drugs as a stimulus in sexual activity or to facilitate intercourse. "Natural and synthetic psychoactive drugs," he has argued (drugs such as cocaine, amphetamines, heroin, Quaaludes, and amyl nitrites and butyl nitrites, or "poppers"), "are the only new pathogens around since the 1970s, and the only new disease syndrome around is AIDS, and both are found in exactly the same populations."

AZT was approved by the Food and Drug Administration (FDA) for general use in combating the effects of AIDS because AIDS patients were dying fast and the drug helped patients live longer and more endurable lives. Still, it is decidedly not for everyone. Some people tolerate it with relative ease, some only with grave side effects. Some tolerate it for a while, then must give it up. Still others cannot tolerate it at all. To my relief, I tolerate AZT fairly easily.

However, in 1988, no one was sure of the optimum dose. I started out taking ten capsules a day—five times every day, I swallowed two white capsules with a blue band around the middle. At that time, many doctors were prescribing a sixth dose of two additional capsules each day. After some discussion, Dr. Murray and I decided that I would not take the sixth dose. Not long afterward, following intense medical scrutiny of patients, doctors began to lower the prescribed daily dosage. Lower doses were proving to be more effective than the higher amounts, with much less toxicity. By fall 1992, I was down to a daily dose of three capsules. I refuse to dwell on how much damage I may have done to myself taking the higher dosage. My sacrifice and that of other patients of my generation of AIDS sufferers hardly begins to compare with the sacrifice of patients in the first years of the scourge. In those days, the scientific community had almost nothing to offer in terms of therapies, and the disease killed mysteriously and almost at will.

Eventually, in addition to AZT, I would also be taking regularly the antibiotic Cleocin, in a prescription that calls for three 150-milligram capsules four times a day. The Cleocin is prescribed to treat toxoplasmosis, but an additional benefit is that I did not have a single cold in four years.

To prevent brain seizures, I take two tablets of leucovorin each day, and one of Daraprim (pyramethamine).

For candidiasis (thrush), one of the most bothersome of the infections triggered by AIDS, I take nystatin pills and liquid suspension, a pleasant, lemon-tasting medicine. Thrush, which is a common infection in infants, can be one of the initial signs that AIDS is present or well on its way. It is caused by a fungus, *Candida albicans*, which often coats my mouth and tongue with a thick, whitish substance, making me quite uncomfortable. Thrush is also capable of invading the digestive system, in which case it becomes more dangerous. Nystatin holds the fungus at bay.

To stave off the likelihood of *Pneumocystis carinii* pneumonia, I started taking aerosolized pentamidine once a month.

Late in the summer of 1992, I started taking the drug ddI (didanosine), which was found to be more effective in combination with AZT than either had been alone. Because ddI tablets are supposed to be chewed but are hardly tasty, I ask my pharmacist to grind them into a powder and I add it to my cereal in the morning.

By 1992, I was taking about thirty pills, including natural vitamins, every day. My annual bill for prescription drugs alone runs to about $18,000. However, the cost fell dramatically after I started getting my drugs from my primary insurance carrier. It pains me to think of the many AIDS patients who must face such expense without adequate insurance.

"ARTHUR," A FRIEND said to me, a note of solicitude in his voice, "I know you must have the best doctors available to treat you for this thing." He cares about me. A figure nationally known for his literary skill, he nevertheless finds it hard to say the word "AIDS" to my face.

"Well, I don't know if they are absolutely the best," I reply. "I know they are very good."

"I don't want to interfere. That's the last thing I want to do. But have you heard about . . . ?"

I have a good idea what is coming next. In the murky, unstable, uncertain, swiftly shifting and evolving world of AIDS, many people have heard of miraculous cures, or of new therapies as yet unsanctioned by the FDA that have shown astonishing results.

Even when only a small circle of my friends knew about my AIDS condition, I had conversations just like this one with several of them. After making my public announcement, I received a torrent of advice and counsel about therapies—I don't say medicine—among the mass of mail that I received every day.

Behind these conversations and letters was a genuine desire to help me and others. There was also, in many cases, a deep-seated suspicion of, and even hostility to, the main forces that control the world of health treatment: the federal government and the mighty drug companies. To many black people, the government means white people who oversee the administration of this country. I have already written about the dominant racial aspects of the controversy surrounding the drug Kemron, the alpha-interferon therapy developed in Kenya by Africans. Kemron is only one of the tantalizing "cures" or therapies that have been brought to my attention. Other treatments ranged from the religious to the physically invasive.

I do not need anyone to convince me about the power of prayer, about the wonders that religious faith can work in all sorts of ways and against extraordinary odds. I have believed in God all my life. But I am still surprised by the way some people see the Bible and Christianity in an almost shamanistic way. One day, one of my telephones rang and there was a woman's voice on the line.

"Arthur Ashe?"

"Yes."

"Arthur Ashe, you don't know me, but I have an important message for you."

"Thank you," I said. "Who is it from?"

"This message is from God."

"I beg your pardon?"

"God sent you a message."

"What is the message?"

"The message is that you are going to be cured. And that you must read, every day without fail, Psalm 40."

"Thank you very much."

"You're welcome. Goodbye."

Psalm 40 is a good psalm. "I waited patiently for the Lord," it begins, "and He inclined to me, and heard my cry. . . . He has put a new song in my mouth—praise to our God; many will see it and fear, and will trust in the Lord." All the psalms are beautiful, I would say. But I do not know why I, or God, should favor one psalm over the others in this particular case. I think too many people confuse religion with magic.

Many of the "cures" that were suggested to me involved the powers of herbs and herbalists. Drinking "red clover flower" tea instead of water, along with other regimens, such as lifting weights in bed (but not out of bed?), would lead me to health. Another person touted the properties of a certain "tea from Brazil," which, blended from the "inner bark" of the longest-living tree there, "basically builds the immune system." A woman wrote from Los Angeles to warn about the dangers of AZT and advise about a herbalist in New Zealand whose potions kill bacteria and viruses.

Several letters told of the peculiar power of African herbs and African herb doctors. I was urged to make a quick visit to Abidjan, in the Ivory Coast, "where you can surely be cured" through the use of "African herbal mixtures." A CNN television viewer in Accra, Ghana, wrote to alert me about the skills of an herbalist "in a remote region" of her country, who was so effective that he had cured "a white man" with AIDS.

Needless to say, few of these cures were free. From Natal, South Africa, came the promise of "a herbal formula" used efficaciously for leukemia, at a cost of only 450 rand. An African living in Brooklyn, who boasted of "certain herbs in Africa that have the power to heal any disease," made me an offer: "I am not going to take a penny from you until you are cured, but you will sign an agreement with me for 5 million dollars payable on recovery."

Letters like these tended to give herbalists, if not herbs, a bad name. But I know better than to underestimate the power of so-called "natural" cures. A doctor in Beijing, in the People's Republic of China, sent me newspaper clippings about her "herbal powder" that had been used successfully, apparently, in treating certain brain tumors. (Because China denies visas to AIDS sufferers, she would have to come to me.) A Swiss virologist offered a cure that involved a drug based on a plant material from which toxins had been removed, and which had been used to treat herpes and cancer; treatment involved the ionization of blood with oxygen by IV for twenty minutes, deep injections into the buttocks, as well as gel and drops under the tongue for ingestion.

Other cures or therapies covered a wide spectrum of science. One serum was said to have "piranha-like effects" on HIV. Some involved the diversion of existing medicines toward the fight against AIDS. The drug reticulose, for example, which modulates the immune system, has been in use for a generation; an old tennis friend wrote to me about its astonishing effects on a patient infected with toxoplasmosis (as I had been) and who had suffered a stroke and been given forty-eight hours to live. Now, on reticulose, he was flourishing.

Another treatment involved what is called RBC–CD4 complex electroinsertion technology, by which full-length CD4 cells are inserted into red blood cells as a therapeutic against AIDS. Still another therapy involved a complicated laboratory process over a period of twenty-four hours, in which blood is purified by distillation and calcination (the application of very high temperatures).

Yet another treatment, sent by a man I had met and coached ten years before at the Doral resort in Florida, called for the introduction of a mixture of ozone and oxygen into the patient's blood. This treatment had even been reported on in *Blood: Journal of the American Society of Hematology.*

Many of the letters I received complained about the stranglehold of the big drug companies on credibility and credit. One man, committed to a process in which the technology involved in the sterilization of bone in bone grafts was applied "to sterilize the blood and organs of the body," wanted my help in establishing a major facility to develop this therapy. He lamented that when the powerful drug companies (for example, Johnson & Johnson and Bristol-Myers Squibb) announce promising treatments, they receive respectful attention from the public, the medical community, Wall Street, and government agencies. However, when a fledgling outfit does the same thing, "it is perceived as 'snake oil' because it is not conceivable that David could achieve what Goliath could not."

Another company spokesman wrote about not having the "200-million-dollar bribe" that he claimed it took to establish a major new drug. I think he was referring to the huge amount of money typically needed in order to gain scientific respectability for a new product.

"Inordinate stress caused you to have two bypass surgeries," a doctor wrote me. "The faulty AIDS transfusion was the organic insult to your immunology system. Your body is overloaded with stress." His approach involved the concept of "colored light therapy" and the use of an "imagescope." Doubtless this therapy, which I think has been used in psychiatry, can be useful. Still, I myself think that stress can be overrated as a cause of illness. I believe that controlling one's anger or rage or sense of being overburdened is much better than blowing up or sagging into depression. I agree with what Carol Tavris wrote in her book *Anger: The Misunderstood Emotion:* "The popular belief that suppressed anger can wreak havoc on the body and bloodstream has been inflated out of realistic proportions. It does not, in any predictable or consistent way, make us depressed, produce ulcers or hypertension, set us off on food binges or give us heart attacks."

I certainly do not believe that stress can lead to AIDS, but I remain eager to hear about the latest developments in the work being done on AIDS by researchers and scientists. Like everyone else who has AIDS, or who knows someone with it, I wait and wait for the news of a medical breakthrough or, at the very least, a new, life-prolonging drug. Late in the fall of 1992, for example, the best news was about a new treatment from Bristol-Myers Squibb, a drug called d4T, or Stavodine, supposedly more effective than any other therapy for AIDS. I want to know more about this new drug. On the other hand, I do not want to delude myself. I do not intend to grasp at straws. That helps no one.

WITH AIDS, I have good days and bad days. The good days, thank goodness, greatly outnumber the bad. And the bad days are not unendurable. Mainly my stomach lets me down and I suffer from diarrhea. I take my pills, and I am disciplined enough to stick to my schedule. Sometimes I become a little tired, but I have learned anew to pace myself, to take short rests that invigorate me. In this matter of AIDS, as in so many aspects of my life, I am a lucky man.

I believe that there are five essential pillars to support the health and well-being of every individual. The first is unhindered access to physicians who will render primary care, listen to and advise the patient, and follow up with treatments in a professional manner. The second is the availability of medicines, treatments, and other therapies. The third is the support of family and friends. The fourth is the determination of the patient to make himself or herself better, to take charge of his or her well-being in cooperation with others. The fifth essential pillar is health insurance, because few people can bear the cost of a serious illness without falling irretrievably into debt. Take away any of these five pillars, I believe, and the structure of individual health and welfare starts to collapse.

I have been fortunate to have all five pillars solidly in place: excellent physicians, perhaps the best that can be had; the most efficacious medicines, no matter what the cost; the loving support of a skilled, intelligent spouse and the most loyal and resourceful group of friends anyone could have; self-reliance taught from my boyhood by my father but reinforced by decades of rigorous training in a sport based on individualism; and no fewer than three generous health-insurance policies.

AIDS does not make me despair, but unquestionably it often makes me somber. For some time I have wrestled with certain of Susan Sontag's ideas or insights in her remarkable books *Illness as Metaphor* and *AIDS and Its Metaphors.* In the former, inspired by her battle against cancer, Sontag writes about "the punitive or sentimental fantasies concocted about" illness, especially illnesses such as leprosy, tuberculosis, and cancer. "My point is that illness is *not* a metaphor, and that the most truthful way of regarding illness—and the healthiest way of being ill—is one purified of, most resistant to, metaphoric thinking." AIDS is not a metaphor for me, but a fact; and yet I find it hard to avoid its metaphoric energy, which is almost irresistible. I reject the notion that it is God's retribution for the sins of homosexuals and drug abusers, as some people argue, but on occasion I find its elements and properties peculiarly appropriate to our age.

I live in undeniable comfort—some would say luxury—in a spacious, lovely apartment high above Manhattan. When I venture out to walk the streets below, I see how others live who have not been dealt as generous a hand. I see poverty, usually with a face as dark as mine or darker, sitting on a box in front of my bank with a cup in her hand; or trudging wearily along the sidewalks; or fallen down into foul gutters. Around the corner, huddled on chilly stoops near the Greek Orthodox church, I see loneliness gnawing at human beings who surely deserve a far better fate. I hear madness crying out in the indifferent streets.

Sometimes, gloomily, I wonder about a connection between AIDS and where we in the United States are headed as a people and a nation as this century moves to a close. Too many people seem determined to forget that although we are of different colors and beliefs, we are all members of the same human race, united by much more than the factors and forces that separate us. Sometimes I wonder what is becoming of our vaunted American society, or even Western civilization, as an unmistakable darkness seems to settle over our lives and our history, blocking out the sun. Our national destiny, which at times seems as bright as in the past, sometimes also appears tragically foreshortened, even doomed, as the fabric of our society is threatened by endless waves of crime, by the weakening of our family structures, by the deterioration of our schools, and by the decline of religion and spiritual values. AIDS then takes on a specially ominous cast, as if in its savagery and mystery it mirrors our fate.

Surely we need to resist surrendering to such a fatalistic analogy. Some people profess to see little purpose to the struggle for life. And yet that is precisely the task to which, in my fight against the ravages of AIDS, I devote myself every day: the struggle for life, aided by science in my fight with this disease. I know that we are all, as human beings, going to our death, and that I may be called, because of AIDS, to go faster than most others. Still, I resolutely do battle with this opponent, as I boldly did battle with my opponents on the tennis court. True, this fight is different. The biggest difference is that I now fight not so much to win as not to lose. This enemy is different, too—dark and mysterious, springing on civilization just when civilization was sure that it had almost rid itself of mysterious beasts forever. But it must be fought with science, and with calm, clear thinking.

I know that I must govern that part of my imagination that endows AIDS with properties it does not intrinsically possess. I must be as resolute and poised as I can be in the face of its threat. I tell myself that I must never surrender to its power to terrify, even under its constant threat of death.

CHAPTER 8

Sex and Sports
in the Age of AIDS

THE MOMENT I discovered, some fifteen years ago, that I suffered from heart disease, I passed out of a world in which sex had its normal place in my life—strong, if conventionally restricted—into a world in which sex and death sometimes seemed to go hand in hand, because of the strain I know the act of sex can place on the heart. Whenever I spoke publicly about my heart disease, the first questions from the audience were almost always about sex. How soon could one indulge in sex after heart surgery? Should one have sex at all with a damaged heart? I tried to assure worried questioners that yes, there definitely could be sex after heart surgery.

However, the moment I discovered, in addition, that I had AIDS, I lost even the slightest hope of ever again enjoying a completely normal relationship to sex. In some respects, this is one of the most haunting aspects of AIDS. But the personal implications for me of AIDS and heart disease are as nothing compared to the questions raised about sex in the lives of the masses of people by the phenomenon of AIDS. The glare of a thousand-watt searchlight has been trained on the most intimate act of our lives. In this way, as in other ways, we are all, the healthy and the sick, touched and perhaps tainted by AIDS.

The association of sex and death is ancient; the French playfully call a climax *le petit mort* (the little death). But the images of death fostered by AIDS have no romantic overtones, only ugliness and pain, grotesqueness and bitter irony. The pictures of the ballet dancer Rudolf Nureyev near the end of his life affected me deeply for this reason, since he was the epitome of power and artistry as a dancer. To think of being contaminated by viruses that can kill one's beloved, or create in her a child who is condemned at birth to a horrible death, can be revolting. Such a situation can almost drive one mad. Perhaps this explains those people, HIV-infected or even with full-blown AIDS, who deliberately and maliciously have unprotected intercourse with unsuspecting partners. Such people do exist, and I think they are driven to their attempts at murder by the depth of self-hatred that AIDS, far more readily than any other disease, can engender.

The power of sex in our consciousness obviously has much to do with its force as a biological drive, a primitive hormonal urgency. The hormonal aspect, however, is probably only slightly more important in many respects than the mysterious, romantic element that surrounds sex and plays off its involuntary, hormonal essence in Western culture. Sex and love are presumed to go together. That romantic element has always intrigued and challenged me. Proud of myself as a rational human being, I have almost always preferred a scientific approach to sex, one that gives up much of its mystery and romance for a cold knowledge of biology, physiology, and psychology. I remember poring over the volumes *Human Sexual Response* and *Human Sexual Inadequacy*, by the team of Masters and Johnson, painstakingly and with complete absorption. I wanted to know about the menstrual cycle and estrogen and ovaries and how sperm is produced and all the other mechanical and biological details of sex. I know that romance as often as not involves an evasion of facts, and can be kin to ignorance, fear, guilt, and shame. On the other hand, I consider myself a romantic man. At times, I have surrendered to romance, and indulged in it freely as one of the blessings of human life.

AIDS has made many people see for the first time the wisdom of a scientific approach to sex and the limitations of romance. As a rationalist, I should feel very good about this change, but in fact I do not—at least, not entirely. We do not need ignorance and fear, but we do need a few ideals and those illusions that help us to attain our ideals. And yet AIDS is laying waste to that mysterious element almost as thoroughly as it destroys the healthy bodies of people, heterosexual and homosexual, who once gave themselves with abandon to sex.

I wonder if we can ever achieve a balance now between the need to know the scientific truth and the need to preserve our sense of mystery, beauty, and trust. Some experts call for the inclusion of fairly graphic sex education in our young citizens' early formal education. As rational as I try to be, I recoil from such a radical approach when I think of my six-year-old daughter and my wish for her to enjoy the innocence of childhood as long as she can. I shudder to think that at six or seven, her childhood, in this respect, may be over. In such moments, I see the full tragedy of AIDS.

ONE MORNING IN December 1992, I picked up a newspaper and read a brief story that brought home, as few other reports had done for me, the fact that AIDS is no respecter of people, that the most exquisitely tuned and toughened bodies could be ravaged and destroyed by its deadly power. According to a report from Canada published in the Calgary *Herald*, at least forty prominent male figure skaters and skating coaches in North America had died of AIDS-related diseases in recent years. In addition, at least a dozen other outstanding American and Canadian male skaters and coaches were infected with HIV. The report was based on two months of interviews with about 125 people connected to the sport, including skaters, coaches, and their families and friends.

The connection between male homosexuality and figure skating had long been rumored. Now, it seems, with those forty deaths, the connection may have been confirmed, tragically so. Nevertheless, not long after the publication of the report, the man whom many regard as the most brilliant of all living figure skaters, Brian Boitano, denounced it as "ridiculous" and "a joke." Boitano bridled especially at the implication that skaters are any more likely to be gay than athletes in other sports. "Just like the majority of people in life," he insisted, "the majority of people in skating are straight. That's a fact. Nobody in skating would deny that."

My sport, tennis, has its own notoriety in the area of sex. As long as I have known it, tennis has always been considered, certainly in the

crudest male circles, a "sissy" sport, one mainly attractive to men of
ambivalent sexuality. While it is difficult to look at today's hard-hitting
players and imagine anything awkward or inept about them ("sissy"
usually implies being awkward if not inept at sports), this image of
tennis has a long history. In addition, Bill Tilden, hailed by many
people old enough to have seen him as probably the most accomplished tennis player ever, was gay. Frank Deford delves into this
subject in his important biography of Tilden, a man who tried to hide
in the closet but got into trouble especially when his sexual preferences
became known.

This image of tennis is enshrined in the play *Tea and Sympathy*, a hit
on Broadway and then later as a film in the 1950s. As I remember it,
the drama is mainly about a young man, a college student, who is
deeply troubled by his sexuality, perhaps by his latent homosexuality.
A college athlete, he is a tennis player. According to the script, his game
is not aggressive—that is, without fast serves and crunching volleys,
relying instead mainly on spin and guile—as if that fact were proof in
itself of his sexual deviance.

I know that some people thought that I must be gay. I am also
aware that some people—perhaps even many people—suspect that I
contracted AIDS from a gay contact, and that quite possibly I am a
closet homosexual. In fact, I first heard the suggestion that I might be
gay several years before I contracted AIDS, and from a member of my
family. In 1977, Jeanne and I, recently married, attended a grand family
reunion in Richmond. My folks on my mother's side came from all
over the United States to celebrate the existence of our family, which
we proudly trace back several generations. The family tree is heavy with
branches, dense with leaves. Arriving with Jeanne, my new bride, I
could not help thinking that I was doing my part to ensure that the
tree would grow thicker and the leaves even more dense.

Most of my relatives had not yet met Jeanne and hurried over to
congratulate us when we arrived. However, one of my uncles, who had
come from California for the celebrations, seemed rather less impressed
than others by the newlywed couple. At one point I sought him out
and struck up a conversation. After we had talked for a while, he finally
spoke what obviously had been on his mind.

"Well, Arthur, my man," he said, "you sure surprised me."

"How's that?" I inquired.

"Marrying Jeanne. You sure surprised me."

I looked at Jeanne across the room. As always, she looked radiantly beautiful, as lovely a woman as I had ever seen. I felt proud to be her husband. "Yes, she's special, isn't she? She's definitely a ten."

"I don't mean that. Sure she's beautiful. But I always assumed you went the other way, if you know what I mean."

"Say what?"

"You know, Arthur. I just thought you were, well, of the other persuasion. Don't take offense, now, man."

"Where did you get that idea?"

"Well, I just never heard of you being involved with any woman in particular. You never told us about your chicks and stuff like that. So I thought, Uh-oh, Arthur is one of *those* people!"

I even faced scrutiny on this question recently on national television. In response to a question from Larry King, I said that my doctors, Jeanne, and I were 97 percent certain that I had contracted AIDS from a blood transfusion. Very smoothly, without the hint of a stir, King responded that there are always certain suspicions when one contracts AIDS—as indeed there always are. Without making the slightest fuss or consulting his notes, he rattled off a checklist of questions about my behavior.

"You have not had an extramarital affair?"

"No."

"You have never had a homosexual experience?"

"No."

He did not ask me about intravenous drugs or hemophilia, because they obviously did not apply. But I had to answer these questions on national television. I do not blame King for being frank, and I appreciate his skill in posing sensitive questions with delicacy. But if I needed any proof that AIDS had transformed my life, public and private, down to its most intimate details, including sex, I had it now.

Tragically, in 1988, only weeks after I discovered I had AIDS, I learned a great deal about the special interplay between sex, death, and the disease from the last days of a friend of mine, Max Robinson. Although Max was five years older than I, he and I grew up together in Richmond. Intelligent and talented, he had earned the distinction of becoming the first black television news anchorman on a national network when he served in that capacity at ABC-TV. Then he seemed to stumble, mainly through incidents of erratic behavior that affected his professional reputation. Because I knew Max and his family well, I was saddened to hear about his troubles. Then word spread, incredibly, that Max had AIDS. Watching television one day, I looked on with tears in my eyes as Max made a farewell speech to the world at a conference at Howard University, where some of his friends had gathered to honor him. A short time later, he died.

Just after his death, one of Max's friends revealed to the world that on his deathbed, Max had asked that people be told he had *not* contracted AIDS from homosexual behavior. "Please tell them I got the disease from being careless," Max had begged this friend (or words to that effect), "but not from having sex with men." I thought this confession sad and unfortunate. To worry, at the moment of one's death, whether or not one is perceived by other people as gay or straight is a cruel additional burden to bear at a time of ultimate stress. And yet it definitely seems to matter to the world whether someone is gay or straight.

Since contracting AIDS, but especially after I became committed to fighting its spread, I have had to learn a great deal about homosexuality, especially male homosexuality. For a long time, unprotected anal intercourse between men was the number-one cause of the transmission of AIDS in the United States. Out of sympathy for AIDS sufferers who are gay, but also in seeking to be an effective AIDS educator, I have set myself the goal of trying to understand the culture of homosexuality in all its diversity and complexity; I say "trying to understand" because only a gay person has a chance of fully understanding the culture, I am sure. I have made it my business to open myself to instruction and guidance on this difficult issue by homosexuals themselves, mainly through books, essays, newspapers, and television shows. I have also tried to examine my own feelings about homosexuality, and to confront the possibility of my own personal, subconscious anxieties about the subject. Knowing that one of my uncles had thought of me as gay made me more alert to the complexity of the issue.

In my lifetime, I have had two confrontations with homosexuals. Both were invitations I declined. The first occurred when I was visiting the home of one of my aunts in Montclair, New Jersey. I was sixteen or seventeen years old at the time. One night, around eleven or so, I was trying to hitchhike a ride home on Bloomfield Avenue when a man stopped and picked me up. He seemed pleasant enough at first, but at the second or third traffic light he made his move. To my consternation, I felt his hand settle on my thigh. I moved my leg, but his hand returned. By the fourth or fifth traffic light I was out of the car. I walked home that night.

My other encounter was about three or four years later, at the Seattle airport. The UCLA tennis team was en route to Los Angeles after playing in Seattle in 1962, probably against the University of Washington. We visited the World's Fair, where coach J. D. Morgan took us all to the restaurant in the landmark "space needle," high above the grounds, to eat lunch. Then we drove to the airport. I was in the men's room, in a stall, when I heard heavy breathing outside the door. I looked up and saw a man peering down at me through a crack. I hollered at him, "Get out of here!" He left quickly. I, too, left the room quickly, and returned to my friends.

I had no difficulty resisting both men. I do not believe I felt any attraction to them, and I do not think that fear of censure kept me from becoming involved with them. Certainly my upbringing, especially my religious instruction, discouraged any involvement in gay activity, but I do not recall feeling any personal interest in gay life. After I left UCLA and began touring the world as a professional tennis player, I entered an environment sometimes hostile to gays. In my first few years on the tour, the locker room was ruled by the Australian players, undoubtedly the finest in the world as a group, and an engaging lot. In almost every area they set the tone, and that tone was the *basso* of stereotypical masculinity. In Australia, where I lived for several months in the 1960s, I found a country dominated by men who thought of themselves as rugged individualists, and masculine to the core. Women there seemed to be mainly second-class citizens who existed to serve men sexually and in any other way that men wished. Homosexuality was beyond the pale. Genially, to be sure, the Aussie players brought this intolerance to the locker room, where a known homosexual would probably not have been tolerated. To admit publicly that you were homosexual would have required bravery of an exceptional order. No male tennis player I knew was ever so brave.

A few players, usually *not* Australian, were crudely homophobic. To gain an edge in a match, or simply to be mischievous, perhaps, Ilie Nastase would sometimes affect what were supposed to be the typical mannerisms of a gay male; Nastase would put his hand up, then let his wrist fall loosely, or he would mince about the court to let you know what he thought of your masculinity. Few players ever went so far. However, terms of derision having to do with homosexuality were commonplace in tennis. In practice, you might tell a friend, after a weak shot, "Oh, you looked a little light on your feet on that one!" And of course there was the common British expression "poofter," which means a gay man. A few players used that term all the time.

I never knew a gay male tennis player in the professional ranks. I knew at least two men who played a tangential role in professional tennis and were gay, but I knew of no gay players. Of the two men, neither ever admitted it publicly. One was a tennis organizer on the European circuit who every year helped to stage a talent show or "follies" for charity, involving tennis players. The other person I knew much better, because he was a high-ranking employee of an important tennis players' organization. An outstanding worker, he gave no obvious outward sign of homosexuality, at least in the way many people look for such signs, according to stereotypes; he was quite "manly" and aggressive. Even his direct superior had no idea that he was gay. But he fell sick with AIDS, and then everything came out, as it often does under those circumstances. He died of AIDS.

IF HOMOSEXUALITY IS limited on the men's tour, it certainly is not on the women's. Two of the most famous players in the history of the game have not only admitted that they are gay or bisexual but have also become involved in bitterly contentious, highly publicized situations involving other women who had been their lovers. Two swallows do not make a summer; but several top women players over the last twenty or thirty years have definitely been gay. Some people insist that no difference exists between the sexes here. If an accurate accounting were taken, they argue, one would find as many gays among the male players as among the female players. The women players are supposed merely to be more open than the men about their homosexuality. In my experience, this is simply not the case. Professional tennis players, men and women, do not have to be consistent in this way, any more than the top female figure skaters must include many lesbians simply because there appears to be a considerable number of homosexuals in the ranks of top male skaters.

This question of the prevalence of lesbianism among the women players interests me from more than one angle. On the surface, lesbianism appears to have little to do with AIDS. The transmission of bodily fluids is not as much of an issue among gay women as it is among male homosexuals, or among heterosexual men and women. However, in December 1992, according to a friend of mine who is a physician concerned with AIDS, a medical conference heard a fascinating report on a study which asserts that as many as 80 percent of lesbians may lead a sexual double life, having male and female lovers separately but concurrently. This means that the lesbian population is almost as much at risk from AIDS and other sexual diseases as is the heterosexual community. The discovery of this lesbian double life, I am told, has come as a shock to researchers and other experts on the subject of homosexuality among women.

Why does lesbianism appear to have more of a place than male homosexuality in professional tennis? The subject is fascinating, and should be explored carefully, rather than remain the stuff of gossip and innuendo; but no one, as far as I am aware, has been doing so. In the absence of facts, suspicions abound. Over the years, I have heard several parents worry openly about their young daughters and their alleged vulnerability in the locker room. They have seemed far more concerned about the dangers posed by other women than by the dangers posed by men, especially older men in positions of authority, such as coaches. Many years ago, when one of the superstars of the last generation was about fifteen, I remember her mother loudly insisting on the right to accompany her into the locker room to ensure that she was not being sexually recruited by anyone there. The parents of several other young players were no less assertive. Many of them demanded that the Women's Tennis Association actually guarantee the safety of their young daughters in the locker room.

What impresses and troubles me above all in looking at this

general question is the fact that women professional tennis players seem to be under far more acute psychological strains and stresses than their male counterparts. Whether sexual behavior is affected by these acute stresses and strains is open to debate; but the increased pressure is clearly present, and distressing. The women's tour is not simply a mirror image of the men's tour plus skirts. There are some crucial differences between the two camps, and some of these differences are paradoxical, at least in part.

On one level, the women are far more sociable than the men; and on another level, they are the opposite. The women players are much more involved in union and association activity than the men. The top women's players, individuals such as Martina Navratilova, Gabriela Sabatini, Arantxa Sánchez Vicario, Steffi Graf, and Monica Seles, for example, are much more likely than their male counterparts to turn out dutifully for union meetings, public-awards ceremonies, and the like. In comparison, the men tend to be undependable at best and sometimes downright loutish when challenged about a sense of responsibility. (This was not true of my generation of professionals, but it certainly is true of many of today's male players.)

Paradoxically, however, the men seem to be on much friendlier terms with one another than the women are. McEnroe or Connors might explode on the court; but the explosions, no matter how vulgar or profane, seem to be relatively controlled and do not reach the locker room with anything like a similar force. The impact of competition on the women—polite as the players generally are on court, in contrast to the men—seems to be much more insidious and destructive. According to Graf in a recent issue of *Tennis* magazine, few friendships exist among the women players. Graf spoke of an almost poisoned atmosphere among the players. "I always had only male friends in the tennis world," she declared. "The rivalry among women tennis players is overwhelming." She contrasted this to the men's tour, where players routinely squabble on court, then go out after the match to drink a beer and talk. Male stars practice together, but not the women. Graf apparently has never once practiced with Sabatini, although they played as a doubles team at one time. As for inviting Sabatini to take a stroll somewhere, "she would probably just stare at me."

Why should the women be less friendly to one another than the men? Interestingly, I have found exactly the opposite to be true about men and women players at the amateur level. In both tennis and golf, women seem to care much more about their friendships with other women than the outcome of their matches together. I have seen this difference repeatedly on the tennis court and the golf course. Aggressively seeking dominance and almost careless about the possible consequences, men tend to challenge one another with macho posturings. Women, on the other hand, seem to take exquisite care not to offend one another and jeopardize their friendships. Frequently, they may even play beneath their top level of skill in order to preserve peace. Not so on the women's tour, according to Graf and several other commentators.

The dynamics of competition among women are excellently discussed, as far I can judge, in Laura Tracy's book *The Secret Between Us: Competition Among Women*, which I rushed out and bought after hearing it discussed on National Public Radio when the work appeared in 1991. Tracy's "secret" is that while women have been socialized by the ideal of femininity (which is not to be confused with feminism) to deny that they are competitive and to resist being openly competitive, they have no choice as human beings but to be competitive for jobs, material possessions, family affection, lovers, and so on. However, the denial of the reality of competition usually forces women to act subversively and destructively, especially against other women, as they make their way through life. Competition becomes a clandestine and often self-destructive activity, one that preys on and exacerbates the elements of vulnerability in a woman.

"Women have been taught that competition is unethical, even immoral," Tracy writes. "We've been socialized against full participation in our economy and our history. We've been taught to be *secret* competitors, and our secret has kept us subordinated members of our society. Most of us recognize competition only when it's practiced by another woman. Even worse, many of us often don't realize we are *in* a competition until we've lost it."

Like men, women compete to get what they want. Unlike men, however, women typically are haunted by fears not simply that they will *seem* selfish, or greedy, or envious but that they will actually *be* selfish, greedy, and envious. "Men don't have this problem," Tracy argues. "When men compete with each other, they compete to identify with a masculine ideal embedded in their competition, to be strong, tough, aggressive, independent—and separate. Unlike a woman, a man can make his competition impersonal because he can detach it from the man who is his current antagonist. Although we may not admire some of the ideals offered to men, all these ideals encourage men to become self-determined individuals."

Obviously, the pressure of professional tennis, where huge sums of money are at stake, creates an environment substantially different from the rest of the world for women. Not only is there no way to escape competition in the tennis world, but competition is of the essence—that is why the women are there. Moreover, competition in this sport is accentuated. Unlike in a team sport, where victories and defeats are shared, the one-on-one nature (in singles play) of tennis demands a sustained competitive drive in anyone who would win consistently. Champions must have the celebrated "killer instinct." But even years of training to win tennis matches probably cannot eradicate in a woman the ideals of femininity that still prevail in the world at large despite the teachings of feminists. And there is money, lots of money, in femininity. Advertisements featuring Andre Agassi exploit his agressive and rebellious image to sell sports gear, while Gabriela Sabatini's image is used to sell a perfume. Chris Evert, who exudes femininity, seems to be the ideal tennis player where advertisers are concerned. Thus, women tennis players must lead a double life if they wish to succeed both on and off the court, according to the normal terms set by society.

In addition to prize money, the prominent position of men in the lives of these women may also be a factor in making professional women's tennis an especially difficult world. Remarkably, it is almost impossible to find a top woman player with a woman coach. The women stars fade fast when they retire. In a recent essay in *Tennis* magazine, Lynne Rolley of the USTA pointed out that only Billie Jean King, Betty Stove, and Hana Mandlikova among the top retired players have gone on to make their mark as a coach. What do the young women players learn from their male coaches about competition, and can they integrate these lessons into their complete lives as women?

Herself a coach, Rolley identified some of the key questions that face a young woman player, and suggests that a woman coach is more likely to have good answers: "Is it acceptable to compete? Is it O.K. to build muscles? Is there a contradiction between the assertive, aggressive athlete and the accepted social role for women?"

(In Graf's frank and intelligent interview, she indeed worried about her muscles and about a photographer who was "enthralled by my muscles." *Interviewer*: "Do you think you look too masculine?" *Graf*: "No, I simply don't like my muscles.")

Add to such pressures the rootlessness and disruptions of tour life, and it becomes quite understandable to me why many players are unhappy on the tour. The existence of these pressures makes me admire even more those women who have made it to the top of professional tennis, individuals such as Billie Jean King, Martina Navratilova, Tracy Austin, Pam Shriver, Steffi Graf, and Zina Garrison—to name a few. Almost all of them have had to struggle as women against many more subtle and complex obstacles than have faced their male counterparts. Some critics of women's tennis like to contend that its stars lack individuality and flair. I think this suggests a personal ignorance of the lives of these gifted women. It is also argued that women should not receive pay equal to men in tennis, because their play is inferior to that of the top men. While I once shared this view, I now believe that women should receive all the prize money they can command. As for individuality, someone could write a book about, for instance, the rivalry between Chris Evert and Martina Navratilova, which was not only glorious and protracted—both were superb players—but also fraught with so many rich overtones deriving from their very different personalities and histories. One was heterosexual, the other lesbian. One was America's sweetheart, the other an immigrant who dearly wanted to be accepted like everyone else. Evert seems to have had a relatively stable social life (even her divorce from John Lloyd was smoothly conducted), while Navratilova has gone through some hellishly difficult times, to which she has responded with courage and tenacity, even as her extraordinary playing flourished. I was pleased to see Steffi Graf in her *Tennis* magazine interview cite both Martina and Chris as shining examples of friendship, courtesy, and respect extended to her in the otherwise rather bleak social world of women's tennis, as Graf experienced it.

As far as I am concerned, Billie Jean King is the most important tennis player, male or female, of the last fifty years. Although she was probably not the best woman player ever, she was the most significant of all the players since World War II, easily more important than Jimmy Connors, the most significant male player. King transcends her sport. We were born only two or three months apart, and I have known about her almost as long as I have played tennis. We won our first national singles titles at Forest Hills only a year apart, in 1967 and 1968, and we both won at Wimbledon in 1975. I am truly saddened by the extent to which her career, both on and off the tennis court, has been overshadowed by one major controversy, involving a woman with whom she once lived.

She and I have had our differences. One was about the future path of tennis as the open era evolved. Although both Billie Jean and I resented the stodginess and snobbery of the international tennis establishment, we had different ideas about how best to proceed. Billie Jean favored the team approach, and she and her husband, Larry King (not the broadcaster), started World Team Tennis (WTT), an innovative league made up of various teams playing according to an ingenious format of shortened matches unlike anything ever seen in tennis. However, I thought their timing was wrong; I didn't think the public was ready to support such a concept. In any event, WTT certainly fractured and segmented those of us who wanted to oppose the old order. I also think team tennis diverted prize money away from the regular tournaments for a long time and kept the prizes from growing more than they did. Nevertheless, Billie Jean and Larry did a fine job in trying to make their concept work, even as she became identified with quite progressive attitudes and positions away from WTT. Using—sometimes sacrificing—her tennis fame, Billie Jean advanced the cause of women and of gay people on a number of fronts, including many where the connection to tennis was not at all apparent. Her victory over the aging male chauvinist Bobby Riggs in September 1973 in their celebrated battle-of-the-sexes challenge match was an enormous boost for feminism *and* for tennis in general.

Energized as much by the feminist movement as anything else, Billie Jean brings energy and imagination to just about everything she touches. She is rare in combining unquestionable brilliance and success as a tennis player with the passion of a crusader for justice. Quick to anger, she once stung me with a remark that many people took a curious pleasure in repeating to my face. "I'm blacker than Arthur," Billie Jean had quipped. I suppose she meant that I was not impulsive or explosive enough; the stronger and longer that one protests, it seems, the blacker one becomes. Her remark startled but did not offend me. And whenever it was repeated to me, I usually responded, "That's just Billie Jean," perhaps proving her point. Maybe I should have called her a name, or slapped her around a little, and thus demonstrated my "blackness." Unfortunately, I don't call people names, and I have never slapped anybody in my life. Besides, she might slap me back.

I understood that Billie Jean's anger comes from an honorable place, and I truly respect her for what she has accomplished as a feminist. To me, she has earned her place in the pantheon of international modern feminists along with intellectuals such as Betty Friedan, Gloria Steinem, and Germaine Greer, and political activists such as the late Petra Kelly of the Green Movement in Germany. So few professional athletes accomplish anything beyond their sport that King's work is quite extraordinary. Billie Jean's criticism of me came out of the fervor of the feminist movement. Because of that fact, I have never felt the need even to discuss it with her, and she has never brought it up. It has had no effect on our friendship, which blossomed after we both retired. We spent some time together, especially when we worked for HBO at Wimbledon, and I saw her sweetly affectionate side as well as the sharp mind that has made her such a force among us.

Billie Jean's feminism and her sexual preference must have cost her a fortune in endorsements, which is often the major way to wealth for the famous ex-athlete. I know that corporate America was slow to exploit women's tennis for the purposes of advertising because, in part, of the fear that details about the private lives of some of the players, if made public, might harm the sponsors. Later, as our moral climate became more permissive, and the popularity of women's tennis grew, the same companies became more comfortable with this aspect of tennis, and with women's tennis in general. But individuals still suffer. Navratilova, like King, certainly has not had endorsements commensurate with her superstar success on the court. The same is true of John

McEnroe and Jimmy Connors (until recently, when Connors became, in his relative old age, the darling of American tennis). As Davis Cup captain, I had more than one company president and chairman look at McEnroe and tell me, in effect: "That guy's a player, Arthur. But my company wouldn't touch him with a ten-foot pole."

The difference, needless to say, is that McEnroe and Connors behaved outrageously in public, while King and Navratilova were almost always polite as players. In a sense, the women were penalized for what they did in private. In reality, however, they were penalized because what they did in private got into the newspapers, although neither woman wanted it there. It makes little sense to take issue with advertisers on this score; they have no obligation to hand out endorsements equitably, without regard to reputation. However, the public may be more forgiving than some corporations. I certainly think that this is the case with both Billie Jean and Martina, who are justly admired by millions of people, and by me.

Then we have the example of Zina Garrison, which has nothing to do with sexual preference. Garrison was once the only player in the top ten in the world who could not find a corporate sponsor. In her case, she was penalized not for bad behavior or bad publicity but, almost certainly, for "bad" skin. She is black.

IN GENERAL, THE sex life of an individual should be nobody's business but his or her own. Nevertheless, the sexual behavior of a famous athlete, when widely publicized, may have a powerful and deleterious impact on young people in particular. Add the factors of AIDS and rampant unwanted teenage pregnancy into the equation, and the sex life of individual star athletes may become a matter of public concern.

Sexual promiscuity has often been a feature of the behavior of athletes, or at least of male athletes. In recent times, in keeping with our collapse of standards, or our increasing commitment to candor, we have had a better understanding of what constitutes promiscuity for some athletes. The former basketball player Wilt Chamberlain, in his autobiography, has numbered his sexual "conquests" at about 20,000 women. (I don't believe him about the number.) By comparison, Earvin

"Magic" Johnson has been almost monkish, with a mere 2,500 partners, according to one estimate. Many women wanted him, he once
explained with his beautiful smile, and he tried to "accommodate" as
many of them as he could. However, Johnson may have made up for
his lack of numbers, compared to Chamberlain, with revelations of
kinkiness. According to him, he has responded to the desire of various
women by having sex in an elevator, sex on a desk in a business office
(while a board meeting was going on next door), sex with six women
in one night.

As much as I like Wilt and Magic, I must say I did not enjoy
reading these accounts. I must also admit candidly that part of my
reaction to Wilt's and Magic's revelations was a certain amount of
racial embarrassment, an affliction to which I hope never to become
immune. African Americans have spent decades denying that we are
sexual primitives by nature, as racists have argued since the days of
slavery. Then two college-trained black men of international fame and
immense personal wealth do their best to reinforce the stereotype. And
Chamberlain and Johnson merely bolstered the substance of an article
in *Esquire* magazine about promiscuity among players in the National
Basketball Association (NBA), which is predominantly black. Magic
even repeated "an old joke in the NBA" in his book. "Question:
What's the hardest thing about going on the road? Answer: Trying not
to smile when you kiss your wife goodbye."

Of course, I also know from experience that men's professional
tennis, for all its white, upper-class associations, is also a haven of
promiscuity and easy sex, as perhaps all male professional sports are.
Even in my day as a player, we had our camp followers. Top players
traditionally stayed not in hotels but in the homes of local patrons of
the sport, and our hostesses now and then gave us bed and board and
insisted on sharing the bed with us. We had our Lotharios and
Casanovas among the players, and group sex was not hard to come by,
if that was your taste. It was never mine.

And, as I said, I did not enjoy reading about Wilt's and Magic's
escapades. I felt more pity than sorrow for Wilt as his macho accounting backfired on him, in the form of a wave of public criticism. This
admission (or exaggeration?) will probably haunt him for the rest of
his life. He did not seem to understand that many people would find

his behavior dehumanizing, or that it might lessen his attractiveness to women. After all, how many would want to be No. 20,001 in Wilt's ledger? I was also uncomfortable watching Magic talk on television about his own sexual adventures, just after the publication of his book. With his insouciant smile, he seemed to be boasting about them, as at least one television reporter suggested to him; and yet Magic had also preached restraint as part of his laudable efforts at AIDS education. Making what he hoped was a careful distinction, he anticipated this criticism in his book. "I'm not writing about the women in my life in order to brag," he declared. "I'm no Wilt Chamberlain."

Along with just about everyone else, I too am fond of Magic as a person, beyond his commanding skills as a basketball player. I was happy for all his successes, from his victories as a college player to his Olympic Games triumph in Barcelona. I was in favor of his return to professional basketball after his retirement following his announcement that he was HIV-positive. I was disappointed by the reaction of those other players, notably Karl Malone of the Utah Jazz, who apparently helped to drive him back into retirement by expressing fears about possible contamination by him. What puzzled me especially, on this score, was a question I did not see raised anywhere. If Malone and others were so fearful of being contaminated by Magic, why were they not insisting on mandatory testing of all athletes? After all, Johnson wrote candidly of sharing the bodies of certain women with other players. Who else is infected in the NBA?

However, Magic may have missed one opportunity in his commendable campaign to fight AIDS. Although he doubtless was caught up in the business of promoting his book (an obligation he certainly owes to his publisher), he probably went too far as a salesman. Unconsciously, no doubt, promotion of the book took momentary precedence over his sense of the dangers of promiscuity. In addition, while Magic is certainly a good, honest man, his discussion of promiscuity seldom had anything to do with morality or religion. As far as I can tell, nowhere in his book does Magic ever address the question of religion and morality in relationship to sex. When he discusses problems concerning promiscuity, they have to do with lawsuits alleging his paternity of children or spreading the AIDS virus, or with embarrassing Cookie Johnson, whom he married in 1991. In his book, he is discreet in not revealing the names of his partners, but he also offers "no apologies." He declares only: "In the age of AIDS, unprotected sex is reckless. I know that now, of course. But the truth is, I knew it then, too. I just didn't pay attention."

I myself do not want to appear self-righteous in writing about morality in the context of sex; I know that I risk seeming pretentious and, worse, out of date. I also know, as Magic does, that to ask typical teenagers to see the moral dimensions of sex in any practical way is an act of futility. "Just Say No" is a catchy but quixotic slogan. The Nike company's "Just Do It" is the call to which most teenagers will respond. Tell the average inner-city kid about sexual abstinence and he or she will guffaw in your face; I feel sure the same is true of most suburban adolescents. That is why I am for praising the Lord *and* passing the ammunition, which in this case consists of condoms and thorough education about sex.

I know what young men and women go through, with even the best of intentions and the best of home training. I remember my own sexual initiation, one night not long after I earned my driver's license. I had proudly driven my father's car to a party, and was even more proud and happy to offer to drive three friends home. The last one, a young woman who was not my girlfriend, decided to reward me in her own way. She suggested a visit to Byrd Park, a lovely woodland setting with a fountain that changed colors every few seconds. I knew Byrd Park only moderately well, because the tennis facilities there were for whites only; but I drove as deep into its recesses as I could.

We stared at the fountain, and no doubt each of us made a wish. I think we wished for the same thing. Before I knew what was happening, my companion had unbuttoned my pants and was sliding the zipper down. Her speed took me by surprise; until that moment, she had been rather shy.

Suddenly I thought about my girlfriend. I had been having a mild and completely chaste flirtation with a classmate. We certainly had never gone this far. What if she found out about us?

"I hope you don't tell my girlfriend about this," I blurted out.

"She won't find out from me, Arthur," my partner muttered impatiently, even as she shoved me up under the steering wheel of Daddy's car. "She won't know nothing unless you tell her. *I* ain't going to tell her nothing, that's for sure."

Only much later, after I got home depleted and in a daze, did I begin to wonder about the police patrolling Byrd Park. Then I began to think about the possibility that my partner might get pregnant. Suppose I became a father? I would have to marry her, and maybe give up my tennis! But when I met her on Monday morning, she seemed not worried at all. Neither did she say anything about seeing me again. I remained nervous for a week or two, then forgot all about the dangers we had courted. I remembered only the unbelievably sweet new feeling of sex.

Facing the problem of young people as ignorant and as unprepared for sex as I had been, I want them to know the moral and religious aspects of sexuality. I want them to be familiar with the teachings of the Bible and with other religious doctrines. Because of AIDS, however, I am equally committed to the policy of giving condoms, as well as the bare, unvarnished facts about sex and AIDS, to students. I want adolescents caught up for the first time in the sizzling heat of sex to know scientifically about the penis, the vagina, and the rectum; about blood, sperm, and mucous membranes; about pregnancy, viruses, and the fatality of HIV. In the midst of an epidemic that will only grow worse, I have no time for evasions and euphemisms or other timidly genteel deceptions in teaching young people who are either sexually active or on the brink of becoming so.

Many people, however, cannot bring themselves to face the facts. When Magic, in a book about AIDS aimed squarely at adolescents, deliberately used certain terms and expressions that many young people would readily understand, more than one bookseller chain and several individual stores refused to sell the book because they considered the language too vulgar. When Dr. Louis Sullivan, the Secretary of Health and Human Services in the Bush administration, moved to institute a complex study of sexual practices among teenagers, an alliance of the religious right and the Republican party killed the idea almost at its birth. And late in 1992 came word that, to avoid offending conservatives, the Centers for Disease Control (CDC) routinely deleted information concerning AIDS from its materials aimed at the public. The CDC censored terms such as *oral sex, anal intercourse,* and *vaginal intercourse;* it even dropped the use of the term *condom* from its announcements. Surely this is discretion gone too far. A spokesman for the CDC declared that they wished to make the material "broadly acceptable"—even if, apparently, these deletions caused people to die.

We need to know all we can about sex and AIDS. A report such as that compiled by the New York State Department of Health, released late in 1992, in which sex acts were rated according to their degree of danger, contains information that can save lives. Some of the findings did not surprise me, but others certainly did. For both men and women, anal intercourse offers the highest risk of infection. Next comes vaginal intercourse for women. Third is vaginal intercourse for men. In vaginal intercourse, women are twice as likely to get AIDS as men. If an infected woman is also menstruating, the man is at greater risk than if she is not. Despite myths to the contrary, oral intercourse presents a risk of infection, although it is slight compared to anal and vaginal intercourse. More open to debate is the risk offered by mutual masturbation and passionate kissing. The report defines the latter as "a kiss lasting a few minutes, with vigorous rubbing of the oral mucosa" (the inside of the mouth) in the process. "In a study of ninety subjects," the report states of researchers, "they found [that] blood was normally present in the saliva of 50 percent of the subjects and increased significantly after teeth brushing and after passionate kissing."

Some people think that only the receptive partner can become infected as a result of anal sex. Not so, according to the report; a man can also become infected in this way even if he is the inserter. And although I have always assumed that AIDS cannot be transmitted in lesbian sex, the report cites two possible incidents of infection that took place by woman-to-woman sexual activity.

The report also discusses such acts as individual masturbation, "dry" kissing, massaging, hugging, and stroking. While these and other activities treated in the report are not normally the stuff of polite conversation, there is nothing polite about AIDS. Around the world, heterosexual contacts make up the majority of infections, and a similar pattern is fast developing in the United States. Nothing is gained by suppressing these essential pieces of information.

For the African American community, as for other communities, condoms can protect against AIDS and also protect against an evil just as dangerous, and possibly more so: the flood of unplanned, unwanted, and insupportable teenage pregnancies that lead in part to the army of delinquents, drug addicts, welfare recipients, and violent criminals who are destroying our community. In my work with youngsters in Newark, New Jersey, our instructors have emphasized and encouraged the avoidance of pregnancy among our teenagers. I am proud that not one of the unmarried young women in our program has given birth.

For Jeanne and me, as parents of a child about to enter the first grade in New York City, these issues are not a matter of theory alone. The clash between religion and morality, on the one hand, and practicality and science, on the other, has come close to a flash point here; I am sure that similar conflicts will arise in other parts of the nation and perhaps the world. Bitter opposition has arisen to the City Board of Education over its proposed elementary- and secondary-school curriculum. Among its goals, this curriculum aims to teach the children tolerance of both homosexuality and heterosexuality. It does so mainly by engaging the question of what constitutes a family. The simple sentence "Heather has two mommies," which introduces a lesson designed to teach tolerance of lesbianism, has enraged many people. Frankly, I myself am not sure that I want my daughter to be taught about lesbian parents in her first year at school, when she is only seven. I am certain, however, that I want her to have a tolerant and enlightened attitude toward homosexuals.

The conservatives are not without supporters on the Board of Education, and elsewhere. At one point, the board voted to require those groups offering AIDS education to New York City schoolchildren to sign an oath stating that they would emphasize abstinence first, and prophylactics and other defenses against diseases only later. Within the health-care apparatus of the Roman Catholic church, on which many people depend for medical assistance, a debate rages about AIDS treatment, AIDS education, and the use of condoms. Late in 1992, a major Catholic hospital in New York City, breaking with years of tradition, decided against observing World AIDS Day. The reason given by administrators was the nature of the information and materials handed out on behalf of AIDS education; they were "not in keeping with the teachings of the Catholic church."

I believe in the wisdom of the Bible and I believe also in ascertaining the moral implications of our actions. I respect the Roman Catholic church; Jeanne, a Catholic, goes to mass regularly. Yet science and statistics tell us that AIDS in America is spread increasingly by hetero-sexual contact. To preach morality *only* and at the same time to ignore the practical aspects of the problem seems to me unwise. The aim of all sex education should be to inform children what it means to act responsibly, and also to convince them that they should do so. The distribution of condoms should be an essential part, but only one part, of the overall effort at education. If the aim is to stop the spread of AIDS, we must have both condoms and moral instruction. One with-out the other will not do the job. The result will be more young people who are HIV-positive in the suburbs, in the city, and in rural areas; poor, middle-class, and rich.

Nevertheless, no one should sneer at the idea of sexual abstinence or of self-control under certain conditions. I believe in abstinence from extramarital affairs. I think such activity is morally wrong, as well as contractually wrong in the context of the vow one takes in a marriage. I absolutely believe in the need to refrain from promiscuity. This is a term almost always applied to women and almost never applied to men, but in writing of promiscuity I am thinking above all of men and the double standard by which we have lived for centuries. Nowadays, it is true, some women measure their freedom in the same way: the ability to be sexually promiscuous. I think that this is not freedom but one of the fantasies of freedom. Both men and women should recog-nize that promiscuity is, as often as not, a condition of violence against our own individual best interests.

Total premarital abstinence, stressed by many churches and by those who would have young people "Just Say No" (although this slogan was first used for a campaign against drugs), is another matter altogether. I and others of my generation or older have lived through extraordinary changes in the level of tolerance about premarital sex. Not very long ago, many hotels would not allow an unmarried couple to register and stay in a room together. Once, for instance, when I went to San Juan, Puerto Rico, with a young woman to whom I was formally engaged at the time, we took separate rooms at our hotel. A couple I know, despite the evidence of their marriage license, was once refused accommodations in a Massachusetts hotel because the wife had not taken her husband's last name. Honestly, I am not always sure how I feel about the new freedom. As I get older, and with a young daughter,

I see increasingly how rules and conventions about behavior help to protect the integrity of the family. I believe that the family, however defined, must be protected. No African American, in particular, watching the deterioration of our culture through the decline of the family, can sensibly wish otherwise. However, I know that rules about appropriate male and female behavior often work to keep women in an inferior place by permitting double standards, as existed flagrantly in the recent past and even in some areas today, as well as to intimidate gay people.

I believe strongly that homosexuals should enjoy equal protection under the law. One of the members of my family closest to me is gay, and I feel for him and the problems he routinely encounters. I am disappointed at the attitude of certain churches toward homosexuals, who are excluded in various ways, sometimes callously. Surely it isn't hard to see the homosexual's point of view on the question of rights. If I am gay and have been so all my life, why shouldn't I be protected equally and given all the rights and privileges of a heterosexual citizen?

Religious opponents of homosexuals regularly cite the Bible to support their position. I am well aware that Mosaic law decreed certain unspecified homosexual acts to be punishable by death (as it also did for several other, to us, ordinary types of behavior). In Leviticus 18:22, in a translation from ancient Hebrew increasingly called into question by scholars, the Bible says (in the New International Version, at least): "Do not lie with a man as one lies with a woman; that is detestable." (The practice is called "an abomination" in the King James version.) Nevertheless, whatever the accuracy of the translation, I believe that Leviticus 18:22 must be read in the more tolerant light shed by other parts of the Bible, including the New Testament. This position is only reinforced when I consider the legal and constitutional issues raised by this question within the context of American democracy.

However, I sometimes fear that a major anti-gay backlash is coming in the United States. The repeal of a statute protecting the rights of gays in Colorado, and the narrow upholding of a similar statute in Oregon, may be warning signs. In Colorado, voters across the state passed Amendment 2 to the state constitution, which prevents the adoption of laws anywhere in the state to protect homosexuals against acts of discrimination. The voters in the resort of Aspen and in the cities of Boulder and Denver voted against the passage of Amendment 2, but anti-discrimination statutes in those communities were automatically rescinded by the passage of the amendment, which took effect in January 1993. The sponsors of Amendment 2, a group called Colorado for Family Values, evidently expressed the opinion of a large number of people concerning homosexuality and homosexuals. "What they want is a special protected status," one of the leaders said. "They just don't deserve it. The majority of America is with us on this."

Even as gays and their supporters, who regard the "special protection" argument as specious, work hard to promote a climate of acceptance, most Americans indeed seem to oppose granting gays protection as a group. A large percentage of Americans take religion and the Bible seriously and claim that both support their anti-gay position. However, a large percentage of gay people also take religion and the Bible seriously. I am in favor of guaranteeing the rights of gays as citizens. Unquestionably, homosexuals are the object of prejudice and discrimination. They constitute a group threatened by special problems and dangers deriving from prejudice, from which they should be protected by law.

I am inclined, further, to support the boycott of the state of Colorado or any other state that acts against the rights of individual gay men and women. I regret that some innocent people, mainly merchants and their employees, will suffer, just as some innocent people suffered with the boycott of South Africa and perhaps suffer when any economic sanction is imposed. Practically speaking, however, opponents of the new amendment, and especially those people outside the state who fear the spread of similar amendments, have few options in making their case. As a leader of the American Civil Liberties Union put it: "People need to know that if they adopt measures that discriminate against gays they will be ostracized."

To refrain from boycotting Colorado is in effect to condone the actions of those who voted yes to the question on the ballot: "Do you want to repeal the Gay Rights Act?" A boycott is usually a messy and divisive affair, but it worked in the state of Arizona after the state voted against making Martin Luther King, Jr., Day a paid holiday. In two years, Arizona lost more than $500 million in business through the cancellation of lucrative conventions and other meetings. It even lost the chance to host a Super Bowl—the most eagerly anticipated football game of the year in the United States—along with the millions of dollars in revenue that it would have made for the state. In 1992, Arizona reversed its decision and established the state holiday honoring King. If the Colorado boycott is pursued with the same vigor, it will hasten the day when laws guaranteeing the same rights to homosexuals as are accorded to heterosexuals are on the books there again. Some people will insist that homosexuality is a sin; I respond that, to me, it is definitely not a crime, and must not be treated as such.

FROM TIME TO time, I find myself thinking about those forty figure skaters and the tragedy of their lives and deaths. They were no doubt, most of them, young men of good family and bright hopes, of powerful bodies and soaring imaginations. Some no doubt were secure in their homosexuality; some must have been furtive, guilt-ridden, ashamed. All had to work brutally to make themselves ready for the challenges of their demanding sport. I think of the long, chilly years of labor when they strove to master their sport, to bring their bodies to the peak of physical perfection, and to learn to seem effortless in creating their designs. Their task, in a sense, was to write their names on ice. Now the ice is melted, and they are gone.

I am moved by the fact that despite their best efforts to achieve fame and fortune, they nevertheless went to their deaths without fanfare. Unlike Magic Johnson or me, they had no electrifying news flash, no emotional press conference, no opportunity to be a hero stoical before the television cameras, no outpouring of sympathy and affection from the loving public. A few had won a measure of fame, but nothing that could adequately recompense them for the way they died. Many had no sporting reputation to speak of, except what they had eked out in minor competitions. What they all had were those years of chilly labor and the endless gliding over ice in search of perfection.

In each case, I hope, his family and friends made sure that he died with dignity and honor, surrounded by love. These young men did not deserve to die so young, and they did not deserve to die unnoticed, to be resurrected only as a statistic in a newspaper report. As a fellow athlete, I mourn them. As an AIDS patient, I feel a kinship to them that goes far beyond the bonds of sport. I wish I had the power to keep their memory alive. I would do so, not least of all, as yet another token of our human determination to live in the face of this terrible disease that has brought death into every corner of our lives, including the world of sport.

CHAPTER 9

Stepping Up

AFTER MY AIDS announcement on April 8, 1992, I was angry for several days. But when Jeanne and I had to tell Camera of my illness, I swallowed my feelings and put on a dispassionate face.

"Precious," I asked her that evening, when Jeanne and I decided that the time had come, "have you noticed anything unusual lately at home?"

"Yes," she said.

"What?"

"The telephones," she replied, not looking up from my computer, which she was using. "They keep ringing all the time."

"Yes. Do you know why? They're ringing because Daddy had to go on television and tell everybody that he is sick, that he has AIDS."

"What's AIDS?" she asked, looking at me now. "Is it like when you have diarrhea? When you don't feel well in the morning? Is that AIDS?"

Her instincts surprised Jeanne and me; she knew more, had noticed and associated more, than we had ever suspected. Five years old, she could understand only a small part of what we said, but we talked to her as best we could about the illness. We also tried to prepare her for the taunts of classmates and other children.

"Camera, what are you going to say to anybody who tells you your daddy has AIDS?"

"What should I say?" she asked.

"Just say, 'Oh, I *know* that.'" We hoped that this simple reply would stop the teasing. We were sure that Camera would master this response easily. After all, like it was for almost every child of her age, "I know that" had become her spontaneous reply to almost anything said to her, even if she didn't have a clue about it. But this piece of information—that her father suffered from AIDS—she would indeed have, and her knowledge would save her from hurt. Or so we hoped.

I also spent an hour and a half at Camera's school, Marymount, the Catholic institution she has attended until recently, after I discovered that many of the girls in the upper school were upset and confused by the news about me. After visiting Camera's classroom, I spoke to a subdued gathering of these older girls in the auditorium. As best I could, I tried to help them understand AIDS as a new force in their lives, and to assure them that they could do much to curb its destructive power.

Although my anger at being "outed" was real and intense, it quickly began to ebb. After all, I am not one to bank and stoke rage; instead, I want its fire to go out as soon as possible, and cool reason to return. Within two or three weeks, anger on this score passed out of me entirely, or almost entirely, as I turned to the new stage of my life. Ever since September 1988, AIDS had been a fact I had integrated into my life. Now I tried to integrate into my sense of self, as smoothly as possible, the public knowledge that I had AIDS.

The world saw me now in a different way. Although I was on guard against paranoia, I thought I detected people whispering and pointing more than before, when I was an ordinary celebrity. Most people are kind to me, but I felt a degree of solicitude that wasn't there before, an element of tenderness and perhaps even of pity. I do not care for pity, but I know that people who pity others usually mean well. Above all, as closely as I looked, I saw nothing of the revulsion I had feared others would manifest because they now knew I had AIDS.

In one respect, I was relieved by my announcement. No longer would I have to make different excuses to different people about lapses in my health, as I had been doing since 1988. Nor did I have to deny being ill, as I had often done. Now I could tell the truth when my body hurt or failed me, and also talk about particular nuances of my illness. For this freedom I was grateful.

Because this latest stage of my life opened almost without warning, at first I felt in danger of being overwhelmed by the publicity. More than ever before, the world wanted to hear from me. Requests for speeches more than tripled. Invitations to meetings, to dinners, awards ceremonies, and the like, also increased dramatically. Here I saw something of a dilemma. On the one hand, the last thing I wanted to do was to dine out on my story of AIDS. On the other hand, I was bent on telling the story of AIDS so that as many people as possible would be aware of its dangers, its myths and realities. I made up my mind not to withdraw from the world nor even to turn bashfully from the limelight. Unless I fell severely ill and became gaunt and wasted, as many AIDS patients do, I would not become a recluse. "You come to the realization that time is short," I told a reporter later that year. "These are extraordinary conditions, and you have to step up."

How much time I had left, I did not know; no doctor could tell me. In the first two or three years of knowing I had AIDS, I could argue to myself that I might defeat it, that with the right combination of medical help and mental and physical toughness, I might be one of the first to beat the odds and survive it. Or survive for so many years that I could claim a victory over the disease. Already, in fact, the medical community saw me as a long-term survivor. However, I could not ignore the fact that AIDS, as well as heart disease, was exacting a heavy toll on my body. My weight was down, perhaps irremediably so; at six feet one inch, I now weighed just over 140 pounds. (In my playing days, I weighed just over 150.) My stamina, too, was impaired. I had no time to waste.

As I settled deeper into this new stage of my life, I became increasingly conscious of a certain thrill, an exhilaration even, about what I was doing. Yes, I felt pain, physical and psychological; but I also felt something like pleasure in responding purposefully, vigorously, to my illness. I had lost many matches on the tennis court, but I had seldom quit. I was losing, but playing well now; my head was down, eyes riveted on the ball as I stroked it; I had to be careful but I could not be tentative; my follow-through must flow from the shot, fluid and smooth. Experience as an athlete had taught me that in times of danger I had to respond with confidence, authority, and calm. So many looming defeats had turned strangely, sometimes even miraculously, into victories as I applied that lesson to the task before me.

It helped, too, that for some time in my life I had been ready for nothing so much as the unexpected. Life, I believe, is a succession of often suddenly realized stages, of fresh beginnings for which one has constantly to be prepared. The death of my mother before I was seven had been one of those surprises, and perhaps had instilled in me the notion of life as a succession of sudden changes. I remember being startled to find this aspect of my sense of life beautifully captured in "Stages," a poem in Hermann Hesse's famous novel *The Glass Bead Game* (or *Magister Ludi*), probably my favorite work of modern fiction. Perhaps Hesse intended "Stages" to be ironic—after all, it was composed in the "student years" of Joseph Knecht, the main character of the novel, which is supposed to be Knecht's biography. Still, the poem seems to me beyond irony. Just as every flower fades, Hesse writes, so too our virtues, our visions of truth, are transitory. Life itself is change, so we must be ready to take leave of the old and familiar and embark on the new. All beginnings, Hesse insists, have a magical force that can guard and empower us. Indeed, even the hour of death may send us on to "fresh and newer spaces," for which we should be prepared.

FOLLOWING MY ANNOUNCEMENT, one of my most urgent decisions was to establish the Arthur Ashe Foundation for the Defeat of AIDS. I was conscious of the possibility that I did not have sufficient time left to mount such a project, but I became determined to move ahead with it, come what may. Although I could have joined an existing organization, I wanted my foundation to be somewhat more international in scope than any I knew, as befits an epidemic that knows no national boundaries and is ravaging some of the poorest countries of the world. According to the Harvard AIDS Institute, by the year 2000 as many as 110 million people around the world may be infected. The plight of patients in Africa is particularly terrible; nations such as the Central African Republic, Uganda, Kenya, Zaïre, and Zambia loom as major sites of AIDS devastation. With death rates soaring across Africa, some experts predict perhaps 10 to 15 million orphans there by the year 2000. With the average cost of treating a patient in the United States now about $100,000 from diagnosis to death, it is clear that many people, perhaps most, will die untreated.

I decided that my foundation would keep these tragic facts in mind, in the hope that it could contribute to lessening the dimensions of this global disaster. Accordingly, I decided that at least half of the money we raise would go to AIDS research and treatment outside the United States. As a matter of policy, we would work with and through respected organizations such as the International Red Cross and the World Health Organization of the United Nations. We would guard our resources carefully, and do everything we could to ensure that the maximum part of each contribution went to alleviate the suffering of AIDS patients, or to promote some vital aspect of AIDS research.

By mid-August, helped especially by my friend and colleague Margaret Mahoney, who selflessly shared her time and expertise as executive director of the Commonwealth Fund, the Arthur Ashe Foundation began to take shape. The extensive legal work was complete, as was my selection of board members. In addition to Jeanne and myself, the members are Dr. Henry Murray, Bill Cosby, Donald Dell, and Frank Craighill, a former law and business partner of Dell's, now with the management firm Advantage International; also, Seth Abraham of HBO, Sheila Foster, a social worker and a family friend (her husband is the former baseball star George Foster), Dr. Irving Chen of the UCLA AIDS Institute, Dr. Machelle Allen, whose practice at Bellevue Hospital in New York is almost exclusively with HIV-positive women, Dr. George Fareed, who has been associated with the U.S. Davis Cup program as a physician, and Dr. Michael Merson, the director of the Global Programme on AIDS of the World Health Organization.

After some searching, I found an executive director with outstanding credentials, given the special relationship of the foundation to the tennis world: Jacqueline Joseph, a young graduate of Stanford University who not only holds an M.B.A. from Columbia University, but also was a collegiate and professional tennis player. She and I are working closely together to plan the future of the foundation.

We have set as a goal the raising of between $2.5 million and $5 million in about two years. How realistic this goal is, I do not know. So far, we have done reasonably well. At the end of August, the day before the start of the U.S. Open, we launched our appeal at Flushing Meadows, New York, with an exhibition featuring John McEnroe,

Andre Agassi, Pete Sampras, and Jim Courier among the men, and Martina Navratilova, Steffi Graf, Pam Shriver, and Arantxa Sánchez Vicario among the women. To entertain the crowd, McEnroe even staged a mock tantrum against the umpire, Mike Wallace of CBS-TV. A few months later, the USTA sent the foundation a check for $114,000, our share of the proceeds.

Above all, I am deeply pleased by the way that the tennis world, often accused of selfishness and snobbery, has responded to the foundation's challenge. Both at the amateur and professional level, we have had the full cooperation of virtually everyone in a position to help. We are currently planning events in connection with the next Wimbledon and U.S. Open.

In other ways, public support has been gratifying. Thousands of kind letters have come in, some with donations, some without. Some of our supporters are interested in tennis, but at least as many are not. At our tennis exhibition, I was absolutely astonished when a man approached me in the stands, casually handed me a personal check in the amount of $25,000, then went on his way. Some days later, a check arrived for $30,000, drawn on a North Carolina bank, from a donor who has remained anonymous. The young American tennis player MaliVai Washington, after a tournament in Antwerp, generously sent a check for $10,000. A fifth-grader in Bradenton, Florida, inspired by reading about Franklin Delano Roosevelt's March of Dimes campaign against polio, sent me a dollar. "Can you find a way," he wrote me, "to ask all of America to send a dollar bill to fight AIDS? I would call it March of Dollars." I wish we could do so; on the other hand, I am well aware that many worthy causes compete for charity.

Whatever happens to me, I hope that people will continue to support the Arthur Ashe Foundation for the Defeat of AIDS. As its name declares, it exists not simply to help fight this terrible disease but to help conquer it. How long the foundation will continue to exist, I do not know. The fight against AIDS may take as much as a generation, perhaps even more, although I look for a cure in the next few years. Whether through my foundation or not, however, we must keep up the struggle until the fight is won. And I know that the fight will be won.

The month of my announcement also saw the formal launching of another project initiated by me and of significance and importance to me. After two years of planning and consultations designed to ensure that the support I needed would be there, I helped to found the African American Athletic Association, of which I am chairman. I conceived of the AAAA in the aftermath of my protracted struggle with other opinionated leaders over academic requirements for black collegians. As the daunting statistics about increased black involvement in sports and the decline in black academic performance mounted, I became convinced that we needed an organization that would create and maintain structures for advising and counseling young black athletes, especially student-athletes. This body would also work to create job opportunities for them in the face of racism and other problems, and to help shape public policy in this general area through both the skilled collection and dissemination of data about sport and the writings of experts on the subject. Aided by Gloria Primm Brown of the Carnegie Corporation, who gave me valuable advice about funding and other financial and legal matters, I began to see more clearly the task that faced me. Dr. Alpha Alexander, a member of the nominating committee of the U.S. Olympic Committee and director of health promotion and sports for the YWCA of America, has been a fruitful source of ideas and opinions about goals for our organization, which she joined as vice-president. Our other officers include Dr. Dick Barnett, the former New York Knicks basketball star, who now holds a doctorate in counseling, and Dr. Roscoe C. Brown, the president of Bronx Community College. Our executive director, Yolanda Jackson, is a graduate of Columbia University and a specialist in public relations. She and I have worked closely together over the last two years to make the association a reality.

I believe that the AAAA is at last poised to begin to make an impact on this troubled aspect of American and African American life. I am convinced that the mentoring of student-athletes is crucial not only to our efforts but to the future of the black community in America, and I am delighted to know that Columbia University proposes to join us in this aspect of our effort. With hard work and adequate support, I think we can make a difference in the lives of a substantial number of young people.

*   *   *

TO MANY PEOPLE, especially to people who meet me or even those who merely find themselves in the same room with me, I probably personify the problem of AIDS. When I am there with them, they can avert their eyes but not for long, and must face the problem that has been facing them for years and will face them even more boldly in the future. I do not like being the personification of a problem, much less a problem involving a killer disease, but I know I must seize these opportunities to spread the word. Talking to audiences about AIDS has become, in some respects, the most important function of my life. To all groups I take the message that AIDS is here and growing both in volume and complexity, that it is no respecter of race or privilege, that our health care is insufficient to its challenge, that we must do all we can to defeat it.

I stepped up my visits to college campuses, starting with a speech and an honorary degree at the end of April from Kalamazoo College in Michigan, where I played many matches in my youth in the annual national junior tennis championships. Before the year was out I had received another degree from Loyola College of Baltimore, and spoken at a host of colleges and universities, including McGill in Canada, Niagara County Community College, Duquesne, Brown, and the universities of Florida, Virginia, and Pennsylvania. I mention these honors and invitations not to boast about them but to underscore the growing concern about AIDS. Everywhere, I found the students eager to hear about my personal experience and about the onerous problems surrounding American health care. Their questions were intelligent, their manner sensitive and mature. In general, I always returned from these visits to colleges and universities impressed by our young people and their teachers and encouraged in my own struggle with AIDS.

I also found satisfying, although sometimes in a different way, my speeches to a wide range of professional groups, from a luncheon gathering of the National Press Club in Washington, D.C., in May to a morning speech to five hundred public-school teachers at the Sheraton Hotel in Manhattan in October. I have spoken to groups of pharmacists and employees of drug companies, to journalists on the issue of privacy and press freedom, and to businessmen wanting to know firsthand about the magnitude of the AIDS problem. Every group seems to have a different perspective on the problem, so that I constantly find myself being educated even as I try to teach. One of my most satisfying speeches of the year started with a simple letter to me from a student at Greenwich High School in Connecticut who was disturbed by the apparently cavalier attitude toward the disease exhibited by many of her classmates. On short notice, squeezing my visit between two flights out of town to more formal speaking engagements, I drove up from Manhattan to address an assembly of students there. I hope my talk made a difference, at least to some of them.

In addition to all my lectures and other addresses, the awards dinners and the like, I kept as busy as ever on my various business interests throughout the year after my announcement. I saw absolutely no diminution in the call for my services from groups such as ABC-TV, HBO, Head USA, Le Coq Sportif, or Aetna; far from it. In a variety of ways, from board meetings to tennis clinics to morale-boosting sponsored public appearances, I continued to work energetically with all of these companies.

AIDS is a formidable enemy, one that can demoralize the strongest individual if it touches that person intimately enough. In November, I had a sad reminder of that power. After Jeanne and I had agreed to host a forum at New York Hospital for hemophiliac AIDS patients and their families, approximately two hundred invitations went out. When we arrived at the hospital, we found almost no one present. In the end, only seven people attended. I was stunned. But I know that it is hard for many people who are caught up in such suffering, either directly or as family members, to expose their emotions. I did my best to make the evening as warm and productive as I could. I tried to draw out individuals who needed to talk about their problems, and I shared with them aspects of my own experience. The evening was a success, I think, for those who came. Nevertheless, the poor attendance was hard to ignore.

I was happy to speak to small groups, but I also sought chances to maximize the impact of what I have to say. Late in the spring, I was in a taxi going to La Guardia Airport when I heard the news on the radio that, with only a few days left before the event, Magic Johnson had canceled an appearance and speech at the commencement ceremonies of the Harvard Medical School, because his wife was about to give birth to their first child. From the taxi I placed a telephone call to the school and offered to replace Magic. Normally I do not solicit speaking engagements, but the Harvard Medical School commencement is such a splendid opportunity to speak about AIDS and health care that I was willing to risk being turned down.

On an afternoon early in June, offering myself "more as a thirteen-year professional patient than just as someone with AIDS," I addressed the graduating class. My talk had its light moments, but its core was serious, as I outlined the most pressing issues as I saw them. Doctors, I argued, need to communicate much more sympathetically with their patients. Health care is far too expensive in America, with much of the expense incurred unethically, in padded bills and other inflated charges. The serious decline in ethics, in fact, has become a pervasive scandal within the profession. As medical costs soar, the huge fees and salaries earned by most physicians might have to be reduced, especially if AIDS continues to spread as expected. Whatever their individual attitudes toward treating AIDS patients (and some, perhaps even many, would refuse such work), doctors must not be aloof from the public discussion of the issue of sex education for young people in the age of AIDS. "You *must* enter the fray," I urged. "You, as healers, must become part of the debate."

The absence of a coherent national health-care policy is, in my opinion, one of the major disgraces of American life. Greed should not blind doctors to the devastating effect of the absence of such a policy on the American poor and the middle class. I offered to sum up, in exactly fifty words, what our goals should be in facing the national crisis in health care: "Through a prudent combination of federal assistance and private enterprise, America will ensure appropriate, adequate, and sufficient physical and mental health care for all its citizens. Furthermore, America acknowledges its preeminent moral position in leading combined global efforts to assist, share information, and seek solutions for our common medical concerns." I urged the graduates to accept all of these challenges and to meet them with all the skill and knowledge at their command.

A few days later, around the middle of June 1992, Jeanne, Camera, and I flew to England for Wimbledon, where I would again broadcast for HBO. I left New York with a happy heart, because I thought of this trip as a true bonus. The previous year, I had flown to London for Wimbledon thinking that it would surely be my last visit to the scene of my greatest triumph in tennis. One misty afternoon, just before the start of the tournament, I had even taken Camera by the hand and strolled with her from one green court to another, telling her (as if at four she could understand me) about my matches on this court and that. Now, in 1992, feeling myself reprieved, I returned once again to a place I dearly love.

The typical HBO day at Wimbledon is grueling. Leaving home at 8:30 in the morning, I usually would not return before 10:30 at night or even later. I found the tough schedule a challenge but also invigorating. Fortunately, our contract does not allow us to broadcast on the weekends. And Wimbledon is a wonderful gathering of the tennis clan. I enjoyed spending time, especially in the long delays brought on by wet weather, with old friends and opponents from all over the world, some back as mere spectators, others, like myself, working for the press. In the HBO facility, I spent many pleasant rainy hours with my colleague Billie Jean King as we waited for play to resume or to start; more than ever I savored the terms of our long friendship, and admired the sharpness of her mind and the resilience of her spirit. On television, I watched Agassi win the men's singles crown, and Graf take the women's; but I was even more pleased that McEnroe, still struggling with his demons but still a marvelous player, won the men's doubles title, with Michael Stich.

On June 27, I took time off from tennis to appear on a television interview show, "Fighting Back," hosted by the actress Lynn Redgrave. I was glad for this chance to speak directly, as it were, to the people of Great Britain, a country I love. A thoughtful interviewer, Redgrave touched me with her questions about my life with AIDS. Toward the end she asked me for a message to the viewers. "Apropos of this show," I said, thinking of its title, "Fighting Back," my message was that "there is always hope, and you must live your life as if there is, or there *will be* some hope." Moreover, this hope "should not be a selfish hope. . . . For me, the hope is that maybe there is no cure for AIDS in time for me, but certainly for everyone else." That fact alone, I suggested, "should be sufficient to maintain this hope." Redgrave ended by quoting Jeanne to the effect that I would never give up. "That's right," I assured her and our audience, "I will never quit."

When I left England this time, I did not feel nearly as pessimistic about my chances of returning next year as I had in 1991. Perhaps I will be back next year, and even the year after. Who knows? London and Wimbledon are special to me. In a real way, my first visit there in 1963, to play Wimbledon, was the beginning of my intellectual and cultural growth beyond my schooling in Richmond and Los Angeles, as sound as that was. England broadened my mind immeasurably, and enriched my sense of culture and civilization. I began to see myself as a citizen of the world, and to understand more fully what that concept might mean. It is hard for me to think of never returning to England.

APART FROM THOSE few days when my medical problems sapped my strength, when my mornings were an ordeal of listlessness and diarrhea, the summer of 1992 was a joy. Of course, my medical problems are seldom far away from my thoughts. I remember last summer for several reasons, but not least of all because I started my treatment with ddI (didanosine), the anti-AIDS drug I am pinning much of my hope on right now, until something more efficacious is discovered. I take it in combination with the more toxic AZT.

My best days of the summer (and the spring and the fall, come to think of it) no doubt found me teeing off on the golf course, preferably at Sleepy Hollow Country Club in Scarborough-on-Hudson, New York. Sponsored by my good friend Gil de Boton of Mount Kisco, I had been admitted in March, just before my news conference about having AIDS. In the few months I have been a member, Sleepy Hollow has probably given me almost as much pure pleasure as anything else in my life during the same time. I love being able to call up the clubhouse and arrange for a foursome, take my car out of the garage, drive forty-five to fifty minutes north out of the city, and breathe the fresh suburban air while I chase the little white ball over the green grass in the company of good friends such as Doug Stein or Eddie Mandeville or perfect (and imperfect) strangers also out for a game. Although I play at other clubs, I am delighted to call Sleepy Hollow home, as a golfer. Best of all, my game has improved almost beyond recognition.

The month of my announcement also saw the formal launching of another project initiated by me and of significance and importance to me. After two years of planning and consultations designed to ensure that the support I needed would be there, I helped to found the African American Athletic Association, of which I am chairman. I conceived of the AAAA in the aftermath of my protracted struggle with other opinionated leaders over academic requirements for black collegians. As the daunting statistics about increased black involvement in sports and the decline in black academic performance mounted, I became convinced that we needed an organization that would create and maintain structures for advising and counseling young black athletes, especially student-athletes. This body would also work to create job opportunities for them in the face of racism and other problems, and to help shape public policy in this general area through both the skilled collection and dissemination of data about sport and the writings of experts on the subject. Aided by Gloria Primm Brown of the Carnegie Corporation, who gave me valuable advice about funding and other financial and legal matters, I began to see more clearly the task that faced me. Dr. Alpha Alexander, a member of the nominating committee of the U.S. Olympic Committee and director of health promotion and sports for the YWCA of America, has been a fruitful source of ideas and opinions about goals for our organization, which she joined as vice-president. Our other officers include Dr. Dick Barnett, the former New York Knicks basketball star, who now holds a doctorate in counseling, and Dr. Roscoe C. Brown, the president of Bronx Community College. Our executive director, Yolanda Jackson, is a graduate of Columbia University and a specialist in public relations. She and I have worked closely together over the last two years to make the association a reality.

I believe that the AAAA is at last poised to begin to make an impact on this troubled aspect of American and African American life. I am convinced that the mentoring of student-athletes is crucial not only to our efforts but to the future of the black community in America, and I am delighted to know that Columbia University proposes to join us in this aspect of our effort. With hard work and adequate support, I think we can make a difference in the lives of a substantial number of young people.

*   *   *

TO MANY PEOPLE, especially to people who meet me or even those who merely find themselves in the same room with me, I probably personify the problem of AIDS. When I am there with them, they can avert their eyes but not for long, and must face the problem that has been facing them for years and will face them even more boldly in the future. I do not like being the personification of a problem, much less a problem involving a killer disease, but I know I must seize these opportunities to spread the word. Talking to audiences about AIDS has become, in some respects, the most important function of my life. To all groups I take the message that AIDS is here and growing both in volume and complexity, that it is no respecter of race or privilege, that our health care is insufficient to its challenge, that we must do all we can to defeat it.

I stepped up my visits to college campuses, starting with a speech and an honorary degree at the end of April from Kalamazoo College in Michigan, where I played many matches in my youth in the annual national junior tennis championships. Before the year was out I had received another degree from Loyola College of Baltimore, and spoken at a host of colleges and universities, including McGill in Canada, Niagara County Community College, Duquesne, Brown, and the universities of Florida, Virginia, and Pennsylvania. I mention these honors and invitations not to boast about them but to underscore the growing concern about AIDS. Everywhere, I found the students eager to hear about my personal experience and about the onerous problems surrounding American health care. Their questions were intelligent, their manner sensitive and mature. In general, I always returned from these visits to colleges and universities impressed by our young people and their teachers and encouraged in my own struggle with AIDS.

I also found satisfying, although sometimes in a different way, my speeches to a wide range of professional groups, from a luncheon gathering of the National Press Club in Washington, D.C., in May to a morning speech to five hundred public-school teachers at the Sheraton Hotel in Manhattan in October. I have spoken to groups of pharmacists and employees of drug companies, to journalists on the issue of privacy and press freedom, and to businessmen wanting to

I travel a great deal now, sometimes flying three times or even more in a single week. But I seldom stay away more than a night from my family. I cannot bear to be away so long from Jeanne and Camera. For the first time in her life, Camera went away without us to Florida for three days, so that Jeanne and I could have a little time to ourselves; we could hardly wait for her return. On another occasion, in November, Jeanne and Camera went off to Disney World, leaving me behind (I was to join them there in a day or two). I missed them, and I was not happy until I set my eyes on them again. I love getting Camera ready for school in the morning, or helping her go to sleep at night. I love sitting on the floor with her and her coloring books or playing games or simply talking with her.

I love the pleasure she finds in our outings as a family together—apple-picking in autumn in Bethel, Connecticut, on a marvelously crisp, sunstruck day; or stepping out together, just the two of us. One evening, when Jeanne was not well, I remember taking Camera, dressed exquisitely in a long-sleeved, flower-print dress with a green sash belt, to the annual *Essence* magazine awards show. Only two days had passed since my AIDS announcement. I entered the hall with her on my shoulders, so she could see everything and everyone, and the crowd kindly gave us a standing ovation as we made our way to our seats near the front. At one point, Denzel Washington, who has four daughters himself, came down from the stage to say hello to Camera, and she slunk in embarrassment to the floor. "Precious," I told her as I helped her up, "your mother is going to be so jealous that you met Mr. Washington and she stayed at home." (She was.)

As Camera grows, I grow; as she lives, I live. I feel strong when I am with her, I feel the power of her youth and vitality. She taxes me at times, to be sure, but I pay the tax willingly. In October, I experienced one of those ordinary miracles of life, an event that left me almost in tears: for the first time, Camera read an entire book to me. She gives me so many reasons to want to live.

In the long shadow of the announcement, family is more important to me than ever. They have rallied beautifully to my side; I feel their love as I have felt it all my life. I am proud of the branches and roots and leaves of the family tree. Jeanne shares this sense of family with me; it helps to bind us. On Mother's Day, she and I went to Chicago to have brunch with her mother, Elizabeth. And on a Sunday in mid-August, we entertained twenty-four members of my family at our apartment, when they drove down from the wedding of one of my cousins in Massachusetts. At first only three persons had been scheduled to come, but the party grew and grew, out of love and caring for me, and I was glad for that. I had no way of knowing when I would see many of them again. My emotions must have been working furiously, because at some point I suddenly became overwhelmed, exhausted. Two of my aunts saw my tiredness; everyone left quickly. But that afternoon was special.

A few days later, Jeanne, Camera, and I went to spend a blissful weekend with my stepmother, Lorene Kimbrough Ashe, at her home in Gum Springs, Virginia, near Richmond. Although I have never lived in that house my father built, I had helped him build it, and I was moved to be back among some of the scenes of my childhood, with the woman who had been a loving stepmother to me and my brother, Johnnie. Away from the heat and the summer sun, we rocked and reminisced easily on the porch, and I also wrote a little; Camera played happily with Granny Lorene's dog, Seiko; and we visited the cemetery where my mother and father are buried.

At Thanksgiving, we flew to Chicago to be with Jeanne's family, which is also large and loving. Her father's sister had come in from Tucson, Arizona, and we had dinner at the home of one of Jeanne's aunts, Bernadette, who is one of my favorite people. I have so much to be thankful for. For someone with AIDS, as with any life-threatening illness, the family is often the main bulwark against embittering anxiety and the darkest depression. On every side, my family supports me.

However, I have not allowed either my illnesses or my desire to enjoy the comforts of home and family to put a stop to my involvement in politics. A few days after our AIDS tennis exhibition at Flushing Meadows in September, I took part in what might well have been my last protest action, although I make no promises on this score. The cause this time was Haiti. After Randall Robinson of TransAfrica informed me that he and Benjamin Hooks of the NAACP had decided to take the drastic step of picketing the White House, I decided to join them in the demonstration. For months I had been outraged by our national policy toward political refugees from Haiti. Vessels of the U.S. Coast Guard, acting on instructions, were intercepting boats carrying refugees from Haiti and returning those people to Haiti without a hearing. The argument behind this policy was that most of the people in those boats were fleeing economic hardship, not political persecution, and therefore had to be sent home at once.

The argument incensed me. Undoubtedly, many of the people picked up were economic refugees, but many were not. According to U.S. law, all were entitled to a hearing, and this step was routinely denied them. Meanwhile, Cubans who reached the United States were welcomed like heroes; newspapers regularly published photographs of Cuban refugees beaming in triumph on the decks of refugee boats. I was certain that race was a major factor in this double standard.

My feelings about Haiti were complicated. I had grown up reading about Toussaint L'Ouverture, Henri Christophe, Jean-Jacques Dessalines, and other black heroes of its revolution against France two hundred years ago, and of the mighty citadel at Cap-Haïtien built as a bulwark against white imperialism. Haiti had been the first independent black republic in the world. At UCLA, one of my closest friends, also on the men's tennis team, was Jean Baker of Haiti. Then, as I grew older, Haiti had become for me a racial embarrassment, a nation known more for its poverty and corruption than its independence. While many black Americans continued to boast about its history, many whites probably saw Haiti as proof that blacks can achieve little on their own. What Jeanne and I saw on our honeymoon there in 1977 only reinforced my feelings of confusion and embarrassment. Our hotel, owned and run by a Frenchman, was lovely. But Haiti in general was a nation in need of help.

Recently, however, there had been signs of hope. After various despotisms, notably under the Duvaliers, Haiti had held relatively free elections. Jean-Bertrand Aristide, enjoying the passionate support of the black poor, if not of all the mulatto elite, took office as president. Then, before he could consolidate his rule, Aristide had been deposed by the military. Essentially, the United States was supporting the anti-Aristide forces by various actions, including the interdiction of Haitians fleeing their country. I was prepared to be arrested to protest this injustice.

On the morning of September 9, I flew from New York to Washington. The demonstration had been planned meticulously. Every detail was known to the police in advance, because the last thing we wanted was disorder. We understood that one hothead—or saboteur—could transform a peaceful demonstration into a melee. At Shiloh Baptist Church, one of the biggest black churches in America, we received our marching orders. We then rode in vans to Lafayette Square, across from the White House, for the main rally. About two thousand people took part in the march, with another three or four thousand standing behind police barricades on the sidewalks. The most dramatic moment was the arrival in a wheelchair of the choreographer Katherine Dunham, who had lived for many years in Haiti and had been on a hunger strike to protest the U.S. actions. I was also glad to see that a large number of Haitians were present. Haitians and black Americans generally do not mix; in fact, this demonstration was probably the first major show of unity between black Americans and an immigrant community so clearly connected to Africa.

Following rules for demonstrations codified mainly during the civil-rights era, we proceeded with our plan. As we knew, our demonstration violated the law forbidding demonstrations within a certain distance of the White House. When the police ordered us to disperse, we refused. After several minutes, they again ordered us to disperse, and again we refused. They then began to arrest us. I was handcuffed and put into a police wagon. The police did their job efficiently and well. I was pleased when a few of them, out of earshot of their officers, told us that we had their support. We were then taken to the U.S. Superior Court in southwest Washington. There I was fined fifty dollars, which I paid. We were detained for about an hour, then released. From the courthouse, I went directly to the airport and took the shuttle back to New York.

The next day, around seven in the evening, I was sitting on my living-room couch watching a newscast when I began to feel a pain in the center of my sternum. The show ended and I started my dinner, but the pain kept coming. Although I did not think that I was in the middle of something serious, I took no chances. Reaching for some nitroglycerin lozenges I keep close at hand for emergencies, I put two or three under my tongue over a five-minute period. Nothing happened. I had kept the lozenges too long; they were outdated and useless. I bit into a Procardia, the football-shaped pill that I take regularly as a vasodilator, to expand my arteries. For about four or five minutes, the Procardia helped me. Then the pain returned, stronger than before.

The sensation of a heart attack, at least of mine, is of a burning, searing, viselike grip in the center of the chest. It feels as if your chest is imploding, that there is a black hole into which some force is trying to pull your entire corporeal being. It leaves you short of breath. It leaves you sweating. It leaves you very frightened.

I still did not know if I was having a heart attack, but I could not take a chance. Back in 1979, I learned that many deaths from heart attacks are caused by the self-delusion of people who take a chance and wait for the pain to pass. Jeanne and I quickly headed for New York Hospital, where I was admitted as a patient. At once, through three intravenous lines, I was fed nitroglycerin, lopressor (to lower the heart's need for oxygen by making it beat more slowly), and morphine for the pain; a fourth line was installed in case I needed a clot-busting drug. I was also given an electrocardiogram, which showed acute ischemia (lack of blood to the heart muscle), but none of the classic telltale signs of a heart attack.

The next day, I was given another test, this time an analysis of enzymes released by the heart when it is damaged. This test revealed that I had indeed suffered a heart attack, the second of my life. It was a very mild version of a cardiac attack, but an attack nevertheless. However, an angiogram, in which a catheter was slipped into the femoral artery in my groin and snaked up to my heart, showed virtually no new damage. This was excellent news.

I had many visitors in the hospital. One day, Jesse Jackson came with his son Yusuf, who had just graduated from law school at the University of Virginia. I told Yusuf how proud of him I was for his success at the distinguished university, where he had also been an undergraduate. When I was growing up in Richmond, I could not think of attending the University of Virginia, a state school, because of segregation. Virginia and the world had changed for the better, and continue to change for the better in so many important ways. I take comfort in that fact.

In the room with the Jacksons were Jeanne, Yannick Noah, and Carole Dell. Before Jackson left, he made us all form a circle and hold hands—Jesse, Yusuf, Yannick, Carole, Jeanne, and me. He asked God to tend to my illness; God could cure me. Jesse spoke of the woman (Mark 5:25–34) who suffered for twelve years from an issue of blood that no physician could stop: "She had spent all that she had and was no better, but rather grew worse." Then she touched the hem of Jesus' garment, and "immediately the fountain of her blood was dried up, and she felt in her body that she was healed of the affliction." Jesus had said: "Daughter, your faith has made you well. Go in peace, and be healed of your affliction." Jesse Jackson prayed that, in these hard times, we might find the faith in God that would guide and shepherd us.

He had chosen his scriptural passage well. It was a touching moment, which I appreciated and fully accepted. Over the years, I have shared in several moments of prayer with the Reverend Jesse Jackson, and even though I am often skeptical about what he says and does, I know that his faith is real.

Whatever the cause of my heart attack, I left the hospital inclined not to curtail my schedule in any way, provided that I could carry out my duties well. I was discharged on September 16. I was at my desk at home that night when Bill Clinton telephoned to wish me well and express the hope that we might meet soon. As I sat in my office after hanging up, I thought of him and Hillary Rodham Clinton and the grueling, sometimes humiliating, and still unfinished campaign they were pursuing simply to have his message heard and believed and his integrity accepted, and I was encouraged to continue to carry on my own campaign. I decided to strike nothing from my schedule but to plunge ahead. Four days later I flew to Atlanta to speak to a gathering of officials of community health centers on "Health Concerns of the Uninsured." Just after my return, I engaged a lively call-in audience on WLIB, the New York radio station. I then flew to Gainesville for a lecture at the University of Florida. The next day I was in Hartford, Connecticut, for an Aetna board meeting, then dined on September 24 at a fund-raiser in Manhattan for Governor Clinton, where I had the opportunity to meet and talk with him. The next day I returned to Hartford by company helicopter for another Aetna meeting, then I flew to Duquesne University in Pittsburgh to give a speech. The last day of September found me in Richmond, discussing with the mayor of the city a project dear to my heart—an African American Sports Hall of Fame to be located there. Then I returned to New York to attend a special showing of the Matisse exhibition at the Museum of Modern Art before heading out that evening to Baltimore, where I was to speak the following day.

All my engagements were satisfying in one way or another, but some were especially appealing. In October, for example, along with Donna deVarona, I was master of ceremonies at a fund-raising awards dinner sponsored by the Women's Sports Foundation at the Marriott Hotel in midtown Manhattan. I was happy to see all the athletes there, and especially in the areas, such as fencing, that give so little back to the women in terms of money and recognition but call for at least the same degree of sacrifice as the major sports. In sports, men have many avenues to big money and fame; for women, tennis stands out almost alone in this respect, although other sports allow a few women a decent financial return. Because I want to see women athletes gain the recognition and prizes they deserve, I was honored to be invited to take part in the event. Among the tennis players, young Lori McNeil was there, and my pal Billie Jean King, whom I had not seen since Wimbledon, and who has done at least as much as anyone else to raise the morale and the prestige of American women athletes. Billie Jean sometimes used to tease me about being too undemonstrative, but this time I gave her a long, close embrace that Jeanne noticed and commented on approvingly.

Tennis, and my own part in its recent history, were very much at the center of a weekend soon after in Jacksonville, Florida, when Jeanne and I attended various events, including a gala dinner, to mark the twentieth anniversary of the founding of the Association of Tennis Professionals. In 1972, I had played a leading role in its formation, and I had served for one year as president of the body that helped to reconstitute tennis in the open era. The event brought together some of the leading names of the past thirty years of the game, including Rod Laver, Roy Emerson, Stan Smith, Charlie Pasarell, Eddie Dibbs, Bob Lutz, Jaime Fillol, Bjorn Borg, and Ilie Nastase. I could not help notice, after a while, that I was obviously one of the special attractions of the hour, that my old tennis comrades were seeking me out and spending time with me; I seldom sat down without a small group gathering around my chair. The companionship of these men meant and continues to mean a great deal to me. I remember one night during my Davis Cup captaincy, about ten years ago, when I spoke at a gala dinner in Portland, Oregon, and broke down in tears talking about the Australian players and my feelings about them as individuals and as a group. I feel that way about so many of the men with whom I battled during my career. I love them for what we have been through together, and for sharing with me so many of the finest moments of my life.

I felt honored by their gestures of friendship; and indeed the fall of 1992 was a season of being honored; bashfully but gratefully I accepted a number of awards. Early in November, I received the Helen Hayes Award, and, a few days later, another award from the National Urban League, an organization that has labored for decades on behalf of economic opportunity for blacks. Later that month, I received the first Annual AIDS Leadership Award of the Harvard AIDS Institute, at the Carpenter Center at Harvard. Senator Edward Kennedy spoke on the topic of leadership in combating AIDS, and Maurice Tempelsman, chair of the advisory council of the institute, presented the award. Early in December, I received the American Sportscasters Association Sports Legend Award. Days later, an afternoon press conference at the Pierre Hotel on Fifth Avenue revealed that I was to receive unquestionably the most publicized of my awards of the year. The editors of *Sports Illustrated* magazine named me its Sportsman of the Year, obviously not because of what I had done on the court but away from sports. The award was presented at a gala dinner that evening at the Jockey Club in Manhattan.

On December 1, at the invitation of Secretary-General Boutros Boutros-Ghali, I had addressed the United Nations on the occasion of World AIDS Day. I considered that speech one of the most significant of my life, perhaps even the most significant. In it, I stressed the formidable power of AIDS but also deplored the weakness of the effort against it. "It has been the habit of humankind," I noted, "to wait until the eleventh hour to spiritually commit ourselves to those problems which we knew all along to be of the greatest urgency." In the face of a pandemic, we could hesitate no longer. Although 80 percent of the new cases would arise in developing countries, 94 percent of the funds to treat AIDS patients are spent in industrialized nations. This imbalance must be corrected, I urged. "All of us world citizens—Eastern and Western, developed and developing, regardless of ethnicity, nationality, or geographic origin—must see AIDS as *our* problem. Developed countries must do more, not only out of a moral sense of purpose but because it is in their own selfish economic interest to do so."

In the United States and around the world, a variety of reactionary attitudes impeded the fight against AIDS. "Nevertheless," I insisted, "we must try and we must succeed or our children and grandchildren will one day rightfully ask us why in the face of such a calamity we did not give our best efforts. What shall we tell them—and their mothers in particular—if we don't measure up? How shall I answer my six-year-old daughter and what do we say to the estimated ten million AIDS orphans by the year 2000? That their parents' generation was so racked with political and cultural and religious discord that it was willing to needlessly condone millions of medical refugees?"

Commending both the United States and the United Nations for recent decisions, however belatedly, to intervene in hunger crises in Africa and Eastern Europe, I reminded the delegates that "the AIDS pandemic has an even greater urgency." I ended by expressing optimism that AIDS would finally be defeated: "We want to be able to look back and say to all concerned that we did what we had to do, when we had to do it, and with all the resources required."

Two days later, in Brooklyn, I announced the creation of the Arthur Ashe Institute for Urban Health at the Health Science Center of the State University of New York there. Earlier in the year, after my AIDS announcement, I had visited the center with the Reverend Paul Smith, who is affiliated there, then met later with him and some other officials, including Donald J. Scherl, the president of the Health Science Center. I found the major aim of the center, to develop innovative approaches to the problems facing residents of Brooklyn and other urban areas across the nation, to be closely in line with some of my pressing concerns. After some deliberation, I agreed to the creation of the institute in my name, and to serve as the first chairman of its board. However, the most unforgettable aspect of that visit was my tour of a ward at the center devoted to children stricken with AIDS. I was touched to see a banner, signed by all of the children, welcoming me.

"I know what you are going through," I told them, "because I, too, have AIDS. I hope we can one day eradicate this disease through the work of the institute."

Aside from my own AIDS foundation and this center, I expect to lend my name to only one other project: the funding of the Arthur Ashe chair in pediatric AIDS research at St. Jude's Hospital in Memphis, Tennessee. This project is independent of the work of the Ashe Foundation for the Defeat of AIDS. Again I must try to persuade friends and well-wishers to contribute money to this fight. Anyone who had been with me at that hospital in Brooklyn, and at any of the hospitals I have visited in the past year, where children stricken with AIDS are increasingly commonplace, would recognize the urgency of this need to conduct research into the effects of AIDS on children.

AS CHRISTMAS DREW near, I had every reason to be happy. The *Sports Illustrated* award brought a spate of publicity, including appearances on ABC's "Good Morning America" show and with Tom Brokaw on NBC. On December 21, Camera celebrated her birthday with a party that I not only attended but also videotaped. The party proved something of a strain, however. Walking through the streets lugging the videocamera proved more onerous than I had thought; at least, I was sure that the weight of the videocamera was the source of my discomfort. I was left feeling weak and tired, so that I did little for the next two days. Then on Christmas Eve, around noon, tired of being housebound, I went out for a walk in the neighborhood. I was startled by how freezing cold the air was. I walked for about twenty minutes, but after five minutes I began to regret having come out at all. I was frozen to the bone and gasping for air.

Christmas found me not very well, but I was buoyed by the joyous reaction of Camera to her presents, and by the telephone calls that came from family and friends. Still, I was not well enough to do what has become for me, in some respects, the most important ritual of the day. When I was a boy, on Christmas, my father always took me late in the day to visit families who were less fortunate than we were. We brought food and toys—and Daddy always insisted that we give away not simply old toys but one or two of the new toys we had just received. I have continued this tradition with Camera. For the past three Christmas Days we have gone to Harlem late in the day and visited the hospitals and given away toys, old and new. But I couldn't do it this year. I was not well enough.

So I was glad the next day, when Jeanne, Camera, and I flew south to Miami and the Florida sun. Down there, at the Doral Resort and Country Club, with our friends and family, we would ring out the old year, which has been so packed with events, some of them momentous. And we would ring in 1993, with kisses and hugs and sips of wine and the hope, always the hope, for a bright and healthy and prosperous New Year.

CHAPTER 10

The Threads in My Hands

THE YEAR 1993 did not start well. In fact, New Year's Day found me ill at ease, hurting, coughing, and feverish, on an airplane bringing my family back a day early from Miami.

I had planned to work hard while in Florida. My main task there would be to teach my annual Christmas tennis clinic at the Doral, where I am now international tennis director—having relinquished my leadership of the main tennis program some time ago. I looked forward to working diligently with the guests. But I also hoped to squeeze in as many rounds of golf as I could, on one or another of the four excellent courses at the Doral.

A cold front was pushing its way south across the eastern United States, but near Miami we were bathed in sunshine and warm weather. Although Camera had been reluctant to leave her Christmas tree and most of her presents behind, she seemed ecstatic to be in the sun. Her happiness made Jeanne and me feel all the more blessed.

In fact, I was out on the golf course with Jeanne's father, John Moutoussamy, and a Canadian friend, Stanley Kivenko, when I first noticed that I was having some difficulty breathing. I couldn't understand why; we were riding comfortably from tee to tee in a golf cart, so there was no reason for me to feel tired. Then I started to cough. The cough persisted. From the seventh green, as I waited to putt, I took out my cellular telephone and called my main AIDS physician,

Dr. Henry Murray, in New York. He advised me to see a doctor as soon as possible.

Later that day, I went to see my AIDS physician in Miami, Dr. Barry Baker. After examining me, he ordered a chest X ray. It revealed nothing out of the ordinary.

The next morning, I went to Miami Baptist Hospital to seek the advice of Dr. Michael Collins. Fourteen years ago, in New York, Dr. Collins had treated me for the heart disease that had started my sorry medical record. He examined me, and ordered an echocardiogram, which uses sound waves to study the action of the heart. At this point, I still assumed that the cause of my shortness of breath was a lack of blood going to the heart, depriving the heart of oxygen. In New York, I had found out that one of the arteries leading to my heart had virtually shut down, and I had thought of having it opened in Miami. Dr. Collins and I would have to decide on one of three procedures. In an angioplasty, he would insert a balloon into the artery and then inflate the balloon. He could use a laser beam to melt the deposits clogging the artery. Or he might perform yet another invasive procedure, using a sort of Roto-Rooter on the deposits.

After his examination and the echocardiogram, however, Dr. Collins decided that the problem was not with my heart but in my lungs. What exactly was wrong, he couldn't say. Clearing the artery should wait until my lungs were healthy again.

The next day, still coughing and short of breath, I tried to get another X ray of my chest. However, when the physician learned that I had just had one, he refused my request; chest X rays are not done every day, he insisted. His refusal actually lifted my spirits, and I went out cheerfully to play a round of golf with a foursome that included former American tennis great Butch Buchholz, whom I have known since my senior year of high school in St. Louis, Missouri. Again I enjoyed the outing in the warm sunshine, but again I was bothered by an inexplicable shortness of breath. I began to think that perhaps a cold was coming on. Perhaps I had simply breathed too much bitingly frigid air on Christmas Eve in New York. I told myself not to worry. With the daytime temperature in Miami resolutely in the eighties, I looked for my symptoms to lift within a day or two.

That night, when we had dinner at what some people call Miami's most famous restaurant, Joe's Stone Crab, I enjoyed feasting on the delicious specialty of the house. Later, I went to bed feeling pretty fine, except for some slight coughing and just a hint of congestion.

On New Year's Eve morning, I went out for my last day of tennis clinics for the Doral. Even with my cough and chest pains, I looked forward to a full two days of golf before we headed back to the wintry cold of New York. After my last clinic, I headed for the links. I played a decent round, but found myself depending on a golf cart to move myself to the ball. I was beginning to recognize that in addition to anginal discomfort, the mere act of drawing air into my lungs was causing me some pain. I certainly could not take any deep breaths.

After finishing my round of golf, I stopped by the hotel swimming pool to catch a glimpse of Camera enjoying the water and the warm weather. Then, feeling drowsy, I quietly retired to my room alone for a nap.

That evening, Jeanne, Camera, and I went to dinner in the hotel coffee shop with Jeanne's parents, two of their friends, her brother Claude, and her sister-in-law. After dinner, we all went over to Claude's home to bring in the New Year. But midnight did not find me there. At some point, after watching me try to breathe without discomfort, Jeanne suggested that we head back to New York the next day, if she could arrange a flight. I agreed to do so, and around ten-thirty we left Claude's so that we could call the airlines and pack.

I was drowsy again when I reached our room, but Camera insisted that we turn on the television and watch the ball drop in Times Square to ring in the New Year. Earlier in the month I had taken her there and painted a festive picture for her of the coming New Year's Eve celebrations. Now, all excited, she was determined to see that ball drop. Although the hour was late, way past her bedtime, Jeanne and I had no trouble giving in to her, and we enthusiastically joined the count-down into 1993. Then we all went happily to sleep.

At five in the morning, I awoke with a start. I was on fire, burning up. I took my temperature: 101.9 degrees. Around eight in the morning, Jeanne called Dr. Murray in New York. He advised that we should see a doctor in Miami, but we both wanted to return home that day.

With the aid of nothing more exotic than Extra-Strength Tylenol, I brought down my temperature and relieved the other symptoms sufficiently to fly back to New York. From the airport, I went straight to New York Hospital, where Dr. Murray was waiting for me. His examination did not settle the matter. Speculating that I probably had a form of atypical pneumonia, he put me on a powerful antibiotic, azithromycin. I started with two huge red capsules, then continued taking the drug through the weekend.

It had no effect on me whatsoever. More feverish than ever, coughing badly, and miserable, I returned to the hospital on Monday. I saw Dr. Thomas King, a pulmonary specialist, who ordered a bronchoscopy; this procedure alone could give the answers we wanted. Dr. King warned me that the procedure, while painless, is extremely unpleasant. A local, topical anesthetic was applied to my nasal passage, and I swallowed a dose to anesthetize my throat. A thick tube, about a third of an inch in diameter, was forced down my nose and into my lungs. At the end of the tube was a tiny television camera. To allow me to breathe, another tube went down my throat into my esophagus.

Dr. King had said that with the tubes in me, I would feel certain that I could not breathe, but in fact I would be able to. He advised me not to panic. I tried to be reassured by his confidence, but a minute or two passed before I gained my own. Listening just outside the door, Jeanne told me later, she heard the most awful gurgling and heavy breathing as I struggled for breath while the camera mucked around my lungs, rummaging in what looked like a dirty sponge.

The procedure lasted between thirty and forty minutes. As he watched the television monitor, Dr. King spoke into a microphone and recorded his observations. That is how I found out I was suffering from the dreaded PCP, or *Pneumocystis carinii* pneumonia, about which I knew something.

Thus far, aside from the toxoplasmosis that uncovered the fact that I have AIDS, I had avoided every one of the opportunistic diseases that, in combination with the presence of HIV in the body, define the condition known as AIDS. Now I had one of the most feared. *Pneumocystis carinii* pneumonia is a very rare form of pneumonia, found in the past mainly among traditionally impoverished East European immigrants with already severely compromised immune systems. The disease acquired a fresh notoriety with AIDS. In fact, my shivering and burning fever were trademarks of PCP infection. In the last stages of their illness, AIDS sufferers often endure raging fevers all day and all night.

Fortunately, Dr. Murray assured me, my case was not particularly serious. I would definitely survive this bout. And New York Hospital–Cornell Medical Center was in the forefront in the world in research on this disease. Eight years ago, I probably would have been dead by this time.

His words encouraged me, but I was still miserable. Sweaty with fever and chills, coughing and shivering, I lay under my blankets, feeling drained and depressed. As if the bronchoscopy had not been enough, the nurses couldn't find a vein from which to draw my blood for a test. They stabbed my arm repeatedly, coming up dry each time. To complete the test, which had to be done as close to the time of the bronchoscopy as possible, I endured a rectal examination, a procedure that has never lifted anyone's spirits.

After an hour or so, Tylenol again brought down my temperature and gave me some relief. Then, intravenously, I was put on a regimen of the drug pentamidine, an anti-protozoal agent that has proven quite effective in treating PCP. At one time, I had taken it regularly in aerosolized form precisely to ward off infection from PCP. Now I was to stay on pentamidine for at least two weeks. This was not onerous; the side effects are tolerable. Perhaps the most common of these is an elevation of one's potassium level above the ideal amount. Another side effect, potentially more serious, is interference with the heart's electrical system. Yet another is the anesthetizing of the taste buds (in this respect, pentamidine is like chemotherapy). Since I entered the hospital, I had been eating by the numbers.

ON THE SIXTEENTH floor of a wing of New York Hospital, I sat in a room named after the late Greek shipping magnate Stavros Niarchos. I didn't ask for the room; it was assigned to me. Undoubtedly it was the most luxurious hospital room I had ever had, and I have had quite a few. Apart from an intravenous feeding stand parked discreetly in a corner, my iron bed, mechanized and grimly practical, was perhaps the sole reminder that I was in a hospital. The elegant wood floors are stained dark; the ceilings are high; the furniture, which includes a sofa upholstered in leather, would hardly disgrace the living room of a fine house.

Dr. David E. Rogers, one of the most eminent teaching physicians there—he holds an endowed professorship in medicine—stopped by to see me one morning.

"A beautiful room," he said.

"Yes," I responded. "It's really special."

"I remember this room from my early days here as a doctor. In fact, I had a patient in here once. A young senator. John F. Kennedy, no less. That was a long time ago."

Through one set of tall windows in this corner room I could see, to the south, the skyscrapers of midtown. I could see the silver chevrons of the Chrysler Building; the blunter summit of the old Pan Am Building, now the Met Life Building; the austere, fluted elegance of the Empire State Building. Directly below my window passes the East River. Mainly a somber brown and green, the dark water glitters and gleams here and there when sunlight flickers off its surface. Moving in each direction, boats ply the river. Downstream, they pass under the latticework of the Queensboro Bridge at Fifty-ninth Street. On Roosevelt Island, directly to the east, the fields were damp green. In the early morning, through the haze of the rising sun, I could see mist rising from the grass. In the evening, darkness swept quickly over the island.

By choice, I had few visitors. At first, Jeanne came three or four times a day; after a few days, when I was better, she came less often but stayed longer, hours on end. I saw Camera only twice. We do not want to disrupt her schedule. Once, after Jeanne and Dr. Murray literally smuggled her into the hospital hidden in their cloaks, I spent a wonderful hour with her in a conference room elsewhere in the building. She was fascinated by a plastic model of a heart I brought her, and by the mice in their cages, used by Dr. Murray and his colleagues in medical experiments. A few friends have come by. Cheerfully bearing belated Christmas presents for everyone, Donald Dell came up from Potomac, Maryland, to see me. My two close physician friends, Eddie Mandeville and Doug Stein, stopped by. Frank Deford visited me, and Alvin Schragis, whose wife's family owns the Doral. Still another friend, Dr. Paul Smith, who is pastor of the First Presbyterian Church of Brooklyn Heights, also came to see me. One day, he brought along Andrew Young, who was visiting New York. Before they left, in a moving moment, Paul, Andy, Jeanne, and I held hands in a circle and prayed.

These are some of my friends, but only a few of my friends, most of whom had no idea I was in the hospital. Jeanne and I kept my illness out of the news, where my name seemed to have been everywhere lately, at year's end. The honors and awards had come thick and fast. They pleased me, but they were not nearly as consoling as the visits of these friends, and the knowledge that people I have known for a lifetime were thinking about me and wishing me well. Whatever happens, I know that I am not going to be alone at the end. That is not to be my fate. Of course, in a sense, we are always alone at the end.

I have invested in friendship all my life. I have been patient and attentive, forgiving and considerate, even with some people who probably did not deserve it. It did not take an enormous sacrifice, however; for whatever reason, it came almost naturally. I made the investment of time and energy, and now the dividends were being returned to me in kindness.

For once, at Jeanne's encouragement (or was it her command?), I had left my cellular telephone at home. I made few telephone calls, and received fewer. I remember calling Randall Robinson to tell him that we had to do more about Haiti; we had to press the initiative we had won with President Clinton's election. The African American community, I thought, had to extend its arms in welcome to the refugees, the same way the Cubans in Miami welcome those refugees fleeing Castro. We had been far too remote from the struggle of the people of Haiti. Randall was in complete agreement with me.

On a table in my hospital room, coincidentally, was an invitation to the inauguration of President William Jefferson Clinton on Wednesday, January 20. I was touched and grateful to be invited, but I did not plan to go. I would not have attended the event even if I had been well, which I was not. I looked forward to going home to Jeanne and Camera and spending a few days in quiet reading and reflection, while my strength returned. I meant no offense or criticism of the pomp and splendor of the inauguration; I was a Clinton supporter and I am happy to see him president. But I wanted to be in my own home.

Of course, I intended to watch the inaugural events on television.

Stan Smith called, and we talked about tennis matters, which had seemed far away until then. We talked about a certain controversial father of a certain promising young woman tennis player; some people find the man offensive, even intolerable, because of his often harsh behavior both to his daughter's opponents and to the young woman herself. Because of him, the tennis establishment may move to curb the behavior of relatives of tennis players.

After the telephone call, I lay in bed and thought about tennis. The behavior of some adults is quite amazing. I remember one day years ago, at the Doral in Florida, almost coming to blows with a father. We had organized an informal tennis tournament for kids staying at the resort. One boy, about eleven years old, fought hard but lost his match. He walked off the court disconsolately. I watched him go up to his father, who promptly punched him in the head. I was stunned.

"Don't do that!" I said, quietly but as sternly as I could.

He turned and glared at me. "Who the hell are you," he said, "to tell me what to do to my kid?"

"Do it again and I'll have you evicted from this place."

"How dare you threaten me?" he shouted. "I'll report you to the manager!"

"I hope you do," I said. "You'll be out of here a lot faster."

People like that sometimes destroy the joy of sport and the joy in the lives of young people. Victory in a tennis match, money won in a tournament: these are not so important as good health, the honest affection and respect of friends, the love of one's wife or husband, and the spicy innocence of one's child or children.

I also remember one evening with Jeanne and Camera at a hotel in Eleuthera, the Bahamas. We were under the stars, the hour was late, way past ten o'clock, and Camera was still up, but what did we care? She was happy after a day in the sun and the sea, and now she was dancing to the music of a calypso band with a little friend she had just met. Jeanne was happy, too, talking easily to the wife of a musician she had met earlier in our stay and liked at once. I was with them, but alone. As I sat in an armchair watching my little daughter dance and my wife's face sparkle with life and joy, a wave of emotion like one of the waves of the ocean a few feet away from us washed over me, and

I started to cry. I cried quietly, but Jeanne turned her face and saw me. The smile left her face but then it quickly returned, not the same kind of smile but another, because she knew that at that moment I was happy. She knew I was crying not only out of sorrow but also out of joy, and that the joy was so powerful that it hurt. My joy was that I was there, on that beach under those stars listening to that music and watching the two people I loved more than anyone or anything in the world, and I did not want that feeling of perfect joy ever to end.

THERE, IN THE corner room on the sixteenth floor of the hospital, as I kept company with the memory or the spirit or perhaps only the ghost of John F. Kennedy, I knew that what matters are the genuine consolations of life. What else will sustain you in the dark hours?

These days I read even more than usual, and I listen to music much of the time. I have always been an avid reader of books and also of newspapers and magazines of all types. I have always craved information, and my strong interest in national and international affairs has only intensified in recent years. I like to know something about everything, from economics and geography to science and philosophy. I want information, not to enliven exchanges at dinner parties or in some other way to show off my collection of facts before less-informed people but because—as I tell myself—if I am proud to be a citizen of the world I must know as much as possible *about* the world. So I love to read several newspapers a day and several magazines a week, and books fascinate me. I read relatively little fiction, but I like poetry. Biography is a favorite area of mine, and politics, sociology, psychology, and anthropology also appeal to me strongly. Lately, however, I have spent more time reading the Bible than any other single book. I began reading the Bible while I was young, a long time before my illnesses. Now, not surprisingly, its words appeal to me more than ever.

I love almost all kinds of music. Certainly I love the symphonies of Beethoven, which comfort and inspire me. I remember an idyllic day many years ago, an autumn day in Essen, Germany, when I spent the long, serene afternoon playing golf, and then listened in the evening, as if I had never heard the strains before, to Beethoven's "Pastoral" Symphony. Germany in the fall, and Beethoven's Sixth: the right music in the right place at the right time. I listen to jazz, too, which I love; the trumpet playing of Miles Davis and Dizzy Gillespie, both of whom I had known personally, both now gone. Also from my past, from the 1960s, when such music gained a hearing in America, I turn to the recordings of the Red Army Chorus singing religious songs of the Russian Orthodox church. I love to listen to Eric Clapton playing his guitar; the man is a master.

In the end, however, the music that moves me most now, as in my youth, is gospel music. To listen to gospel music is to be invited deep into the roots of African American history and culture, past the blues and the spirituals of the nineteenth century and beyond even that era into our African past. My grandmother used to tell me that some of the black elders in her youth would gather in a circle for what they called a "ring-shout," accompanied by the beating of a drum in a slow, steady cadence as the elders slowly shuffled about, releasing their rage and frustration in music and dance. I hear those sounds, that rage and that beauty, in gospel music.

Music links me effortlessly to religion and philosophy, or at least to reflection and meditation, which I prize. When I played the trumpet as a boy, I used to think of its place in the Bible, of the playing of Joshua, whose trumpets made the walls of Jericho fall down, and of Gabriel, whose trumpet would announce the end of the world and the coming of Judgment Day.

In the end, as much as I love reading and music, and although love given and received by human beings is perhaps the only sure token of God's love and God's grace, I understand that the deepest consolation comes from one's relationship to the divine.

Some people have curious ideas about God. Many letters I receive speak of passages in the Bible that are supposed to have almost miraculous potential. Read this chapter or this verse and you will surely be saved! Study this book of the New Testament and feel the power of God sweep over you! In the summer of 1992, I had just finished dinner at the Sleepy Hollow Country Club when a man came up to our table. Holding a baby in his arms, he knelt down beside me.

"You are Arthur Ashe, aren't you?"

"Yes, I am."

"Arthur, have you taken Jesus Christ as your savior?"

"I beg your pardon?"

"I sincerely hope that you have, Arthur. Only Jesus can save you."

"The church is a very strong influence in my life," I said.

"Are you a Christian, Arthur? I hope you are a true Christian."

"I've been a Christian all my life. A practical Christian. All my life. I'm fine, thank you."

With the qualifying word "practical," I slipped past that man's zealotry, which was possibly the zealotry of the recently converted. He may be burning with more religious zeal than I can muster, but I do not believe he is any more of a true Christian than I.

As I told him, religion has been a part of my life since my youth. Before I finished high school, I had worshiped for appreciable lengths of time at the churches of at least four different denominations. I had started at my father's church, First Presbyterian, at the corner of Monroe and Catherine streets in Richmond. At the same time, while my mother was alive, and later, when she was dead, I often went out to her church, Westwood Baptist in Westwood. Shortly after she died, my father brought in a respectable woman of mature years, Mrs. Otis Berry, to take care of us. Mrs. Berry was Episcopalian—not AME, but Episcopalian—and even more devout than my father and mother. She often took me to St. James Episcopal, at that time one of a handful of Episcopal churches in Richmond. Then, in my senior year in high school, in St. Louis, Missouri, I attended a Roman Catholic church. I did so because the people with whom I lived, Richard Hudlin and his family, were Catholic.

I don't think I was more devout as a child than any other normal boy. I chafed at going to church on Sunday when the sun was shining and summer was at its height, but I had no choice; my father, who himself went only from time to time, and my stepmother, who never missed a Sunday, insisted that I go. At home, the Bible was always at hand.

As I grew older, but still a boy, class and race began to affect my religious zeal. The class divisions among the black denominations and within the black denominations began to bother me. If God and religion were involved, how could churches divide along socioeconomic lines? Why were the Episcopalians more prestigious than the Presbyterians, and the Baptists less? I was also perplexed by the fact that the lower one went on the economic scale, the more demonstrative and impassioned the worshiping often became.

Every Sunday morning I could see and hear on television Dr. Theodore F. Adams, minister of the huge, white First Baptist Church. That church confirmed its domination and its strict racial identity by its presence on Richmond's Monument Avenue, the avenue of Confederate heroes, with its statues of Stonewall Jackson, Jefferson Davis, J. E. B. Stuart, and Robert E. Lee. Didn't we in the black churches read the same Bible as the whites in First Baptist? Didn't the whites know how Jesus felt about the equality of human beings, about justice, and about the meek inheriting the earth?

By the time I reached junior high school and took the ponderings of our Sunday school more seriously, such thinking began to complicate my faith, though not to wreck it. Still later, I reached the point where I knew I was hearing nothing new spoken in the pulpits, that the preaching had ceased to provoke me intellectually or emotionally. At some point I decided that all the moral instruction of the churches I attended, especially the Protestant churches, came down to loyalty to the Golden Rule: Do unto others as you would have others do unto you. If one needed that rule developed, turn to the Ten Commandments. If one wished a deeper explication, read and study the Sermon on the Mount. However, I know that I was never so arrogant as to disparage the preachers or their churches. I simply put them into perspective, while continuing to respect their authority.

When I started playing tennis seriously, I tried to follow my father's wishes about churchgoing and made it my business to be aware of the place of religion in the lives of most of the people I played with. I found out that American players were mainly Episcopalian, Presbyterian, or Methodist. I couldn't play in the South, where the preponderance of white Baptists lived, so I didn't meet many Baptist players. Of course, almost all the Latin American players, and many of the Europeans, were Catholic. Because of my year in St. Louis, I thought I understood something of their lives away from the tennis court. I thought I had some degree of entry into their psychology; certainly they were more familiar for my having attended mass.

My first trip abroad as a player, to England to play at Wimbledon in 1963, was the beginning of years of religious exploration for me. I discovered for the first time the close connection between the Church of England and the Episcopalians back home. However, the fact that Queen Elizabeth II was not only the head of state of Great Britain but also the head of the Church of England jolted me into my first true bout of religious skepticism. How could a secular ruler also be, *ex officio*, the head of a religion? It made little sense to me, but this seemingly illogical arrangement was part of the grandeur of Great Britain and its culture, which I greatly admired.

On the tour, I made a point to visit not only museums but also historic places of worship. I went to St. Paul's in London and St. Peter's in Rome. I visited celebrated Islamic places of worship in Cairo, Teheran, and elsewhere, and Buddhist temples in Thailand. The more non-Western the religion, the more I was fascinated by its places of worship and its tenets. My good friends and fellow tennis professionals Torben Ulrich of Denmark and Jeff Borowiak, an American like me but one gifted (he is a fine pianist) and curious, were crucial to my development of a broader understanding of religion. Borowiak and I read *The Three Pillars of Zen* and sought to probe into its meanings. We even tried to apply the lessons of Zen to tennis, as did a popular book, *The Inner Game of Tennis*; I certainly think it helped me to concentrate.

I was able to compare the beliefs of other peoples in other parts of the world to what I was taught growing up in Richmond. I think I grew, but I also came to know the feeling of alienation, when you come home and your family and friends expect you to be the same but you are not.

As powerful and persistent as the African American church has been in my life, its influence has been tempered by my own life experiences. That is an essential part of the pragmatism I try to bring to my life. I do not have the rock-solid, literal belief of my aunts, but I do not think of myself as being incapacitated as a result. My aunts had probably never known anyone who was Buddhist or Shinto. Like my aunts, I believe in God, in a Supreme Being, and I believe in the Bible. I also choose to dwell on the common areas shared by the religions I have known, rather than their differences. Meditation, contemplative states of mind, personal reflection, prayer—all are part of Catholicism and of Buddhism, Methodism, and other religions.

I suppose that the religion I practice now is some mixture of all these influences. I do not place dogmatic faith in any single religion. Each one claims authenticity and uniqueness, as far as I can tell; which means that many of them are bluffing, since they cannot all be *the* religion of God. I do not hold their grand claims against them, but I cannot imagine shifting from Presbyterianism to another on the basis of its credibility. No; I would rather see myself as open to all religions, even if each religion seems to demand my exclusive attention.

One thing I know for certain is that I cannot know much. My mind clearly has a scientific bent but I know the limits of both science and my mind. Some time ago, *Life* magazine published a feature story about religion. "Is there a God?" the cover asked. Chosen as one of the respondents, I tried to make two main points.

First, I believe that I am part of a continuum of life that has existed, exists, and will exist into future generations. At most, I am only a ripple in this mighty river of life, but I am nevertheless a part of it, and a unique part, as well. Second, I cannot believe that life started haphazardly. Life must have come out of a design, from a First Mover, a Prime Cause. I believe in an original source or cause of life, which we call God, and which may have evolved over the billions of years of time. I do not believe that because we cannot scientifically and objectively prove the existence of God, we can therefore dispense with religion and the Bible. I know that I turn my back on God only at my peril. This I shall never do.

IN RECENT YEARS, Jeanne and I have found true solace in the teachings of the preacher, mystic, philosopher, and theologian Howard Thurman. I was introduced to the writings and tape-recorded sermons of Dr. Thurman by my good friend the Reverend Jefferson Rogers, with whom I later worked to help save Thurman's birthplace from destruction and to restore it as a memorial to him. One day, we hope, it will be on the National Register of Historic Places. I certainly believe that Thurman deserves such recognition. Andrew Young is also a devotee of Thurman's writings, as is Dr. Paul Smith of the First Presbyterian Church in Brooklyn Heights. In the past months, I have spent some happy hours talking with Paul about Thurman and his works.

Thurman was born in Daytona Beach, Florida, in 1900. His childhood was marred by the death of his father and by Thurman's sense of being out of place in the world; he took refuge in nature, in the woods near his home, the Halifax River, and the mighty Atlantic itself. However, he shone as a student in high school and at Morehouse College in Atlanta, from which he graduated in 1921. Later, he trained for the ministry at the Rochester Theological Seminary in New York. In 1926, he took his first position, as minister of Mt. Zion Baptist Church in Oberlin, Ohio. In 1932, he joined the faculty at Howard University as a professor of theology and, later, dean of Rankin Chapel.

In 1944, Thurman gave up his professorship to co-found the Church for the Fellowship of All Peoples, in San Francisco. By all accounts, this was the first integrated congregation in America—that is, integrated in its leadership as well as in its following. Then, in 1953, in a daring move, Boston University selected Thurman to be dean of its Marsh Chapel. That same year, his influence was so wide that a panel of judges at *Life* magazine named him one of the twelve greatest preachers in America. Martin Luther King, Jr., it is said, always carried in his briefcase a copy of Thurman's *Jesus and the Disinherited*. Toward the end of his life, Thurman returned to San Francisco. A prolific writer and lecturer, he published more than twenty books before his death in 1981.

For me, Thurman is the supreme example of the black American's capacity for achieving spiritual growth and maturity despite the incessant blows of racism. Born in the shadow of slavery, black and poor, he developed his understanding of the human and the divine to such an extent that he influenced thousands of people; Thurman became, as Jesse Jackson accurately and elegantly called him, "a teacher of teachers, a leader of leaders, a preacher of preachers." He did so by opening himself to a wide range of ideas and influences unlimited by race or nationality, borrowed gratefully from this religion or that philosophy. From his childhood, his sense of religion was brilliantly colored by poetry and mysticism. When he found an intellectual basis for this tendency in the book *Finding the Trail of Life* by Rufus Jones, a Quaker philosopher-mystic on the faculty at Haverford College, he sought out Jones for guidance. In 1929, Jones accepted him as a special student.

His months at Haverford, Thurman later said, were "a crucial experience, a watershed from which flowed much of the thought and endeavor to which I was to commit the rest of my working life."

In 1935, a visit to the "colored" lands of Burma, Ceylon, and India in a delegation of African Americans also proved powerfully influential. In a meeting with Mohandas K. Gandhi, the Mahatma sharply questioned Thurman and his companions about black America, its acceptance of Christianity in spite of the destructiveness of Christians, its need to accept nonviolence, or *satyagraha*, and to emphasize morality in its quest for justice. At the Khyber Pass, Thurman also underwent a mystical experience, "as close to a vision as I ever had." This visit to the East was crucial in Thurman's development of his identity as a Christian mystic and preacher dedicated to the exploration of the complexities of the self and of the divine, as well as to exposing the spurious nature of most of the barriers that separate human beings.

Little in Dr. Thurman's teaching is clearly original. Like most ministers, he borrows readily from the work of other ministers and thinkers. His power lies, on the one hand, in his eloquent fusions of ideas concerning the self, society, and the divine, and, on the other hand, in the appropriateness of his teachings to the problems that we face every day. Although Thurman was an African American, his writings make few references to race, or concessions to the idea of race. Like Rufus Jones, he spurned social divisions based on race, class, and gender. And yet his mysticism is of a practical, active kind, rather than one that leads to seclusiveness and denial. Spirituality for him must be a dynamic force, gathered and refined in solitude but applied in the world for the betterment of humanity.

The epigraph to one section of his book *Meditations of the Heart* captures something of both the substance and style of his ministry. In graphic images, Thurman describes the integrity of the self and the determination that should move each individual to guard and nurture that self, which is our one sure conduit to God. Thurman wrote:

There is in every person an inward sea, and in that sea
there is an island and on that island there is an altar and
standing guard before that altar is the "angel with the
flaming sword." Nothing can get by that angel to be placed

upon that altar unless it has the mark of your inner authority. Nothing passes "the angel with the flaming sword" to be placed upon your altar unless it be a part of "the fluid area of your consent." This is your crucial link with the Eternal.

Aside from the Bible, Dr. Thurman's two dozen or so volumes are the most important books to me both in my moments of crisis and in my extended struggle with disease. First, Thurman confirms my faith in God. "There is in God," he insists, "strength sufficient for all my needs whatever they may be." He notes how virtually all the religions of the world affirm this point, no matter how each religion interprets or represents God. Divine power is sufficient to aid every human being, no matter what his or her trials and needs. This belief is true of all the major religions, including Judaism, Islam, Christianity, Taoism, and Buddhism. One may doubt one's acceptance of God, or one's under-standing of God, but one must never doubt God's sovereign power.

Dr. Thurman's concept of "centering down" also appeals to me. It is both a practical process I try to employ and an idea about the mind, the soul, and the world. In one of his many prayer-poems, he wrote:

How good it is to center down!
To sit quietly and see one's self pass by!
The streets of our minds seethe with endless traffic;
Our spirits resound with clashings, with noisy silences,
While something deep within hungers and thirsts for
    the still moment and the resting lull.
With full intensity we seek, ere the quiet passes, a
    fresh sense of order in our living;
A direction, a strong sure purpose that will structure
    our confusion and bring meaning in our chaos. . . .

Resembling Zen Buddhist teachings about meditation, but also akin to the Christian meditative tradition, centering down is the pro-cess of bringing oneself to the state of serenity that would permit the believer to gain insight for the purpose of drawing closer to God. Centering down is not the same as prayer. Rather, it often precedes prayer. Dr. Thurman speaks approvingly somewhere of a rabbi who once suggested to him that genuine prayer is less an agency than the consequence or *result* of an inward journey or a centering down inside oneself. Prayer then has a chance of developing into a genuine dialogue with God, rather than the whining and importuning that it often becomes.

Much has happened in my life, but Dr. Thurman's teaching helps me to maintain control despite these changes. In fact, he insists we remember that the self is not static but constantly changing in accordance with new episodes and facts involving the individual. The self is not a purely ethereal or a purely physical entity but one composed of earthly as well as transcendental properties. Thus any journey into the self, any effort at centering down, must take into account new facts and events in the individual's life; all important new "self-facts" must be integrated harmoniously into one's self-image. Such exploration must not be undertaken in willful avoidance of these facts, as if they did not exist. As a devoted pragmatist, I relish the practicality of this teaching, how it respects the concrete aspects of existence even as it facilitates a search for divine grace. In my case, heart disease and AIDS are absolute facts that I must integrate into my sense of my own reality, my self. Mysticism is not escapism, in Dr. Thurman's view. Mysticism is aware of its own evanescence, its slippery, delusional nature, which can prevent someone seeking grace from ever attaining it.

As I face heart disease and AIDS, perhaps the most important concept offered by Dr. Thurman is the idea of the sacrament of pain, or the ministry of pain, as he calls it elsewhere. No doubt this is his attempt to answer the most haunting and perplexing question of Christianity and of many other religions: Why does a benevolent God tolerate or even encourage the presence of suffering in the world? Collectively, black Americans (and other oppressed peoples) have often asked God this question. "What did we do to deserve slavery? What did we do to deserve a century of segregation? Didn't our famed love of religion, our adoration of God, count for anything with the divine?" Those questions are woven into the fabric of historical African American religion and religious music. In the spirituals or sorrow songs, mainly in coded ways, they are posed again and again.

Dr. Thurman distinguishes between pain and suffering that might be deserved, as a response to evil deeds, and the more enigmatic kind, which seems unearned, gratuitous. He believes that humanity is protected and enfranchised by its participation in this innocent suffering. In his meditation "Pain Has a Ministry," he raises the possibility that "pain has a ministry which adds to the sum total of life's meaning and, more importantly, to its fulfillment." Nevertheless, he sees as a danger the idea that a specific kind of pain might be sent into the life of an individual in order to perform a ministry in his or her life. Indulged, this idea can lead to fatalism and despair. God certainly did not give me AIDS. Still, Thurman writes, "any tragedy has inherent in it positive good. . . . The pain of life may teach us to understand life and, in our understanding of life, to love life. To love life truly is to be whole in all one's parts; and to be whole in all one's parts is to be free and unafraid."

Believing that pain has a purpose, I do not question either its place in the universe or my fate in becoming so familiar with pain through disease. Quite often, people who mean well will inquire of me whether I ever ask myself, in the face of my diseases, "Why me?" I never do. If I ask "Why me?" as I am assaulted by heart disease and AIDS, I must ask "Why me?" about my blessings, and question my right to enjoy them. The morning after I won Wimbledon in 1975 I should have asked "Why me?" and doubted that I deserved the victory. If I don't ask "Why me?" after my victories, I cannot ask "Why me?" after my setbacks and disasters. I also do not waste time pleading with God to make me well. I was brought up to believe that prayer is not to be invoked to ask God for things for oneself, or even for others. Rather, prayer is a medium through which I ask God to show me God's will, and to give me strength to carry out that will. God's will alone matters, not my personal desires or needs. When I played tennis, I never prayed for victory in a match. I will not pray now to be cured of heart disease or AIDS.

I do not brood on the prospect of dying soon. I am not afraid of death. Perhaps fear will come to haunt me when the moment of death is closer. On the other hand, perhaps I will be even less fearful, more calm and at peace. I think of my lack of fear as being, in some ways, different from true courage. My bouts of surgery have made me a veteran in fighting death. Familiarity has not bred contempt of death but has given me practice in learning to face it calmly. In any event, the courage I yearn for is that described by Dr. Thurman: "There is a quiet courage that comes from an inward spring of confidence in the meaning and significance of life. Such courage is an underground river, flowing far beneath the shifting events of one's experience, keeping alive a thousand little springs of action."

I think that we must do our best to face death with dignity. I hope that I can be strong when my time comes. A true hero in facing death was Senator Hubert Humphrey of Minnesota, once vice-president of the United States and, in 1968, candidate for the presidency against Richard Nixon. Ten years later, as he faced the final onslaught of death by cancer at his house on the shore of Lake Waverly, near Minneapolis, Senator Humphrey's glowing optimism, even ebullience, was an example of true heroism I will never forget. I remember how it was said of him that in his splendid career as a liberal he taught us how to live, and that in his magnificent battle with cancer he taught us later how to die. I hope that I learned something from his example and can emulate it when my time comes.

I believe with Dr. Thurman that "death is an event in life. It is something that occurs *in* life rather than something that occurs *to* life." Death is but one of many occurrences in life, "none of which exhausts life or determines it." I believe, too, "that what a man discovers about the meaning of life . . . need not undergo any change as he meets death." So I go calmly on with my life. Keeping as busy as my health allows, I press on with my modest efforts at striving and achieving.

Above all, I have faith in God. Dr. Thurman has looked at the fear of death and reminded us of the infinite power of divine grace. "When I *walk* through the *valley* of the *shadow* of death," he writes, alluding to the Twenty-third Psalm, "I will fear no evil because God is with me." God's presence "makes the difference, because it cancels out the threatening element of the threat, the evil element of evil." God does not promise a pleasant end; far from it. "Of course I may linger, or I may die; I may suffer acutely, or all my days may rest upon an undercurrent of muted agony." Nevertheless, God is sufficient: "I shall not be overcome; God is with me. My awareness of God's presence may sound like magic, it may seem to some to be the merest childlike superstition, but it meets my need and is at once the source of my comfort and the heart of my peace."

Thus far, I have been steadfast. At night, I get into bed and I go straight to sleep. Is this bravery, or only denial? My wife, Jeanne, thinks that I practice denial a fair amount of the time. Wisely, she makes a distinction between good denial and bad denial. The latter is when I walked around with a pain in my chest but brushed off the hurt and declined to go to my doctor. Good denial is my refusal to dwell on the idea of death, or even to accept as a fact the notion that I will die soon from heart disease or from an illness related to AIDS—to me, this is not denial, but a simple acknowledgment of the facts of my case.

I am a fortunate, blessed man. Aside from AIDS and heart disease, I have no problems. My stepmother, about whom I care deeply both for my sake and for my dead father's, is in fine health; my wife is in fine health; my daughter radiates vitality. I have loving friends in abundance. I have the support of skilled doctors and nurses. I need nothing that money can buy. So why should I complain? And beyond them, I have God to help me.

Perhaps my favorite prayer-poem by Howard Thurman is "The Threads in My Hand." The speaker of the poem says that he holds only one end of a number of threads, which come to him from "many ways, linking my life with others." Some threads come from the sick and troubled, some from the dreaming and the ambitious; still others are knotted beyond the speaker's power to understand and unravel. But one thread is different from all others:

> One thread is a strange thread—it is my steadying thread;
> When I am lost, I pull it hard and find my way.
> When I am saddened, I tighten my grip and gladness glides
>   along its quivering path;
> When the waste places of my spirit appear in arid confusion,
>   the thread becomes a channel of newness in life.
> One thread is a strange thread—it is my steadying thread.
> God's hand holds the other end . . .

CHAPTER II

My Dear Camera

BY THE TIME you read this letter from me to you for the first time, I may not be around to discuss with you what I have written here. Perhaps I will still be with you and your mother, sharing in your daily lives, in your joys and in your sorrows. However, I may be gone. You would doubtless be sad that I am gone, and remember me clearly for a while. Then I will exist only as a memory already beginning to fade in your mind. Although it is natural for memories to fade, I am writing this letter in the hope that your recollection of me will never fade completely. I would like to remain a part of your life, Camera, for as long as you live.

I was only a few months older than you are now when I lost my own mother. Eventually I had no memory of what she was actually like, how her voice sounded, how her touch felt. I wanted desperately to know these things, but she was gone and I could not recover that knowledge. For your sake, as well as mine, I hope that I am around for a long time. But we cannot always have what we want, and we must prepare for and accept those changes over which we have no control.

Some of my most important thoughts about you are in this book, only as far away as your bookshelf. And your mother will be with you, alive and well, for a long time, and she knows exactly how I feel about most matters. If you ever want to know what I would think or say, ask her.

Coincidentally, Camera, I am writing this letter to you on the same day as the inauguration in Washington, D.C.—January 20, 1993—just a few hours after William Jefferson Clinton became the new president of the United States of America. I have been watching much of the pomp and pageantry on the television in my study. I especially loved listening to Maya Angelou, tall and dignified and with a rich, melodious voice, read the poem that our new president asked her to write especially for this occasion.

Tears came to my eyes as I watched her conjure up symbols and allusions generations old in the African American world as she sought to describe the nature of life and to challenge humanity to do better. She spoke of "a rock, a river, a tree" as sites in and of the earth that over time have witnessed the sweep of recorded and unrecorded history. For me, the river and the tree hold special significance as symbols because they are so much a part of African American folklore and history, our religion and culture in the South, where I was born and grew up, and where so many other black folk have lived in slavery and freedom.

When I was a boy not much older than you, one of the most haunting spirituals I heard on many a Sunday morning in church spoke movingly of a "rest beyond the river." These words and music meant that no matter how harsh and unrelenting life on earth may have been for us as slaves or in what passed for our freedom, once we have crossed the river—that is, death—we will find on the other side God's promise of eternal peace. The river is death and yet it is also life. Rivers flow forever and are ever-changing. At no two moments in time is a river the same. The water in the river is always changing. Life is like that, Maya Angelou wisely reminded us today at the inauguration.

What is sure to be different for you will be the quickening pace of change as you grow older. Believe me, most people resist change, even when it promises to be for the better. But change will come, and if you acknowledge this simple but indisputable fact of life, and understand that you must adjust to all change, then you will have a head start. I want you to use that advantage, to become a leader among people, and never to lag behind and follow the selfish wishes and snares of others.

On the other hand, Camera, certain things do not change. They are immutable. Maya Angelou's tree stands for family, both immediate and extended. She had in mind, I imagine, some towering, leafy oak, with massive and deep roots that allow the tree to bend in the fiercest wind and yet survive. The keys to the survival of this big tree are the strength and the depth of these roots, and especially of the taproot far down in the earth, sprung from the original seedling that long ago gave life to the tree. When you see a magnificent tree anywhere, you know it has had to fight and sway and bend in order to survive. Families that survive are like that tree. Even larger groups of people, such as those of an ethnic group, are also like that.

You must be like that, too, Camera, although your fighting must always be for morally justifiable ends. You are part of a tree. On Grandpa's—my father's—side of our family, we proudly display our family tree carefully painted by Grandpa's cousin Thelma, who lives in Maryland. On that side, we are descendants of the Blackwell clan. Your name, Camera Elizabeth Ashe, is one of the freshest leaves on this old tree. You are the daughter of a tenth-generation African American. You must never forget your place on that tree.

Mommy is a third-generation American. Like nearly all African Americans, Mommy is of mixed background. Her father's father was born in Saint François, Guadeloupe, of East Indian heritage. He came to America through Louisiana, where he married a black American woman who was herself born in St. James Parish. She was the daughter of a man born a slave in 1840. Then Mommy's grandparents moved to Chicago at the same time many other blacks in the South did, as part of what we now call "the Great Migration" that changed the North forever. They had children. One was Mommy's father, John Warren Moutoussamy ("Boompa" to you, as you are "Miss Camera" to him). He is an architect, so you can see where Mommy gets her talents as an artist. Everyone asks her about her last name, Moutoussamy, which puzzles them. It is only an English version of the Indian name "Mou-tou-swami."

Mommy's mother, your grandmother, Elizabeth Hunt Moutoussamy (some people call her "Squeakie"), was born in Hot Springs, Arkansas. We gave you your middle name, Elizabeth, in her honor. Each of her parents was an only child. Her maternal grandfather was a Cherokee Indian whose ancestors were driven out of Virginia and North Carolina by white men pursuing an idea they called "Manifest Destiny," which meant in effect their right to take whatever land they wanted from anyone who had it. Mommy's grandmother is still with us. On March 17, 1993, she will be one hundred years old. Can you imagine living for one hundred years, and having your mind and memory still work very well? She has outlived three husbands and all but two of her eleven children. She is a living symbol to all of us of the strength of families in the face of unrelenting racial discrimination, as well as the other hardships of life.

As of now, you surely do not know exactly what I mean when I tell you about racial discrimination. If I could present you with one gift, it would be a life free of that burden. I can't, and you must learn to deal with it and remain happy and good. In the past, racial discrimination was especially hard for any black man who aspired to the same heights as any other man in his place. Grandpa, my father, suffered in this way. Like so many Negro men in the South just after World War I, he grew up in a large family but one troubled by poverty and division. He grew up in a place called South Hill, Virginia, on U.S. Route 1. His father, Edward "Pink" Ashe (nicknamed because of his complexion), was born in Lincolnton, North Carolina, in 1873. His mother, Amelia "Ma" Johnson Ashe Taylor, grew up on a farm in Kenbridge, Virginia, not far from South Hill.

Unfortunately, Pink Ashe left his wife and children in the 1920s, when my daddy was not much older than you are now. Sometimes marriages end that way, when one person or another decides that he or she has to leave. But Ma never forgot Pink, who died in 1949, when I was six years old. In fact, when your mother and I visited her a few months before she died in 1977, she still insisted that Pink had been "the great love of my life." Her favorite song was "This Little Light of Mine," which she played for us on her record player as we visited with her. She gently swayed to the music, moved no doubt by her memories of the generations gone by.

I myself loved her very much. As a boy, I spent many summer days visiting her in her big house on the farm in Kenbridge. That's where I first saw a mule; it frightened me. I remember that if I was a good boy, she would give me tall glasses of cool lemonade in the afternoons. She looked forward to our visits. When it was time for Daddy and my brother, Johnnie, and me to go back to Richmond, she would often burst into tears. We would hear her sobbing as we drove off in Daddy's car. Love is strange and powerful, the most wonderful force in the world; and family love may be the most wonderful of all.

My mother's side of the family was a little more fortunate than my father's. Her parents, Johnnie and Jimmie Cunningham (we called her "Big Mama," but her real name was Jimmie), came to Richmond from Oglethorpe, Georgia, and settled in Westwood, a small enclave of blacks on the western fringe of the city. Johnnie died in 1932, leaving Big Mama ten children to bring up by herself. With dignity, faith, and discipline, she did the best she could. In 1938, their daughter Mattie (nicknamed "Baby") and my father, Arthur Ashe, were married in Big Mama's living room, and they even lived for a time with her.

I will never forget Big Mama. A deaconess at Westwood Baptist Church, she proudly wore her starched and immaculately white uniform with white shoes and a lacy handkerchief in her left breast pocket. I also remember the daily dollops she took of her beloved snuff, a kind of powdered tobacco, which she slipped under her bottom lip, and the empty Maxwell House Coffee can she kept close by to use as a spittoon. We all loved her. At her funeral in 1972, Uncle Rudi called out, "Goodbye, Mama," as her casket went by up the aisle. Then something in me simply burst open and I cried uncontrollably, as I had never cried before or have cried since. Her grave is only about a hundred yards from my mother's grave at Woodlawn Cemetery in Richmond. You must visit it some day.

I saw my father lose his own father and his wife—my mother—in less than one year. Those were terrible blows, and ever since then, family has meant more to me than you can imagine. When I think of the many horrors of slavery, the destruction of the family strikes me as probably the worst. We are still facing the consequences of that destruction. What excitement there must have been in 1863 when word arrived that President Lincoln had freed the slaves. Historians tell us that thousands of black men then took off on journeys to find members of their family who had been traded away or sold like cattle. Can you imagine the depths of joy or of sorrow when these searches proved fruitful or fruitless? Suppose you and Mommy had been taken from me, and I had tried to find you for ten years, only to discover in the end that you had died of typhoid fever and Mommy had simply disappeared.

Stories like this were true of many people. Maybe now you better understand why Grandmother Elizabeth and Granny Lorene send so many cards and presents to you. Or why Uncle Johnnie volunteered for a second tour of duty in the war in Vietnam, where many people died or were seriously wounded. He went again to Vietnam not simply because he was a brave and dedicated Marine but also so that I, his brother, would not have to go there as a soldier.

In all likelihood, you too will one day have your own family, which will enrich your life and bring you so much pleasure in knowing that the tree is still alive, still growing. Marriage will probably be the second most important decision of your life. The most important, I think, will be your decision about having a child. Today, about half of all marriages end in divorce, which is a sad and frightening thought. This means that you must choose a husband carefully, Camera. Two parents are usually better for a child. If you had children out of wedlock, as an increasing number of women have chosen to do, I would not be pleased, although I would still love you.

I only wish that you could be as fortunate in your choice of a spouse as your mother and I were when we chose each other. No marriage is without problems, as two individuals learn to adapt their ways for the sake of harmony. But your mother and I loved one another passionately; and we were never more in love than when you came into our lives to enrich and complete our sense of family.

Nowadays, people break up marriages over the slightest of differences, which is a pity. On the night before your mother and I were married, Jean Young, the wife of Andrew Young, the minister at our wedding, gave us some good advice. The most important ingredient in a marriage, she said, was forgiveness: the willingness of each partner to forgive the other. Forgiving takes courage, but it is the key. Now, every time I see Jean, I say, as we part, "Let's hear it for forgiveness!" No marriage or truly important human relationship can survive, let alone flourish, without both partners willing to forgive.

A marriage needs some basic principles upon which it can grow and blossom. When I was a boy, my father was the head of the household, without question. The man of the house made the major decisions; his wife was, as the Bible tells us, his "helpmate." Some wise, brave women in the 1960s and 1970s challenged this attitude, and now many people are confused, and others are experimenting with new roles. Mommy and I agree that my primary role is to protect and provide for the three of us. Her primary role is to see to our welfare, including her own. When you are a little older, and she has more free time, she will become even more involved in her profession of photography. You and your husband, if you choose to marry, must agree on the right formula for both of you.

My advice is not new. Our family elders have tried to pass on to my generation their collective wisdom and values. I am always aware of them. To my embarrassment, Cousin Thelma painted my name on the family tree in gold, the only leaf so colored. That gold paint reminds me always that I must not bring dishonor to the family, as if one diseased leaf might kill the whole tree. We are being watched by our ancestors, as I am watching you. We possess more than they ever dreamed of having, so we must never let them down.

Camera, because of the color of your skin and the fact that you are a girl, not a boy, your credibility and competence will constantly be questioned no matter how educated or wealthy you are. At the same time, your brown skin may bring you a few advantages. You should be wary of them. When the Supreme Court Justice Thurgood Marshall was asked if he should be replaced on retirement from the Court by another African American, he replied emphatically: "No, it should go to the best qualified person the president can find!" That is as it should be.

But many people in the world are not color-blind. I sometimes feel angry and disappointed when, because of stereotypes about the competence of people of color, some worthy man or woman is passed over for a position, just as I am frustrated when an unworthy person cries out about racism the moment he or she is denied a position or a prize. Unlike you, I grew up under the laws of segregation. My classmates and I were reminded every day that we had to resist the worst temptation facing us: despair. If racism was so pervasive, why should we try to do our best at anything? Why study hard? I tell you, Camera, racism and sexism must never be an excuse for not doing your best. Racism and sexism will probably always exist, but you must always try to rise above them.

You must also learn to feel comfortable in any company, as long as those people are good people. Traveling the world as a tennis player, I discovered that deep friendships with an infinite variety of people are not only possible but can definitely enrich one's life beyond measure.

Do not hem yourself in, or allow others to do so. I am still dismayed when I go to some college campuses and find out that in the cafeteria, for example, black students, by choice, sit separately at a table with only other black students. Whether from force of habit, thoughtlessness, or timidity, this practice is usually a waste of time—time that should be used by these students to get to know people of other cultures and backgrounds. This mixing is an essential part of education, not something extraneous to it. I hope you will summon the courage to forge friendships with as many different people as you can. Some African Americans may tease or even scorn you, and some other people may rebuff you, but I want you to persevere anyway.

You must do more. Mommy and I will insist that you try to learn at least two other languages besides English. Spanish must be one, and another may be of your own choosing. Although my French is passable, I never mastered a second language, and I have always regretted that failure. Fluency in a language makes possible a depth of communication for which there is no substitute. Do not succumb to our American fear and ignorance of languages other than English; in Europe, the children learn foreign languages easily. And you may yet see, sometime soon, an American president who will speak English with an accent, even though she, or he, was born here.

The United States of America is your country, Camera. Some people will tell you it is theirs alone, not yours to share. Don't believe them. I remember the presidential election of 1960 when the Protestant denominations feared that if John F. Kennedy, a Catholic, won, he would force his religion on everyone else (which, by the way, is precisely what the Protestants have tried to do since the founding of the republic!). Certain Americans believe that they have an almost divine or historical right to determine our nation's future. As the free-thinking adult I hope you will become, you must not back off from this debate. When the right-wing demagogue Patrick Buchanan stood up at the 1992 Republican National Convention and implored those assembled to "take back our country" from people who look like you and me, I became more determined than ever that he should not succeed. And he will not. America is not *his* country. His vote is not more worthy than mine, or yours when you come to vote. You must resist any group that believes it has a proprietary right to guide the ship of state.

In addition, black demagogues, spawned by the poor conditions under which many African Americans are still forced to live, will try to advance their own narrow political careers by fomenting artificially deeper and deeper schisms among ethnic minorities of goodwill. You will hear of conspiracies against black people and the term "genocide" loosely used. As much as you can, Camera, see people as humans and as individuals first who have been socialized into their cultural claims. As a young boy, I was well aware that whites judged me not as an individual but according to what they believed about blacks in general. You must not do the same to others.

Despite racism, Camera, because of the money I have made through tennis you will have many more material advantages than almost all of the other children in the entire world. Growing up, I never had much money, although we were not poor. My father taught me to be prudent and temperate with money. Use money; do not let money use you. Spend wisely. Your income and wealth should provide for these basics: a comfortable home, the best education that you can afford, health insurance for your family, charitable donations to those in need, and a sum of money saved and never touched except for emergencies. However much you have or make, beware of living beyond your means.

Pay attention to your health, Camera, and do not take it for granted. Mommy exercises every day for an hour after you go to school and I encourage her to do so. Whatever else you learn in school, I would like you to master at least two "life sports," those you can play long after you are out of school. Sports are wonderful; they can bring you comfort and pleasure for the rest of your life. Sports can teach you so much about yourself, your emotions and character, how to be resolute in moments of crisis and how to fight back from the brink of defeat. In this respect, the lessons of sports cannot be duplicated easily; you quickly discover your limits but you can also build self-confidence and a positive sense of yourself. Never think of yourself as being above sports.

Not right now, but in a few short years, you will begin to take an increasing interest in boys. Not long after that, if I am not around, you will think Mommy is cruelly ruining your social life because of the restrictions she will place on you concerning them. In your rush to be treated as an adult, you may want to try supposedly adult things:

driving, staying out late, drinking alcohol, indulging in drugs, gambling, and sex. As your father, I am particularly concerned about alcohol, drugs, and sex. I have seen so many lives ruined by alcohol and drugs that they must be mentioned separately. Because it is so widely accepted and so easily available, alcohol in particular can be a curse. In our family, Camera, several people were alcoholics, and they and others suffered terribly as a result. Sex is one of God's precious gifts, which is not to be treated cavalierly by men or women. When it is time, choose your partner and the occasion with care. Do not allow yourself to be seduced and then cast off and forgotten, as many women tragically are.

I want you to nurture an appreciation of music and the arts. When I was young, I played in my junior-high-school and high-school band for six years and developed a love of music and a persisting wonder that human beings can create and execute such wonderful melodies and harmonies. In my high-school concert each spring, we dressed in formal white jackets and bow ties and played music from Duke Ellington to Beethoven. In our collection of record albums at home you will find music from around the world, collected by me in my travels. Often, when I think of a place, music comes to mind: trumpets for Great Britain, violins for Austria and Germany, flutes for the Middle East, pianos for France, and finger pianos for West Africa; I think of drums for the American Indians, mandolins for Italy, castanets for Spain, cymbals for Japan, fiddles for our slave forebears. Each sound is like the signature of a place and its people. Each is a part of the harmony of the world.

I have always been moved by art, and by poetry. Don't let anyone tell you that either one is frivolous or expendable, or inferior to making money. Without either, and music, life would be dry and without feeling. Art comes from an urge as primal as that of survival itself. While I resist the idea that European art is the sole standard for the rest of the world, some of its works move me to tears. The Pietà at St. Peter's Basilica in Rome, for example, captures in its sculptural complexity about as much sorrow as can be invested in a piece of stone. Great art makes the inanimate live. This gift is from God, and you should revere it in others and in yourself, if you should have it.

Camera, have faith in God. Do not be tempted either by pleasures and material possessions, or by the claims of science and smart thinkers, into believing that religion is obsolete, that the worship of God is somehow beneath you. Spiritual nourishment is as important as physical nourishment, or intellectual nourishment. The religion you choose is not nearly as important as a fundamental faith in God. As a child, I went to Episcopal, Presbyterian, and Baptist churches; later, I went to a Catholic church because I was living with a family who worshiped there. Mommy herself is a Catholic and goes to mass, as you know. These and other religions, some of them outside of Christianity, are all roads that lead to God. Beyond the different dogmas must be a sense of yourself as created by God for a purpose, and as being under God's law at all times. Be ruled by that rule called golden: Do unto others as you would have others do unto you. Do not beg God for favors. Instead, ask God for the wisdom to know what is right, what God wants done, and the will to do it. Know the Bible. Read the psalms and the Sermon on the Mount and everything else in that timeless book. You will find consolation in your darkest hours. You will find inscribed there the meaning of life and the way you should live. You will grow into a deeper understanding of life's meanings. Religions sometimes clash and compete, but there is a reservoir of truth and guidance in the Bible that is beyond controversy and is always available to you.

Camera, as frenzied as is my world, yours will feel even more hurried and frantic. Technology is expanding as never before; the instruments of change are everywhere. You will often feel that you don't have enough time to do what you want to do. Make time. Control time; do not let time control you any more than it must. Balance the activity of your life. My father lived a simple yet pleasant life. A happy man, he worked hard but looked forward to fishing when the season rolled around. Of course, he wasn't faced by as many temptations as I have been or you will be. Don't try to do everything. Choose carefully, and then give your all to what you choose. And please try to become expert at something, so that others will look to you as a human resource.

I end, Camera, as I began, with family. In nearly every civilization of which I have heard, the family is the central social unit, the base and foundation of the culture. You are a member of the eleventh identifiable generation of a family on my side and the fourth generation on your mother's side. We have tried to prepare you as best we can to lead as happy and productive a life as possible. Along the way you will stumble, and perhaps even fall; but that, too, is normal and to be expected. Get up, get back on your feet, chastened but wiser, and continue on down the road.

I may not be walking with you all the way, or even much of the way, as I walk with you now. Don't be angry with me if I am not there in person, alive and well, when you need me. I would like nothing more than to be with you always. Do not feel sorry for me if I am gone. When we were together, I loved you deeply and you gave me so much happiness I can never repay you. Camera, wherever I am when you feel sick at heart and weary of life, or when you stumble and fall and don't know if you can get up again, think of me. I will be watching and smiling and cheering you on.

Index

ABC-TV, 26, 104, 121, 227, 257
Abraham, Seth, 13, 253
academic standards, 169–73
  for student-athletes, 30, 147–51,
    168, 173, 255
acquired immune deficiency
    syndrome, see AIDS
Adams, Brock, 21
Aetna Life and Casualty Company,
    25, 88, 184–90, 195–6, 257,
    266
affirmative action, 152–3
African American Athletic
    Association (AAAA), 255
African American Sports Hall of
    Fame, 267
African National Congress (ANC),
    119, 121, 122
Agassi, Andre, 233, 254, 259
AIDS, 46, 54, 57, 59, 87, 110,
    126–30, 189–91, 202–27,
    239–44, 248–54, 256–62,
    272–3, 289, 290, 292
  in Africa, 124, 132
  alternative therapies for, 215–18
  children with, 269–70
  diagnosis of, 195–203
  homosexuality and, 132, 136,
    205–7, 225–7, 229, 230

life expectancy after diagnosis of,
    210–11
  opportunistic infections and,
    202–4, 214, 275
  public announcement of, 7–20,
    24–9, 31–2
  public speaking on, 169, 256–8
  race and, 131–6, 141
  sex and, 222–4, 237, 239–44
  suicide and, 207–8
  treatment of, 212–15, 219
  United Nations address on,
    268–9
AIDS Leadership Award, 268
Alexander, Alpha, 255
Alexander, John, 84
Ali, Muhammad, 40, 43, 175
Allen, Machelle, 253
Allen, Peter, 11–12
Amdur, Neil, 81
American Foundation for AIDS
    Research (AmFAR), 29
American College Test (ACT), 148,
    150
American Society of Newspaper
    Editors, 23
American Sportscasters Association
    Sports Legend Award, 268
Anderson, Warren, 187, 189

Angelou, Maya, 294
apartheid, 30, 102–13, 117–23,
    168
Arias, Jimmy, 90, 92–4, 96–7
Aristide, Jean-Bertrand, 263
Army, U.S., 114, 115, 145, 170, 178,
    180, 185–6
Arthur Ashe Foundation for the
    Defeat of AIDS, 128, 191, 193,
    252–4, 270
Arthur Ashe Institute for Urban
    Health, 269–70
Artists and Athletes Against
    Apartheid, 110
Ashe, Arthur, Sr. (father), 6, 50, 52,
    54, 57–8, 65, 81, 99, 112, 262,
    270, 282, 296–7, 301
    and African American leaders,
        155
    and civil-rights movement,
        116–17
    Jeanne and, 4
    Jews and, 161–2
    work ethic of, 42
Ashe, Arthur, Jr.
    on Aetna board, 184–90
    affirmative action questioned by,
        152–3
    and alternative therapies, 215–18
    ancestral roots of, 166–7
    anti-apartheid activism of,
        103–12, 115–23
    as art lover, 37–9
    and Black Power movement,
        145–6
    childhood of, 60, 116, 137
    Christmas traditions of, 270–1
    and civil-rights movement, 112–16
    college teaching by, 169–73
    Davis Cup captaincy of, 44,
        62–103, 111, 168
    on Davis Cup team, 61–2, 137–8,
        179

diagnosis of AIDS, 195–203, 205,
    207–10
at Doral Resort and Country
    Club, 60, 168–9, 271–4
educational standards supported
    by, 146–51
and electoral politics, 118–19,
    155–61, 165–6
entrepreneurial ventures of, 181–4
as father, 56–8
finances of, 42–3, 176–81
foundations supported by, 191–4,
    252–5
and Haitian refugees, 262–4
as HBO commentator, 13, 258–9
heart disease of, 15–16, 33–6,
    52–3, 87, 88, 203, 209, 212,
    222, 264–6
history of black involvement in
    sports by, 173–5
homosexual overtures to, 227–8
honors awarded to, 268, 270
last hospitalization of, 276–80
importance of family to, 261–2
and Jews, 161–4
letter to Camera, 293–304
living with AIDS, 219–21
marriage of, 51–2, 55–6, 225–6
and mother's death, 3–4, 48–50
and music, 280–1
in psychotherapy, 49–51
public announcement of AIDS,
    6–32, 249–52
public speaking by, 169, 256–8
and racism, 126–41
relationship with father, 4–6
religion of, 281–92
retirement from competitive
    tennis, 33–6, 40–5, 60
sexual initiation of, 240–1
source of HIV infection of,
    206–7
treatment of AIDS, 211–15

United Nations addressed by,
   268–9
Wimbledon victory of, 48
Ashe, Camera (daughter), 7, 54,
   57–8, 128–30, 174, 195, 197,
   203, 258, 259, 261, 262,
   270–2, 274, 277–9
   and AIDS, 14, 16–17, 21, 28,
   31–2, 209–10, 249–50
   birth of, 56–7
   birthdays of, 211, 270
   letter to, 293–304
Ashe, Johnnie (brother), 50, 58, 99,
   183, 262, 296, 298
Ashe, Lorene Kimbrough
   (stepmother), 42, 99, 262
Ashe, Luchia (niece), 58, 99
Ashe, Mattie Cordell Cunningham
   (mother), 3–4, 48–50, 53, 54,
   81, 282, 297
Ashe, Sandra (sister-in-law), 58, 99
Ashe-Bollettieri Cities program
   (ABC), 191–2
Association of Tennis Professionals
   (ATP), 66, 72, 84, 97,
   119–20, 267
Athletes Career Connection (ACC),
   191–3
Athletes for Jesse Jackson, 158
Australian Open, 35, 72, 92, 93
azidothymidine (AZT), 135, 212–14,
   216, 260

Bailey, William "Bill," 185–7
Baker, Barry, 273
Barnes, Wallace, 187
Barnett, Dick, 255
Becker, Boris, 64, 97–8, 109
Belafonte, Harry, 110, 111, 117
Berry, Mrs. Otis, 282
Bhopal disaster, 189
Bible, the, 140, 243, 245, 280–2

Black Congressional Caucus, 110
Black Panthers, 113
Black Power, 145–6, 153
Blatz, Randolph, 187
Boitano, Brian, 224
Bollettieri, Nick, 191–3
Bond, Julian, 157
Borg, Bjorn, 73, 82, 107–9, 193
Borowiak, Jeff, 284
Boutros-Ghali, Boutros, 268
Bracamonte, Orlando, 61
Bradley, Bill, 43–4, 118
Bradley, Ed, 144
Branch, Kip, 174
Brawley, Tawana, 155
British Hard Court Championships,
   65
Brown, Gloria Primm, 255
Brown, Jerry, 21
Brown, Roscoe C., 255
Brown, Willie, 156
Brown v. Board of Education (1954),
   131, 142, 145
Buchanan, Patrick, 300
Bush, Barbara, 13, 14
Bush, George, 14, 29, 54, 117–19,
   123, 165, 183, 187, 241

Carlos, John, 40, 43
Carmichael, Stokely (Kwame
   Toure), 145–6
Caronna, John, 200
Carrico, Joseph E., 62
"CBS This Morning," 196–7
Centers for Disease Control (CDC),
   134, 205, 207, 241
Chamberlain, Wilt, 237–9
Chaney, John, 149, 150
Chang, Michael, 63, 176
Charity, Ron, 60, 61, 111
Chatrier, Philippe, 79, 84
Chen, Irving, 253

Civil Rights Act (1964), 142
civil-rights movement, 112–16
Clark, Kenneth, 131
Clerc, Jose Luis, 77–80,
    85–6
Clinton, Bill, 21, 157, 165–6, 266,
    278, 293–4
Coetzee, Gerrie, 108
Coffey, Raymond R., 22–3
Collins, Bud, 97
Collins, Michael, 34, 273
Committee for the Freedom of the
    Press, 22
Commonwealth Fund, 211, 253
Compton, Ron, 189
Connors, Jimmy, 6, 62, 68, 71–5,
    77, 82, 89–90, 92–4, 96, 97,
    104, 237
Cordell Village housing
    development, 183
Cosby, Bill, 253
Courier, Jim, 85, 254
Cox, Mark, 65
Craighill, Frank, 180, 253
crime, 141–2
    celebrities involved in, 160
Crown Heights (Brooklyn), 161
Cullman, Joseph, III, 25, 185
Cunningham, Jimmie, 297
Curren, Kevin, 109

Dailey, Quintin, 160
Davis, Brad, 11, 12
Davis Cup, 44, 61–104, 107, 109,
    111, 137, 163, 168, 169, 179,
    186, 268
de Boton, Gil, 260
Deford, Alex, 58
Deford, Frank, 13–15, 29, 58, 176,
    225, 277
de Klerk, F. W., 119
Delatour, Hunter, 94

Dell, Carole, 106, 196, 266
Dell, Donald, 10, 13, 15, 89, 93, 115,
    118, 127, 178–80, 182, 196,
    277
dementia, AIDS-related, 204
Democratic party, 119, 157, 165
Denny, Reginald, 143–4
Dent, Phil, 76
didanosine (ddI), 214–15, 260
Dinkins, David, 14, 15, 17, 121, 156
Dixon, George, 178
Doe, Samuel K., 182
Dole, Robert, 117, 118
Donahue, Jack, 187
Donaldson, William, 187
Doral Resort and Country Club, 25,
    54, 60, 168–9, 184, 271, 272,
    274, 279
Dryden, John, 79
Drysdale, Cliff, 103–4, 109
Du Bois, W. E. B., 42
Duesberg, Peter, 213
Dukakis, Michael, 165
Dunham, Katherine, 264

Ebony magazine, 149, 172
Edberg, Stefan, 93
education, discrediting of, 146–51
Edwards, Harry, 147–8
electoral politics, 118–19, 165–6
    African Americans in, 155–61
entitlement, ethos of, 150–2
Erving, Julius, 160
Evans, Richard, 76
Evert, Chris, 20, 233, 234

Falk, David, 180
Fareed, George, 253
Farrakhan, Louis, 132, 161
Fauci, Anthony, 134–6
feminism, 235–6

figure skating, 224, 247
Fitzgerald, William G., Tennis
    Center, 10
Flach, Ken, 96, 97
Fleming, Peter, 63, 70, 74, 76–80,
    84, 85, 86, 93, 95
Florida Memorial College (FMC),
    170–3
Food and Drug Administration
    (FDA), 212, 213, 215
Ford, Gerald, 23, 29
Forest Hills, 63, 235
Foster, Sheila, 253
Fox, Allen, 162, 163
Franklin, Barbara, 187
free agency (sports), 178
Free South Africa Movement, 111
French Open, 35, 63, 82, 85, 191
Freyss, Christophe, 33

Gandhi, Mohandas K., 287
Gantt, Harvey, 160–1
Garrison, Zina, 237
Gates, Henry Louis, Jr., 169, 170
Gerulaitis, Vitas, 63, 64
Gibson, Josh, 175
Gonzalez, Pancho, 61, 63, 65, 70
Goodman, Ellen, 22
Gorman, Tom, 99
Gottfried, Brian, 82–3
Gottlieb, Michael, 205
Gould, Dick, 84
Graebner, Clark, 35
Graf, Steffi, 231, 232, 234–5, 254,
    259
Grand Slam tournaments, 35, 64,
    108, 128, 139, 176
    See also specific tournaments
Green, Bill, 118
Gregson, Randolph, 94, 99, 103, 111
Griswold v. *Connecticut*, 23
Gulf war, 123, 165, 183

Haiti and Haitians, 131, 262–4, 278
Hard Road to Glory, A (Ashe), 8, 121,
    174–5
Harris, David, 58
Harris, Francis, 174
Harris, Loretta, 52, 54, 58
Hart, Gary, 21
Harvard AIDS Institute, 268
Harvard Medical and Dental
    School, 258
Hasidic Jews, 161
Hazzard, Walt, 115
Head USA, 25, 184, 257
health care, national crisis in, 258
Heckler, Margaret, 206–7
Helen Hayes Award, 268
Helms, Jesse, 161
Henderson, Edwin B., 173
herbalism, 216–17
Hesse, Hermann, 46, 252
HIV, 11, 12, 26, 28, 133, 201–2, 211,
    213
    and alternative therapies, 217
    in blood supply, 16, 17, 27, 207
    identification and isolation of,
        205
    sex and, 223, 241
    see also AIDS
Home Box Office (HBO), 12–13, 15,
    25–6, 236, 257, 259, 260
homosexuality, 224–30, 243
    AIDS and, 132, 136, 205–7,
        225–7, 229, 230
    civil rights and, 245–7
    outing and, 22–4
Hooks, Benjamin, 262
Hopman, Harry, 67
Howard, Rodney, 174
Howard University, 106
Hudson, Rock, 11
Humphrey, Hubert, 291
Hunter-Gault, Charlayne, 4
Hutchinson, John, 35, 87

Inkatha, 119
International Commercial Resources, 181–2
International Jewish Congress, 164
International Lawn Tennis Federation (ILTF), 66
International Management Group, 192
International Tennis Federation, 79
International Tennis Hall of Fame, 98–9
intravenous drug users, AIDS among, 205, 206

Jackson, Isaiah, 171
Jackson, Jesse, 111, 115, 117, 149, 157–9, 164, 265–6, 286
Jackson, Maynard, 156, 159
Jackson, Yolanda, 255
Jackson, Yusuf, 265–6
James, Henry, 127
James, Sharpe, 156, 193
Jamison, Sandra, 174
Jarryd, Anders, 83, 93
Jeffries, Leonard, 155, 163, 164
Jenkins, Bob, 79
Jet magazine, 102, 111
Jews, 139, 153
    African Americans and, 161–4
Jockey Club, 174
Johnson, Earvin "Magic," 11, 17, 20, 26, 28, 29, 237–41, 247, 257–8
Johnson, Jack, 175
Johnson, Robert Walter, 116
Jones, Ann Haydon, 99
Jones, Rufus, 286, 287
Jordan, Michael, 160–1, 180
Jorgensen, Gordon, 79–80, 99
Joseph, Jacqueline, 253
Justice, Barbara, 132–3, 135–6

Kachel, Chris, 33
Kaffir Boy (Mathabane), 120
Kain, Bob, 192
Kaposi's sarcoma, 205–6
Karenga, Ron, 113
Kelleher, Bob, 61, 65
Kemron, 132–6, 215
Kennedy, Edward M., 268
Kennedy, John F., 300
Kennedy, Robert F., 114, 118
Kentucky Derby, 174–5
Kenyan Medical Research Institute, 132
King, Billie Jean, 20, 75, 233, 235–7, 259, 267
King, Coretta Scott, 111
King, Larry (broadcaster), 226
King, Larry (tennis), 235
King, Martin Luther, Jr., 114, 138, 141, 145, 154, 155, 158, 286
King, Thomas, 275
Kiphuth Fellowship, 169
Koech, Davy, 132–4
Koop, C. Everett, 204
Koppel, Ted, 121
Krickstein, Aaron, 96–8
Kriek, Johan, 109
Ku Klux Klan, 112, 116, 117, 140
Kuhnke, Christian, 83
Kwanzaa, 113

Laver, Rod, 29–30, 34, 185
leadership
    African American, 153–9
    political, 165
Leconte, Henri, 84, 85
Le Coq Sportif, 25, 184, 257
Lee, Spike, 132, 154
Lendl, Ivan, 71, 73, 74
lesbianism, 230, 243
Levinsohn, Ross, 15
Levinson, Daniel J., 45–8

Lewis, John, 156, 157
Liberia, 182, 183
Los Angeles riots, 143, 156
Louis, Joe, 177
Louisiana-Pacific Corporation, 94, 97
Lozano, Jorge, 70
Lutz, Bob, 69, 70, 73, 74
Lynn, Jim, 189

McEnroe, John, 62–4, 68–71, 73–97, 107–9, 186, 236–7, 253, 259
McLeod, Derilene, 174
McMillan, Frew, 103, 109
McNamara, Peter, 76, 83
Mahoney, Margaret, 253
Malcolm X, 154–5
Malone, Karl, 239
Mandela, Nelson, 28, 120–4
Mandela, Winnie, 106
Mandeville, Edgar, 15, 201, 211, 260, 277
Mandlikova, Hana, 233
Manning, Bayliss, 187, 189
Marshall, Thurgood, 299
Masters tournaments, 64, 91
Mathabane, Mark, 120
Mattera, Don, 106, 123
Mayer, Alex, 85
Mayer, Gene, 75–6, 84–6
Mayer, Sandy, 84
Merlo, Harry, 94, 97
Merson, Michael, 253
Middle-Atlantic Junior Championships, 5
Mills, Alan, 93
Moi, Daniel Arap, 132
Moore, Ray, 103, 109, 122
morality, 166, 167
  decline of, 141–5
  sex and, 239, 241, 243–4

Morgan, J. D., 43
Moutoussamy-Ashe, Jeanne, 7, 36, 64, 87–8, 99, 128–30, 168, 171, 243, 258, 267, 271, 272, 274, 275, 277–80, 292, 295, 297–303
  and AIDS, 10–12, 14–18, 21, 31, 54–5, 195–7, 200–3, 209–11, 249, 253, 257, 260
  art expertise of, 38
  and Arthur's heart disease, 52–4, 265–6
  Arthur Sr. and, 4
  importance of family to, 261–2
  marriage of, 51–2, 55–6, 225–6
  as mother, 56–8
  religion of, 244, 285
  and retirement process, 44–5
Moutoussamy family, 52–4, 262, 274, 295
Muhammad, Abdul Alim, 132–3
Murray, Henry F., 15, 134, 210–12, 214, 253, 273–7

Nagler, Larry, 162–3
Nastase, Ilie, 72, 91, 109, 229
National Association for the Advancement of Colored People (NAACP), 149, 262
National Baptist Convention, 149
National Basketball Association, 238
National Collegiate Athletic Association (NCAA), 147–9, 173
National Commission on AIDS, 13
National Institutes of Health, Office of AIDS Research, 134–6
National Tennis Center, 73, 128
National Urban League, 268
Nation of Islam, 132, 136, 154, 161
Navratilova, Martina, 234, 236, 237, 254

Nestlé corporation, 193
Newcombe, John, 103
Newsweek, 29, 141, 159
New York City Board of
    Education, 243
New York Community Trust, 25
New York Hospital–Cornell
    Medical Center, 16, 34, 131,
    199–201, 276–80
New York Newsday, 207
New York State Department of
    Health, 242
New York Times, The, 21–3, 99, 102,
    149
Nippon Electric Company (NEC),
    67
Nixon, Richard, 29
Noah, Yannick, 84, 85, 266
North Carolina State University,
    148
Northern Westchester Hospital
    Center, 57, 197
Nureyev, Rudolf, 12, 223

Obel, Arthur, 132
Off the Court (Ashe), 81
Okker, Tom, 66
Olesker, Michael, 22
Olympic Games, 120
Operation PUSH, 149
opportunistic infections, 202–4,
    214, 275

pain, sacrament of, 289–90
Pasarell, Charlie, 29, 72
Paterno, Joe, 149
Patterson, Russell, 200, 202
pentamidine, 214, 276
People magazine, 126–7
Philip Morris company, 185
Pietrangeli, Nicola, 86
Pilic, Nikki, 66

Player, Gary, 30, 109–10
Players Enterprises Incorporated
    (PEI), 180
Pneumocystis carinii pneumonia (PCP),
    204, 205, 214, 275
Poage, George, 175
Policinski, Gene, 8–10, 19, 22
pregnancy, teenage, 237, 243
Price, S. L., 31
Prichard, Peter, 19–21
privacy, right to, 9, 16, 19, 21–4,
    29, 126
promiscuity, 237–40, 244
"Proposition 42," 147, 149
"Proposition 48," 147–51
ProServ, 180–3, 196

Quayle, Dan, 159–60
Queen's Club tournament, 103
Quindlen, Anna, 22

racism, 101, 126–41, 179
    and academic requirements for
        athletes, 148–9
    and AIDS, 131–6
    cumulative cultural impact of,
        141–3
    and religion, 283
    South African, *see* apartheid
    in tennis, 61
Rainbow Coalition, 159
Ramirez, Raul, 69–72
Redgrave, Lynn, 259–60
redistricting, 165
Reese, John, 25
religion, 281–92
    and alternative therapies for
        AIDS, 216
    commitment to, 167
    and homosexuality, 245
    and sex, 239, 241, 243–4

Rembrandt, 37–8
reparations, 151–2
Republican party, 117, 119, 157, 165, 241, 300
Richmond, Marvin P., 62–3, 79–80
Riessen, Marty, 69, 70
Riggs, Bobby, 235
Riordan, Bill, 72
Robeson, Paul, 44
Robinson, Jackie, 44
Robinson, Max, 226
Robinson, Randall, 110–11, 117, 123, 262, 278
Robinson, Sugar Ray, 177
Roche, Tony, 35
Roderick, David, 187
Rogers, David E., 277
Rogers, Jefferson, 114, 145, 170–2, 285
role models, African American, 153, 159–61
Rolley, Lynne, 233–4
Roman Catholic church, 243
Roper, William L., 134
Rowe v. Wade, 23
Russell, William, 197–200

Sabatini, Gabriela, 233
Safe Passage Foundation, 10, 191–3
St. Jude's Hospital (Memphis), Arthur Ashe chair in pediatric AIDS research at, 270
Sampras, Pete, 254
Sánchez Vicario, Arantxa, 254
Savitt, Dick, 163
Scheidt, Stephen, 15, 199, 200, 211, 212
Scherl, Donald J., 269
Schmoke, Kurt, 156, 159
scholarships, athletic, 151
Scholastic Aptitude Test (SAT), 148, 150

Schwaier, Hansjörg, 98
Scientific American, 210, 211
Seasons of a Man's Life, The (Levinson), 45–8
segregation, 61, 101, 111–12, 128, 137, 140, 142, 171
    black-imposed, 154
    reparations for, 151–2
    in South Africa, *see* apartheid
Seguso, Robert, 96, 97
sex
    AIDS and, 222–4, 237, 239–44
    assaults by athletes, 160
    promiscuous, 237–40
    see also homosexuality
sex education, 224, 241, 243–4
Sharpton, Al, 155
Shriver, Pam, 29, 254
Shriver, Sargent, 118
Simon, William E., 94
slavery, reparations for, 151–2
Sleepy Hollow Country Club, 260
Smid, Tomas, 73, 74
Smith, Austin, 128–29
Smith, Doug, 7–8, 17–18
Smith, Marjory, 128–30
Smith, Paul, 269, 277–8, 285
Smith, Stan, 5, 6, 10, 69, 70, 72, 73, 74, 91, 120, 128, 279
Smith, Tommie, 40
Smith, Virginia Bouchard, 34
Smith, Willi, 11
Smith, William Kennedy, 21
Sontag, Susan, 220
South Africa, 9, 28, 30, 102–12, 115, 117–23, 168
South African Open, 103–5
Southern Christian Leadership Conference (SCLC), 145
Southern University, 148
Soweto uprising, 104
Sports Illustrated, 268, 270
STASH clothing importer, 182–3

State University of New York
   Health Science Center,
   269–70
Stein, Douglas, 36, 182, 201, 211,
   260, 277
Stevens-Johnson Syndrome, 210
Stewart, Donald M., 25
Stewart, Sherwood, 69, 70
Stich, Michael, 176, 259
Stolle, Fred, 99
Stove, Betty, 233
student-athletes, academic
   requirements for, 30, 147–51,
   168, 173, 255
Student Nonviolent Coordinating
   Committee (SNCC), 145
suicide, AIDS and, 207–8
Sullivan, Louis, 13, 134–6, 241
Sundstrom, Henrik, 93, 94
Supreme Court, U.S., 23, 44, 131,
   142
Surtee, Yusuf, 121, 123

Tanner, Roscoe, 69–71, 78
Tavris, Carol, 218
Taylor, Elizabeth, 28–9
Taylor, Amelia "Ma" Johnson Ashe,
   296
Taylor, Charles, 182
Taylor, Hobart, 187
Taylor, Marshall, 175
Tea and Sympathy (play), 225
teenage pregnancy, 237, 242–3
Teltscher, Eliot, 82, 96–8
Tempelsman, Maurice, 268
Tennis magazine, 184
Thalhimer, William, 162
Thomas, Clarence, 29
Thompson, John, 30, 149–50
Thurman, Howard, 285–92
Tilden, Bill, 225
Till, Emmett, 116

Tiriac, Ion, 91
Tolbert, William R., 182
Toure, Kwame (Stokely
   Carmichael), 145–6
toxoplasmosis, 202–4, 214, 216, 275
Trabert, Tony, 62–4, 68, 76, 80
Tracy, Laura, 232–3
TransAfrica, 110, 117, 123, 262
Tulasne, Thierry, 84
Tyson, Mike, 160

Ulrich, Torben, 284
United Nations, 104, 108, 110, 117,
   268–9
United Negro College Fund
   (UNCF), 173
U.S. Open, 34, 35, 62, 65, 72, 97,
   103, 108, 128, 139, 185, 196,
   201, 253–4
United States Tennis Association
   (USTA), 62, 72, 94–5, 97,
   102–3, 111, 128, 254
University of California at Los
   Angeles (UCLA), 8, 30, 43,
   45, 137, 170, 171, 179, 200,
   228
   black nationalists at, 113
   Jews at, 162–3
US (black nationalist organization),
   113
USA Today, 7–10, 17, 19–20, 22–3,
   29

Vilas, Guillermo, 77–9, 85–6, 193
Voting Rights Act (1965), 142

Wallace, Lee, 34, 198
Washington, MaliVai, 254
Washington *Post*, 111, 114, 184, 201
Washington Tennis Patrons, 10

Waters, Maxine, 156
Weaver, Mike, 108
West Side Tennis Club, 61
White, Byron, 44
Wickham, DeWayne, 22
Wilander, Mats, 82–3, 92, 93, 186
Wilder, Douglas, 14, 118, 156
Wilkins, Dominique, 177
Wimbledon, 6, 12, 13, 26, 33, 35, 48,
    63, 64, 66, 72, 73, 82, 89, 93,
    97, 99, 103, 104, 108, 109,
    127, 163, 211, 235, 236, 254,
    258–60, 267, 283, 290
WLIB radio, 134, 158, 266
Women's Sports Foundation, 267
Women's Tennis Association, 230
Woods, Sam, 111, 137
Woolfolk, Butch, 158

World AIDS Day, 268
World Championship Tennis
    (WCT), 5
World Cup, 185
World Health Organization, 133
World Team Tennis (WTT), 235

Yale University, 169–70
Yardley, Jonathan, 23
Young, A. S. "Doc," 174
Young, Andrew, 14, 51, 56, 115, 156,
    278, 285, 298
Young, Jean, 51, 56, 298

Zulu, 119

A NOTE ON THE TYPE

The text of this book was set in Centaur. Originally designed by Bruce Rogers in 1914 as a private type, it was named for the book in which it was first used (*The Centaur*, by Maurice Guérin). Monotype made it generally available in 1929.

Rogers based his design upon the 1470 font of Nicolas Jensen, the Venetian printer, introducing refinements lacking in the original. Typographers consider Centaur to be one of the finest roman types currently available, a superb revival of the Jensen letter, which has served as an inspiration for all designers of roman type.

Composed by ComCom,
a division of Haddon Craftsmen, Allentown, Pennsylvania

Printed and bound by
The Haddon Craftsmen, Scranton, Pennsylvania

Designed by Cassandra J. Pappas